CASS SERIES: STUDIES IN INTE
(Series Editors: Christopher Andrew and M

THE AUSTRALIAN SECURITY INTELLIGENCE ORGANIZATION: AN UNOFFICIAL HISTORY

Also in this series

Codebreaker in the Far East
by Alan Stripp

War, Strategy and Intelligence
by Michael I. Handel

A Don At War
(revised edition) by Sir David Hunt

Controlling Intelligence
edited by Glenn P. Hastedt

*Security and Intelligence in a Changing World: New
Perspectives for the 1990s*
edited by A. Stuart Farson, David Stafford and
Wesley K. Wark

Spy Fiction, Spy Films and Real Intelligence
edited by Wesley K. Wark

*From Information to Intrigue: Studies in Secret Service
Based on the Swedish Experience 1939–45*
by C.G. McKay

Dieppe Revisited: A Documentary Investigation
by John P. Campbell

Intelligence and Strategy in the Second World War
edited by Michael I. Handel

*Policing Politics: Security Intelligence and the
Liberal Democratic State*
by Peter Gill

THE AUSTRALIAN SECURITY INTELLIGENCE ORGANIZATION: AN UNOFFICIAL HISTORY

FRANK CAIN

University of New South Wales

SPECTRUM PUBLICATIONS
1994

First published 1994 in Great Britain by
FRANK CASS AND CO. LTD.
Newbury House, 900 Eastern Avenue, Newbury Park,
Ilford, Essex IG2 7HH, England

and in the United States of America by
FRANK CASS
c/o International Specialized Book Services Inc.
5804 N.E. Hassalo Street, Portland, OR 97213-3644

First published 1994 Australia by
Spectrum Publications P/L
PO Box 75 Richmond Victoria 3121
Tel (03) 429 1404   Fax (03) 428 9407

National Library of Australia
Cataloguing-in-publication entry:

Cain, Frank, 1931 -
A.S.I.O. an Unofficial History

Includes index.
ISBN 0 86786 347 1.

1. Australian Security Intelligence Organisation - History. 2.
Intelligence service - Australia - History. 3. Internal security -
Australia. 4. National security - Australia. I. Title. II. Title:
Australian Security Intelligence Organisation.

327.120994

Printed by Allanby Press Printers
1 Crescent Rd Camberwell Victoria 3124

By the same author:
Origins of Political Surveillance in Australia (1984)
*The Wobblies at War: A History of the IWW and the Great War
in Australia* (Spectrum 1993)

Contents

List of Illustrations

Acknowledgements

This book could not have been written without access to Australia's greatest historical asset – the Australian Archives. To its dedicated staff, particularly in Canberra, and there, particularly Moira Smyth, I express my thanks. For their help at the University I thank Barbie Robinson, Elizabeth Greenhalgh and Pauline Green, and for her advice at Frank Cass, Norma Marson.

Grateful acknowledgement is due to the following for permission to reproduce photographs: *Age*, Melbourne; the Australian Security Intelligence Organization; the *Canberra Times*; the Harry S. Truman Library; Tom Mangold; the National Library of Australia; the Royal Military College, Duntroon; the South Australian Law Institute; the University of Melbourne Archives.

Abbreviations

AA   Australian Archives
ADB   Australian Dictionary of Biography
AONSW Archives Office New South Wales, Sydney, Australia
ASIS   Australian Secret Intelligence Service (Australia's foreign intelligence service)
AWM   Australian War Memorial
CIA   Central Intelligence Agency
CIS   Commonwealth Investigation Service (precursor of ASIO)
CPA   Communist Party of Australia
CRS   Commonwealth Records Office (a prefix to Commonwealth Files held in Australian Archives, Canberra)
CSIRO   Commonwealth Scientific and Industrial Research Organization
DSD   Defence Signals Directorate (collects and deciphers foreign radio traffic)
JIO   Joint Intelligence Organization (collects and analyses information of strategic interest to Australia)
NARA   National Archives and Records Administration (National archives system for the USA)
NLA   National Library of Australia
ONA   Office of National Assessments (collects and evaluates information of economic and political importance to Australia)
RCE   Royal Commission on Espionage (inquired into Petrov affair)
SANACC State Army Navy and Air Force Coordinating Committe (controlled release of US military information to foreign countries)

Foreword

Since the ending of the Cold War, the intelligence community in Australia has been confronted by drastically changed times. Cutbacks and belt-tightening have reduced the staff numbers as with other intelligence communities in the post-Cold War years.

But the Australian Security Intelligence Organization (ASIO), the counterpart to MI5 and modelled on its lines when established in 1949, is in deep trouble. Ever since its establishment it has been regarded as hostile to the Australian Labor Party (ALP) which was out of government for 23 years between 1949 and 1972. Many Labor Party activists blamed the electoral losses on the Cold War activities of ASIO. They saw it as being too close to the Liberal Party (Australia's counterpart to the British Conservative Party).

When Labor eventually won office in 1972 it established a Royal Commission into ASIO and significant changes were made. ASIO is now reviewed by a Joint Parliamentary Standing Committee and an ombudsman has been appointed to oversee it. But ASIO has continued to make mistakes, as in 1983 when it falsely reported the former secretary of the ALP as being entrapped by a KGB agent in Canberra.

And now it has found a possible mole in its ranks. One of its agents for twenty years and a Russian expert is to stand trial in the Supreme Court for taking files out of the office. He said that he was concerned about his future employment conditions with the reduction in counter-espionage work. He is friendly with staff in the Russian Embassy. The Labor government has appointed a troubleshooter to investigate what damage has been done and whether there are other moles. This is because ASIO remains a member of the West's intelligence club and appearances have to be maintained. It is possible that ASIO will never be the same again. The last decade has seen a plethora of other intelligence services and investigatory bodies established in Australia to look into modern criminal activity relating to drugs, white-collar crime, police corruption, terrorists and crime generally. Will there be much work left for Cold War intelligence bodies like ASIO?

Another unforeseen factor is the phenomenon reflected in a recent CIA desertion where a counter-espionage agent was found to have been paid $US 2.5 million for information. This man felt he was underpaid and he put the money towards smart cars and a fashionable house. He obviously enjoyed the extra payment. In Australia, too, remuneration is the important issue with the agents of the national spy service, the Australian Secret Intelligence Service (ASIS), who have become disgruntled about dismissals, compensation payments and pension rights and have complained to the media. A judge has been appointed to investigate their complaints.

With the driving force of ideology now exhausted, spies and counter-espionage agents now seem to have lapsed into being ordinary public servants carefully attuned to salary increases and pension payments. This study of the history of ASIO reminds us how different this situation was until recent times.

FRANK CAIN
March 1994

1

Origins of ASIO

The Australian Security Intelligence Organization (ASIO) is often perceived as a new and unusual institution in the field of Australian public administration and to have been established as a direct result of the tensions of the Cold War. Although it is an institution that departs from the usual norms of governmental administration in that it is a totally secret body, its expenditures are not subject to normal auditing arrangements, its various addresses are not revealed, and to disclose publicly the name of any of its employees (other than its Director-General) is to attract a heavy fine or prison sentence, it is not a wholly new-style institution. Indeed, its roots are to be found in the years of the First World War. Certainly it developed out of the early Cold War years, but the Chifley government, which established it in 1949, never expressly intended that it would be such a secret and clandestine arm of the government's administration. This chapter explores how ASIO has evolved from the various intelligence-collecting organizations that developed during and after the First World War, and how the targets that provide the administrative rationale for its intelligence-collecting and functional activities have likewise evolved in a tandem-like arrangement.

Radical political groups have always provided the targets for intelligence collection and surveillance in the decades before the Great War, but such operations were conducted by the police forces of the several Australian states. The militant trade unionists, radicals, Fenians and anarchists were the targets for these policing activities which were later to lead to the establishment of police Special Branches which took over the intelligence-collecting activities in these areas.

WARTIME INTELLIGENCE ACTIVITIES

The outbreak of war in 1914 led to the hasty establishment of several intelligence bodies by the Australian government under the sweeping wartime powers it exercised under the regulations of the War Precautions Act, which, in turn, was copied from the British Defence of the Realm Act. This intelligence apparatus consisted of three interlocking organizations designed to detect and eradicate enemy activity. At its centre was the postal censor who opened letters in all central post offices to obtain intelligence about the activities of enemy aliens or trade directed to Germany by the many neutral countries. The postal censor was responsible to both the British postal censor in London and the head of Australia's Military Intelligence whose organization compiled the intelligence on possible and actual enemy activity and where necessary called on the third wing of this trinity, the states' police forces, which often conducted the prosecutions of the offenders under the regulations of the War Precautions Act. A fourth but independent arm was added to this trio in January 1916 when MI5 in London instructed the Australian government to establish the Counter-Espionage Bureau, later known as the Australian Special Intelligence Bureau. This was based in the office of the Governor-General and run by his secretary, Major Steward, so that he could use the British government cipher to communicate with Vernon Kell, then head of MI5. This Bureau had an uneasy ride during the war years because Military Intelligence, Naval Intelligence (established early in 1917), and the police forces resented Steward establishing a new intelligence empire in what was becoming a field overcrowded with intelligence operatives. Because this Bureau had no legislative measure to support its activities, Steward had to rely on the request of the Prime Minister to police and military chiefs to obtain co-operation from these larger and more powerful institutions.[1]

The first functions of these intelligence groups were to round up German immigrants suspected of supporting the enemy and to stop German trade. After this was quickly accomplished the intelligence agencies began watching the growing groups of dissenters against the war. Initially no one objected to the war except the Industrial Workers of the World (IWW). As the poor Allied generalship led to increased carnage of Australian soldiers, opposition became more widespread. The IWW, however, remained a vanguard of this mounting opposition. Sales of its newspaper, *Direct Action*, expanded to 6,000 per week by the middle of the war.[2] Other anti-war material published by the IWW, such as *War – What For?* by the American author, George Fitzpatrick, was sold in large quantities.

Emboldened by the IWW example, other groups were formed to oppose the war. The Women's Peace Army was established by the Women's Political Association. The pre-war pacifist and peace groups emerged from their self-imposed silence and along with the No Conscription Fellowship led by R.S. Ross swelled the growing opposition. This provided further grist to the intelligence mills. Division over the war in Australia led to division in the government. It split in 1916 and the new Nationalist government, led by the former Prime Minister, W.M. Hughes, began to suppress the anti-war groups. The axe fell on the IWW immediately. The government passed the Unlawful Associations Act to ban the IWW late in 1916 and strengthened it by further amendment in July 1917. This provided work for the MI5 branch in Australia, the Special Intelligence Bureau. The Act provided that IWW members remaining active could be jailed for six months and, if not Australian-born, deported on release from jail. The Bureau rounded up and deported these members with the assistance of the army and the police.[3]

Opposition to the war expanded when the trade union movement generally moved towards supporting the anti-war cause. The army greatly increased its letter openings and the various intelligence organizations expanded. The Australian Navy established its own intelligence section under Lieutenant Commander J.G. Latham. The outcome was tension and rivalry between the intelligence agencies to preserve their domain. When a merchant ship, SS *Cumberland*, sank off the coast with a cargo of frozen lamb bound for the UK, the mishap was immediately ascribed to the IWW. It had support and members in the Queensland meat works from which the frozen lambs came. The MI5 Bureau tried to monopolize the subsequent inquiry, much to the chagrin of the new naval intelligence. A move was launched with police support to dissolve the Bureau and distribute its work among the existing agencies. It was subsequently discovered that the sinking was caused by a mine laid by the German raider, the *Wolf*.[4]

The most enduring factor to develop out of these years of intelligence surveillance was the emergence of a considerable team of operatives trained in the skills of intelligence collection and assessment. Admittedly, many of these were self-taught and had acquired their experience against the background of the emergency of war years and under the sweeping measures of the War Precautions Act. Their skills and organizing abilities remained, to provide the experienced officers to fill the positions in the ongoing surveillance body to be known as the Investigation Branch of the Attorney-General's Department.

POST-WAR INTELLIGENCE ORGANIZATION: THE INVESTIGATION BRANCH OF THE ATTORNEY-GENERAL'S DEPARTMENT

After the conclusion of the war, the question arose of not whether there would be a continuing civilian intelligence organization, but what shape it would take. After a conference arranged by Robert Garran, Solicitor-General and head of the Attorney-General's Department, it was decided to establish an Investigation Branch in his Department. This would conduct political surveillance work and investigate offences against Australian government laws such as counterfeiting. It would also investigate people applying for immigration visas and applications for naturalization.[5] This Investigation Branch took over the records of the MI5 office, which was dissolved, and some of its officers. Major Steward's deputy head, Major H.E. Jones, was appointed head of the Branch. He held the MI5 cipher for communication with Sir Vernon Kell, the MI5 chief in London. He also became the contact point for the Special Investigation Branch at Scotland Yard and its head, Sir Basil Thomson, until he resigned in 1921, when Jones continued to communicate with its new head, the commissioner of the Metropolitan Police into which the Special Investigation Branch was absorbed. The Investigation Branch had a staff of 31 by 1920 with officers in each Australian state.[6]

INTELLIGENCE TARGETS 1919–39

The Russians

The pattern of intelligence-gathering between the wars began with emphasis on the Russian immigrants because of their Bolshevik connections. This was not a new interest for intelligence agencies. The radical Russians had been watched, in Queensland in particular, for some years previously. The majority of Russians came from Vladivostock and with Queensland often the first port of call, 4,000 of the estimated 6,000 who migrated to Australia settled there. Political activists were numerous among this group, one such being Fedor Sergeyev, with the *nom de guerre* of Artem, who arrived in 1911 aged 28, already an activist in the 1905 revolution and a friend of Lenin. He established a modest Russian newspaper, *Echo of Australia*, which was soon closed down for not being a registered paper. The second paper he established, *Izvestiia of the Union of Russian Emigrants*, was suppressed in 1916. After the February 1917 revolution, Sergeyev quickly returned to Russia in July 1917 where, after a rapid rise through the administration, he died in a monorail train accident in 1921.[7]

Another Russian immigrant who attracted considerably more attention of the intelligence authorities was Peter Simonoff, who arrived in Australia in 1912, aged 29. He was fluent in English and worked at various labouring jobs including the ore mines at Broken Hill. By June 1917 he was editing another Russian paper in Brisbane, *Worker's Life*. It was suppressed early in 1918 for refusing to publish solely in English. The Russians wished to have their Consul-General, A.N. D'Abaza, replaced by a Bolshevik officer and sent a representative, A. Loktin, to negotiate with Trotsky who was prepared to appoint the Bolshevik official, Lagutin. Lagutin declined, and Loktin suggested Simonoff who was thereupon appointed by Litvinov, the agent in London for the new government. Simonoff approached the Australian government on 20 February 1918 for recognition. Documents were sent by Litvinoff which the censor seized, but in any event Hughes refused to acknowledge him because he had been connected with the IWW in Broken Hill and Brisbane.[8]

The Australian government chose to exercise little authority over consular and diplomatic affairs, relying passively on decisions made in London by the Secretary of State for Colonies. Decisions about Russian affairs there moved very slowly. When issues intervened about recovering British soldiers and civilians and repayments on loans and investments in Russia, events came to a standstill. Hughes was told by London first, that Simonoff could be regarded as an agent of the Soviet government, and then to watch Simonoff and hold him for possible hostage bargaining.[9]

Finding in September 1918 that he was unable to leave Australia for Vladivostock via Japan, because his ship was calling at Manila and the US Consul refused him a visa, Simonoff engaged in an active writing and public-speaking campaign. His pronouncements on the virtues of the Bolshevik revolution were proclaimed under his new but still unacknowledged consular status. Military Intelligence reported on his utterances, and the government placed an order on him under the War Precautions Act to desist from speaking or risk a $100 fine or six months' jail in default. He chose jail in order to demonstrate the government's abuse of diplomatic privilege. The left-wing and trade unions in Australia rallied to his cause, and he was released in July 1919. By 30 September 1920 the government was reluctantly moving to accept him as Soviet Consul-General, although he was never accorded official recognition.[10] During this time he helped to establish the Communist Party of Australia (CPA). By March 1920 he was publishing a journal, *Soviet Russia*, which the intelligence specialists condemned because it might lead to the 'unthinking people . . . longing for a like Utopia here'. H.E. Jones wanted to see the sub-title of 'Official Organ of the Russian Soviet Government Bureau' removed. Simonoff returned to the Soviet Union on 2 June 1921.

Simonoff did not fade rapidly from the purview of Australian intelligence after his departure and by March 1922 H.E. Jones was advised by a 'reliable source' (often a euphemism for MI5) that he had married a New Zealand girl in Naples and was intending to return to Australia. The port authorities were warned of his intentions, but unfortunately he was to suffer a different fate. His association with Trotsky would have led to his subsequent downfall and it is believed that he was executed in 1938.[11]

Diplomatic relations with the Soviets were not re-established until 1942 and intelligence interests thereafter were confined to watching the relationships between the CPA and Moscow although fluctuating trading relationships were also monitored by intelligence. The attitude of the non-Labor governments was not to follow the British pattern of developing extensive trading arrangements with the Soviets. The MacDonald government in Britain had established a form of diplomatic relationships with the Soviet Union in February 1924 when a *chargé d'affaires* was appointed in Moscow with similar Soviet representation in London.[12] An offer was made by the British government to Australia to become involved in the new Soviet trade treaties, but Australia declined. As was demonstrated over the Simonoff affair, the Australian non-Labor governments felt insecure and uncomfortable in dealing with the revolutionary Soviet state. The conviction prevailed in both the government and intelligence circles that the distant Bolshevik state posed a continuing threat to Australia, if only through the propaganda it might distribute in Australia.

The Arcos raid in May 1927 on the Russian Trade Delegation offices in London by the Special Branch of New Scotland Yard had a small echo in Australia. Some names of Australian communists were discovered as well as a secret cover address for communicating with the Australian party, but these contained few surprises for Jones and his Investigation Branch. Canada reacted by informing the Soviet official Agent in Ottawa that the 1921 Trade Agreement between the two countries was terminated. Of probably greater surprise to intelligence officialdom was the news of the raid by the Chinese (Beijing) government in April 1927 on premises occupied by the Soviet military attaché in Beijing which revealed the nature and amount of support in arms and equipment provided by the Soviet for the Nationalist forces, which included the communists, in Canton. This somewhat partisan report put the value of the aid for the year 1926–27 at 10 million dollars in gold. For both the Prime Minister, S.M. Bruce, and R.G. Casey, his unofficial intelligence officer in London, there was some surprise at the extent of Soviet covert aid.[13]

Full diplomatic relations between Britain and the Soviet Union were resumed with the exchange of ambassadors in December 1929, and after the election of the Scullin government in October 1929 negotiations were instigated through the Foreign Office in London for the Soviets to establish consular representation in Australia. On 14 May 1930, G. Sokolnikoff, on behalf of the

Soviet Union, agreed to exchange consular offices subject to the agreement made between the UK and the Soviets on 20 December 1929 for the Soviets not to distribute propaganda, but nothing seems to have come of it on that occasion.[14]

When the Soviets did become interested in trade with Australia, however, intelligence questions intervened to hinder it. In August 1932 the Soviet Union was seeking to expand its sale of oil through its British marketing subsidiary, Russian Oil Products Company (ROP). A former leader in the IWW, Tom Barker, visited Australia early in 1931 on behalf of the Soviet company, which of itself threw a shadow of suspicion over the enterprise from the viewpoint of the intelligence agencies.[15] A different dimension was added, however, when H.C. Sleigh, a large oil importer, approached John Latham, the Attorney-General, when seeking to replace his US oil imports with Soviet oil. Alarmed at the possibility of the Soviet Union making inroads into Australian economic life, Latham asked the Investigation Branch to review the implications. At the same time a report had been sent to the government by Sir George Macdonough of the Shell Oil Company in Britain urging it to prevent the ROP from being established in Australia.

The Investigation Branch, ever suspicious where it detected evidence of Soviet activity, reported that the ROP tankers and their crews would become the means of introducing and distributing Communist propaganda in Australia and that British intelligence should be asked to report on the dangers ROP had presented in Britain. MI5 was accordingly called upon to report in August 1932 and Sir Vernon Kell returned a brief to Australia painting an alarming picture of menace and subversion in the UK. The ROP had started there in 1923 and imports by 1930 were 8.7 per cent of total imports of crude oil and products, in 1931 they were 12.1 per cent and for the first six months of 1932 were 8.7 per cent. The threat, as MI5 saw it, was that the ROP funded the British Communist Party, it gave employment to party members, it collected intelligence for Soviet intelligence (GPU) and was seen as a 'useful instrument' for mobilizing 'revolutionary disturbances'.

MI5 also obtained reports 'emanating from an especially secret and confidential source' describing the Soviet oil-selling organizations in Sweden and in Germany where they were alleged

8

John Latham, Attorney-General and scourge of the Industrial Workers of the World (IWW) and, later, the Communist Party of Australia. He was political head of the inter-war intelligence organization, the Investigation Branch. He had perceived the effectiveness of using intelligence bodies to harass radical groups while head of the war-time naval intelligence. (Australian Archives)

also to be posing a subversive threat, particularly in Germany, where the organization was established in 1928 and 'where the revolutionary situation, from the Russian point of view, is more developed'. Armed with these alarmist reports Latham put the matter to the Cabinet in December 1932, and that was the last to be heard of the ROP question.[16]

The Communist Party of Australia

The CPA provided the principal target for the intelligence agencies and the Investigation Branch began reporting on it frequently from 1921, soon after it was established. Although such reports accurately reflected the divisions, splits and expulsions that seemed to mark the inter-war CPA, the Branch believed that it was observing the growth of the Australian end of a large international conspiracy. Against this assumption it was not surprising that it greatly overestimated its membership at 2,000 plus 'many hundreds more [who] are Communists save in actual membership'.[17] In fact there were little more than 700 members at this time. The names of the IWW leaders and Russian activists who appeared years previously in intelligence reports cropped up again as forming the nucleus of the new CPA. Curiously, it was these 'old lefties' who were among the first to be expelled or deported in the party's early years, which places in question the optimistic membership figure earlier quoted.

The Branch placed considerable importance on monitoring the radical newspapers and journals to collect information about the Communists. It was a tactic familiar to the investigation officers from their war years. This monitoring, along with reports from informers within the CPA, plus reports from New Scotland Yard and other British intelligence sources, helped to flesh out the periodical reports that Jones prepared for his minister, the Attorney-General, who distributed them to other senior ministers.

When John Latham was appointed Attorney-General late in 1925 the thrust of the Branch to contain the CPA was widened on all fronts. Latham had the Crimes Act amended. He drew on the concepts that were contained in the legislation prepared by Robert Garran, designed to suppress the IWW by having radical bodies simply declared unlawful associations by the Governor-General (acting, of course, on the advice of the government). This had a positive effect on the CPA which, with a membership down to 249 by then, had practically collapsed in all states except New South Wales and Queensland, in that they hid their books and papers at other addresses to avoid incrimination by them.[18] Latham's actions also included the tightening of Customs regulations to prevent radical papers arriving from overseas. By October 1927 the list of 'prohibited importations' included 129 titles and new ones kept being added to them after inspection by Robert Garran, the Solicitor-General, and later his successor, G.S. Knowles.

The Scullin Labor government maintained and extended these bans on imported material and following its defeat, the returning non-Labor government implemented plans in January 1932 to curtail the CPA once and for all. Jones made suggestions to amend again the Crimes Act and with Latham's draftsmanship the Act was expanded in May 1932. It turned round the concept of 'unlawfulness' so that instead of the government having to prove guilt, the Attorney-General was now to have the power by application to Supreme Courts in the States or the High Court to 'call upon any bodies of persons' to show cause why they should not be declared unlawful associations. If they were found to be so their papers, funds and property would be confiscated and those not born in Australia deported. In August 1932 the government implemented this Act by charging F.H. Devanny, publisher of the Communist paper *Worker's Weekly*. The matter came before the full bench of the High Court, but the case was rejected by five to one on the grounds that the charge was insufficient to sustain the allegation of being an unlawful body.

Jones saw this as only a minor setback and optimistically reported in November 1933 that other legal provisions were effectively curtailing the CPA. These included amendments to the Arbitration Court Act to deregister unions which affiliated with Communist bodies; the amendment to the Immigration Act to deport non-Australian-born agitators; the deregistration of Communist papers using the post; the strict control of the foreign language press; the closer supervision of people obtaining passports to travel to Russia; and the closer investigation of people applying for naturalization to exclude the politically undesirable.

11

While a large wall of legalese was being erected to contain and if possible suppress the CPA both the times and the party were changing which combined to make the party more relevant and its suppression no longer appropriate. Fascism was now identified as the far more threatening enemy, and much of the effort to suppress the CPA was reversed. The postal ban, for example, which had been imposed on the Friends of the Soviet Union (FOSU) and their journal, *Soviets Today*, some years previously at the height of the surveillance of the CPA, was abandoned. This ban had been challenged in the High Court by the FOSU and was heard by Justice H.V. Evatt in April 1937. Rather than attempt to defend what now seemed to be an exaggerated charge that the FOSU was intending to 'overthrow the state', the government withdrew the case, and *Soviets Today* again passed through the post. By November 1938 the CPA was leading a protest movement against the Nazi atrocities imposed on Jews in Germany, and Ralf Gibson appealed to Prime Minister Lyons on behalf of the party in Melbourne, and Lance Sharkey on behalf of the party in Sydney, to make strong protest to Hitler and boycott German trade until the atrocities ceased.[19] Lyons did neither, but the event did show that a new foe was facing Australia. The overt suppression of the CPA lessened and the covert monitoring of it by the army and the Investigation Branch increased.

Private Right-Wing Armies

In contrast to the wide-sweeping surveillance maintained on the CPA and the Soviet connection, the intelligence agencies seemed to monitor the activities of those phenomena of the Depression years, the private right-wing armies, very much at a distance. The rationale behind the formation of these armies was a disenchantment with the democratic and parliamentary processes that brought about the election of Labor governments at the State and Commonwealth level. The middle class and former army officers, who led these private armies, were convinced that the economic crisis that was sharpening the class divisions and breeding enmity, hatred and jealousy would bring to fulfilment all that the CPA preached – the seizure of the state by the proletariat. The election of Labor governments was the harbinger, they believed, of this eventual outcome.

Inspector R.S. Browne of the Melbourne office of the Branch first raised the matter with Jones on 24 January 1931 in an indirect fashion. Instead of using the correct title, the League of National Security, he adopted the non-specific euphemism in reporting that a 'law and order movement' consisting of 7,000 to 8,000 and led by a senior military officer had been established in Melbourne. Jones replied with a slight note of panic that 'we cannot directly or indirectly be associated with any movement of this description unless instructed by our Minister'.[20] Ironically, however, it was the attention the CPA began paying to these armies that compelled the Branch to abandon its disinterested policy. The Branch discovered an instruction emanating from the CPA office in Sydney to Brisbane indicating 'that a move is on foot in Australia to form local Fascist organizations by name of Citizens League. These organizations are direct branches from Mussolini and are preparing to attack the workers, just as has been done in Italy'.[21]

By means of highly secret communications obtained from his state offices, Jones read reports of one private army in Brisbane and two in Adelaide, the Citizen League of 1,300 men and a former special constabulary group of 1,000 to 5,000 men. The New Guard was very prominent in Sydney and was planning to seize the principal governing centres in order to topple the Lang Labor government. The monitoring of this private army was mainly in the hands of the State police force, which raided the Guard's headquarters on 7 and 10 May 1931 and took away many documents, which they were compelled to return after Lang was ousted by a non-Labor government.[22]

Another and more secret private army in Sydney was the Old Guard of 30,000 men led by the principal business managers and investors in Sydney. On this army the Branch collected little information, in spite of the US Consul-General and the trade representative of the British government in Sydney each sending reports to their respective governments. Why was Jones so reluctant to compile intelligence on these subversive bodies? It could be that he believed them to be kindred spirits – together pursuing, with a view to suppressing, the dreaded Communists.[23] It could be that Jones was anticipating the successful seizure of power by the radical right in Australia, similar to what had occurred overseas, and wished to avoid

13

the potential embarrassment of possessing official dossiers on people who could become his new masters.

This disinclination to collect and distribute intelligence on right-wing armies was matched in the early 1930s by a similar disinclination to watch the activities of the Italian Fascists, and later the German Nazis. Not until war was imminent did these attitudes in intelligence circles change. The Italian Fascist movement was promoted from the early 1920s by the Italian Consul-General in Sydney and his consular offices in other cities, as part of Italian government policy. Once members were enrolled, their details were sent to Rome for registration and they were given the party-card bearing the Fascist oath. Anti-Fascist groups were likewise formed, but on a far less grand scale, but these were monitored closely by the intelligence agencies. These groups were composed of people who had escaped from Italy in the early days of Fascism or left-wing Italian immigrants who naturally drifted into the ranks of anti-Fascism. They were predominantly men of little education with no finances and few organizational skills.[24]

Italian and German Groups

It was not easy for the anti-Fascists to mobilize support. Their first paper, *Il Risveglio* (The Awakening), established by Frank Carmagnola in Sydney in 1926 was closed by the police for not being a 'registered newspaper'. Its successor, *La Ricossa* (Liberation), and a second paper, *L'Avanguardia Libertaria* (Anarchist Vanguard), obtained permission to print, but this was withdrawn in November 1932 by the Australian government.[25] These anti-Fascist activists came under attack from the Italian consular offices and its intelligence arm OVRA and from the Investigation Branch. Sometimes they faced a combined attack. The several Consuls-General serving in Australia, aware of the various restrictions on radicals and their papers, provided information to the Branch about the anti-Fascists and their publications and sometimes provided copies of the papers and their own translations to assist the Branch's investigations.

The anti-Fascists were forced to rely to an increasing extent on assistance from the CPA, as the consular offices successfully expanded their influence among the Italian immigrants. One of its intellectuals, Ralf Gibson, spoke Italian and acted as a liaison officer to assist with printing and other tasks.[26] This damned the anti-Fascists even more in the judgement of intelligence agencies. Applications for naturalization from Italians who were associated with the Directory of the Fascist Movement received preference from the Investigation Branch in being given a clearance. For the active anti-Fascist, Omero Schiassi, an Italian intellectual and not a member of any Communist party, it took two years and representations from ministers of the Scullin Labor government to obtain his naturalization clearance.

It was a point of unhappy irony that, whereas before the war the intelligence services were able clearly to differentiate the anti-Fascist from the Fascist Italians, during the war when Italians were interned this differentiation was no longer made and the two warring groups were placed in the same internment camps. At the Loveday camp in South Australia this led to F. Fantin being attacked by a Fascist inmate and killed.[27]

The German Nazi movement in Australia was similarly sponsored by the German government. Its paper, *Die Brucke* (The Bridge), was financed largely from Berlin and its membership consisted mostly of German nationals, especially businessmen, who had commercial ties with Germany. Colonel Eric Campbell, a leader of the private army the New Guard, was treated as an honorary member being invited to Nazi functions. The Nazi organizations began in Australia in 1934, centred on Dr J.H. Becker, an agent of the Gestapo and the *Landeskreisleiter* (a party agent) who had arrived in Tanunda in South Australia in 1927. After a visit to Germany in 1934 he became so fanatical in his anti-Semitism and anti-Communism that the leadership was transferred out of his control to the Consul-General's office in Sydney.[28] Much of what we know about the early Nazi Party activities in Australia was reconstructed from records in Germany after the war was nearly concluded, and it is not entirely clear when the intelligence organizations started surveillance on the Nazis. Some reports on the Concordia Club (a club for German businessmen) in Sydney date from 1936. By December 1937 Jones was pressing for his Branch to be the principal compiler of intelligence on the Auslands Organization of the NSDAP because the army and naval intelligence organizations were at loggerheads. Even so, Paul Beckman, the *Stützpuktleiter* (District

15

Stronghold leader) of the local Nazi party was found to be an honorary member of the Staff Corps Officers' Mess at Keswick Barracks in Adelaide in 1939. He discreetly resigned soon after this was discovered, indicating that intelligence-collecting about the Nazis had its deficiencies.

There were no anti-Nazi groups similar to the anti-Fascist Italian groups; that role was assumed more by the CPA particularly through its Movement Against War and Fascism. Its New Theatre Group in Sydney staged an anti-Nazi play, *Till the Day I Die*, to which the German Consul-General, Dr Asmis, strongly objected in July 1936. It was probably more the disenchantment of non-Labor with the anti-Nazi stance of the CPA than its actual support of the Nazi cause that led the non-Labor NSW Premier, B. Stevens, to have the play banned. The Prime Minister notified other State Premiers of this ban, thereby indicating his total support for the measure, but again it could probably be assumed that Lyons did this because he disliked the Communists more than he supported the Nazis.[29]

CIVILIAN INTELLIGENCE DURING THE SECOND WORLD WAR

At the outbreak of war in September 1939 the army immediately established postal censorship under its Military Intelligence corps, re-appointing some of the army officers who had been censors during the Great War. The army also rounded up the enemy aliens, interning over one thousand, and obliged several more thousands of them to report to the police or the army.[30]

On the political surveillance side, events were less well-planned. The Investigation Branch was on the verge of being swallowed by Military Intelligence in a pre-war intelligence planning proposal. But R.G. Menzies, then both Prime Minister and Minister of Defence Co-ordination, was more deeply concerned about the Communist Party and its affiliates at that time, and called a conference of all intelligence sections (police, military and the Investigation Branch) to discuss the problem of controlling it. Little emerged from the meeting and the military services thereafter proposed a defence security organization. Menzies mooted a Ministry of Internal Security, and W.M. Hughes, again the Attorney-General, proposed

16

a Local Security Officers' Force, but the outcome was the establishment on 31 March 1941 of the Security Service operationally under the army, but functionally under the control of the Attorney-General's Department. Jones remained in charge of the Branch and his former subordinate, E.E. Longfield Lloyd, became head of a new service. Thus was solved for the immediate future the question of who, other then the military services, would control the civilian population during the war.

Once the enemy aliens were rounded up and interned, the intelligence agencies had little to do other than watch internal dissenters – that is, the CPA. The army feared that the war between Finland and the Soviet Union could lead to a war between Britain and the Soviet Union in which the local Communists would support the Russian side. The CPA made a virtue out of the German–Soviet non-aggression pact by issuing thousands of pamphlets arguing that had Britain and France made a genuine effort to join with the Soviet Union in confronting Hitler earlier, instead of attempting to establish proposals 'they would wriggle out of', the war would never have happened.[31]

The CPA was aware that it was on the verge of suppression and on 21 March 1940 it advised its members on how to continue operating when it went underground. The banning of their papers was gazetted on 24 May and on 27 May the Cabinet agreed to suppress the party. The Subversive Associations Regulations were promulgated on 15 June (they were similar to the legislation banning the IWW in 1916 and 1917) and the police forces moved in to seize all property, printing presses and then raided members' homes to collect any leftist literature.

In Western Australia, Detective Sergeant Richards led the Special Branch in arresting four party members who were subsequently jailed. They applied to Prime Minister Menzies to be treated as political prisoners, but they were informed that the classification did not exist. Suppressing an active political party is never simple, and fraternal groups of the CPA such as the Friends of the Soviet Union (not banned although its paper, *Soviets Today*, was) continued with a new vigour. In November 1940 it attracted a crowd of 700 people to an open-air meeting in Sydney. After Germany invaded the Soviet Union in June 1941 the FOSU agitated to have the ban on the party lifted, and after the Labor government took office in October 1941 its senior minister, Dr Evatt, removed the suppression order in December 1942.[32]

Intelligence-gathering, as in the First World War, was rapidly becoming an overcrowded field. Longfield Lloyd was eager to carve out a niche for his Security Service. He functioned mainly under the aegis of the army who provided most of his staff and shared reports from army sources of information in London, Ottawa, Singapore, Pretoria, Cairo, Shanghai, Hong Kong and Delhi. The army also gave him access to their reports on the Japanese situation and other foreign reports from Washington, the Dutch East Indies and British Intelligence in Singapore. When he asked for material from the army's jealously guarded postal censorship he was rebuffed. Postal censorship was at the heart of the army's monitoring of wartime Australia. It is not known how much the government was given access to this material and certainly what the army would have regarded as Longfield Lloyd's superfluous organization would have had little chance of sharing its secrets. The army's postal censor was not only opening Communists' and other radicals' mail but was dipping into the general mail to read and report upon the private thoughts of the average Australian about the war.

The army's dominance of intelligence-gathering was becoming resented by others in the field. The navy and the air force refused to be associated with the Security Service and its domination by the army, preferring to establish their own civilian intelligence-gathering groups. H.E. Jones and the Investigation Branch were also displeased at the army's attempt to take over the Australian pipeline to MI5 by gaining possession of the all-important MI5 telegraph cipher. W.M. Hughes, as well as the Minister for the Army, P. Spender, tried to resolve this army dominance by having an inquiry conducted into the Security Service and army intelligence. Cabinet selected for that purpose a visiting MI5 officer on an SOE training operation in Australia, Lieutenant-Colonel J.C. Mawhood. There was a fierce reaction against these events by the army who tapped Mawhood's telephone and sent a signal to the British Army demanding his recall. In spite of going over the government's head, the army won the day and the government replaced Mawhood with A.M. Duncan, Chief Commissioner of Police in Victoria, to conduct the inquiry.[33]

Duncan's report was of little relevance for settling the problem because he recommended that the police forces assume more of the intelligence security work, but by then the new Labor government had taken office. It decided on 9 March 1942 to raise the status of the Security Service by making its head a Director-General and appointing to it W.J. MacKay, the NSW Police Commissioner. MacKay's first initiative was to collect together in Canberra all the intelligence files. But this again aroused the resistance of the army which did not wish to share its collection of dossiers with any department. MacKay had in mind making the Service the Australian version of the FBI and (giving events a modern-day currency) making a security check of ministerial staff, but his term of appointment concluded before he could initiate these proposals. He was replaced by W.B. Simpson on 23 September 1942. By then the service had become more independent of the army. It had been given a new executive branch and had offices in all states and was engaged in enforcing the Regulations of the National Security Act relating to security affairs. It vetted employees in defence industries and looked to widen its scope of intelligence-collecting in such areas as foreign affairs analysis or security analysis in the development of post-war relationships.

Although the CPA by then was no longer banned, much of the Service's dossier collection related to Communists, their newspapers, now printed on new presses and in larger numbers because of their greater popularity, and their connections with other groups such as the Italian and Greek anti-Fascist bodies. The army too was watching the many Communists who were enrolled within its own ranks. By early 1945 it was estimated that there were 6,000 Communists in the army. Besides fighting the war, they were engaged in holding discussions about Australian social, political and economic questions as well as recruiting new members. They distributed CPA publications sent from Australia (Professor Bland alleged that some of this was included in Soldiers' Comforts Fund parcels) and saw themselves as offering a far more meaty intellectual diet about the important questions of war and society than the soldiers' other source of information, the Army Education Corps and its bland publications. The CPA also engaged in a campaign guaranteed to win more soldiers' hearts and minds, if only through their pay books, by demanding that a battle bonus of $1.20 per day be paid to all fighting in the front line. The CPA was also collecting funds from soldiers for transmission to Australia, and it was noted that the ninth division donated $100 to the CPA before it fought the battle at Tarakan.[34]

Like the CPA, the world of civilian intelligence by this stage was also looking towards and planning for a post-war era. By 23 October 1945 Simpson had resigned from the Service, to become a judge, Jones had retired from the Investigation Branch to be succeeded by Longfield Lloyd in December 1943 and the Pinner Committee, acting on a brief to wind down wartime departments, recommended that the Service and the Branch be combined to be known as the Commonwealth Investigation Service. The Security Service during its heyday had provided relatively safe wartime billets for 679 people (of whom 374 were military personnel), who collectively compiled nearly 200,000 files many of which found their way into the Investigation Service and later into ASIO's high technology data-base. Thanks to Australia's intelligence-gathering in two world wars, ASIO was to begin administrative life with extensive dossier-collecting, stretching from the IWW and anti-conscriptionists of the First World War to the Communists and the anti-Fascists of the Second.

NOTES

1. AA, CRS A3932, file SC298; NLA 696/1337, 1531.
2. Frank Cain, 'Opposition to the Great War in NSW: The Case of the Industrial Workers of the World', *Journal of the Royal Historical Society*, Vol. 74, Part 3 (Dec. 1988), pp. 201–12.
3. Frank Cain, 'The Industrial Workers of the World: Aspects of its Suppression in Australia 1916–1919', *Labour History*, No. 42 (May 1982), pp. 54–62.
4. AA, MP1048/1, file 16/014.
5. AA, CRS A3932, file SC298.
6. AA, CRS A3932, file SC294.
7. Tom Poole and Eric Fried, 'Artem: A Bolshevik in Brisbane', *Australian Journal of Politics and History*, Vol. 31, No. 2 (1985), pp. 243–5; ADB (Eric Fried), Fedor Sergeyev.
8. AA, CRS98/1, Item 240.

9. AA, CRS A456/1 Item W 26/241/84.
10. AA, CRS A98/1, Item 60.
11. ADB, (Eric Fried) Peter Simonoff.
12. AA, CRS A98/1, Item 60.
13. AA, CRS A98/1, Item 138, Pt. 1.
14. AA, CRS A98/1, Item 42.
15. AA, CRS A6126 XM, Item 70.
16. AA, CRS A458/1, Item K500/22.
17. AA, 3932, Item SC292.
18. AA, Special file No. 42, bundle 84, Item 6.
19. AA, CRS A461, Item R420/1.
20. AA, CRS A369, Item 585.
21. See Michael Cathcart, *Defending the National Tuckshop: Australia's Secret Army Intrigue of 1931* (Melbourne, 1988).
22. AONSW, 10/1829, file S11718/554.
23. AONSW, 10/1829, file 531/11757.
24. Gianfranco Cresciani, *Fascism, Anti-Fascism and Italians in Australia 1922–1945* (Canberra, 1980), pp. 97–112.
25. AA, MP707/1, Item V6864.
26. Cresciani, op. cit. p. 129.
27. AA, CRS A373, file 3744.
28. AA, AP20419, Item 14/1.
29. AA, CRS A467, Item 62.
30. AA, MP729/6, Item 729/6, 10/401/36.
31. AA, CRS A467, bundle 93, file 19.
32. AA, MP729/6, Item 29/401/407; CRS A472, Item W2425.
33. AA, A1608, Item SCG39/2; CRS A1196, Item 36/501/105; CRS A2671, item 238/1941.
34. AA, CRS A6122, Item 222.

2

The Background to Establishing ASIO

Intelligence agencies in their enlarged and post-war forms are located on foundations in several areas of government administration. These include defence, foreign affairs, immigration, continuing defence intelligence arrangements and politics – particularly radical and Communist politics. This chapter discusses how those administrative elements, sometimes independently and sometimes collectively, contributed to the establishment of ASIO.

INTELLIGENCE ACTIVITIES IN POST-WAR AUSTRALIA

The combined Security Service and Investigation Branch was formally established on 17 November 1945 with the title Commonwealth Investigation Service (CIS), within the Attorney-General's Department. The military Deputy Directors were demobilized and the chief officers of the Investigation Branch became Deputy Directors of the new service.[1] The former Commonwealth Police, now known as the Peace Officer Guard, came under the control of the service and its Director-General, Longfield Lloyd, and these together with the Special Branches of the State police forces resumed their intelligence-gathering operations against what were considered the radical threats. These threats assumed much the same dimensions as they had in the pre-war years, with the exception that the trade unions had become more militant and the CPA (now named the Australian Communist Party, but for consistency will continue to be referred to as the CPA) larger in membership and finances.

Another significant intelligence development was the continuation of the wartime Sigint operations to monitor radio traffic in

22

the Australian environment. Such operations dated back to April 1942 when the Central Bureau was established to monitor radio traffic from stations in Queensland, Victoria and the Northern Territory. Although these were all manned by military staff, three of them were controlled by the Security Service. After the war this organization was known as the Defence Signals Division, and in 1977 it became a Directorate.[2] In November 1947 the Chifley government ratified the UKUSA Agreement, also known as the UK-USA Security Agreement or 'Secret Treaty', which was a compact to record and exchange radio traffic collected by the USA, identified as the First Party in this covenant, and the UK, Canada, Australia and New Zealand, collectively identified as the Second Party. This Agreement divided the world into zones in which the various countries were to collect radio traffic and it also determined security criteria by which this information was to be exchanged and by which staff would be employed in such work.[3] The success of this highly secret compact, which continues to function to this day, has led to co-operation on intelligence collection and sharing in other areas, which will be discussed in other chapters.

These Sigint operations were directed at ensuring the security of Australia's defence and diplomatic transmissions. But more importantly they were established to collect radio traffic emanating from foreign embassies in Canberra and from countries in the Asian region as well as from other countries whose radio traffic by normal patterns of radio-wave distortions can be readily collected in Australia. As during the war, when Sigint became highly developed, secrecy and personal security clearances for people engaged in such work were essential, and the CIS added these duties to its post-war activities. ASIO was to conduct the vetting for these Sigint operations when it became established. ASIO was not directly established because of this secret Sigint operation in Australia. But the fact of its establishment led those in high office to the ready perception of establishing a civilian intelligence agency that was to become ASIO.

COMMUNISM RE-EMERGENT

The re-emergence of the Communist Party in Australia significantly contributed to the establishment of ASIO. Its party membership declined after the war, but it remained very active in theatrical, cultural, art, youth and women's affairs. It also became a leading force in the peace movement formed in response to the Cold War.[4] It was even more active in union affairs and led the opposition to the Labor government's refusal to improve wages and working conditions forgone by the workers during the war. The government sought to dampen the economy and tightly control labour costs. The Labor government turned on the CPA, imprisoning some of its more active union leaders.[5] The press and public media became hysterical over what they portrayed as CPA-driven union militancy, and, encouraged by the government's strategy of suppressing those challenging its economic policies, cast the CPA as the nation's enemy. The actions of the USSR and the success of the Chinese Revolution set a supportive tone for the establishment of a large and secret monitoring intelligence agency, as ASIO became.

IMMIGRATION AND INTELLIGENCE AGENCIES

Immigration has been a growth area for intelligence agencies in Australia. Immigrants have to be checked before entry and their sponsors too. When they seek naturalization they have to be vetted again. The dossier numbers generated in such procedures have become enormous. The CIS had done much of this vetting after the war until ASIO took it over to occupy the time of its otherwise idle agents.

However, the involvement of intelligence in immigration affairs received a considerable boost when immigrants arrived in Australia from Communist-governed countries or when established migrants began identifying with their Communist homeland. In the case of Communist-governed Yugoslavia it was found that agents of the Yugoslavian security service, Bureau of People's Protection (OZNA), were reported to be watching these activists in Australia because of their connection with a terrorist campaign in 1947 to attack Yugoslavia from Austria. The CIS rather than monitor the terrorists began monitoring OZNA.[6] Greece was occupied in a civil war in these years where the Communist-backed guerrillas who had fought against the German invaders were opposing an Athens-based regime being imposed on Greece by Britain aided later by the US. Greek immigrant groups were therefore monitored for signs of Greek Communist Party influence.[7] The Polish groups in Australia divided into those supporting the former and now powerless Polish government and those supporting the new Communist government.[8] Macedonians, Bulgarians, Hungarians and of course Russian immigrant groups were all monitored by the Service and their various newspapers, now allowed to be published more freely in their own language, collected, translated and filed away in CIS dossiers.

Another and far less savoury side of the intelligence/immigration link has been revealed in Mark Aarons' book, *Sanctuary: Nazi Fugitives in Australia*.[9] This shows how many Nazi quislings responsible for the killing of their fellow nationals under the Nazi occupation managed to be assisted to migrate to Australia. Their names were usually in lists of wanted war criminals and their selection and entry may have been undertaken with the connivance of the CIS officers. These officers were stationed in Europe and were supposed to monitor the selection of migrants in order to exclude these ex-Nazis. There was little excuse for them to claim that they were ignorant of the background of these war criminals because private groups monitoring Nazi immigrants to Australia reported their presence in Australia to the government. It should be acknowledged, of course, that several Ministers for Immigration refused to act on these issues when brought to their attention. The East European governments had also documented the cases against these Nazi collaborators and provided copies of these to British and US governments. The Western Allies released these offenders from the camps, often in response to representations from the Vatican or because they could be used as intelligence agents after being infiltrated back into what were now Communist countries. In the cursory examination they did conduct on these offenders, both the CIS and ASIO agents made no mention of their war criminal backgrounds documenting instead the protestations of their anti-Communist beliefs and commending them for holding such attitudes.[10]

In the atmosphere created by the Cold War tensions, the intelligence agencies easily tolerated a blurring of important moral issues. The guilt of having murdered many of their fellow nationals while working for the Nazi occupation regime in their home countries was regarded as unimportant by the officers of the Australian intelligence agencies. The immunity of these war criminals seemed to be strengthened, in the judgements of the intelligence agencies, by their becoming leaders of migrant groups that adopted strong anti-Communist postures.

THE RUSSIAN CONNECTION

While the Soviet Union and its embassies in the West were to become the main focus for intelligence agencies in post-war years, the tradition of maintaining an intelligence watch on all things Soviet had become a well established practice in Australia. The establishment of a Soviet embassy in Canberra in 1943, however, did appear to be a further justification for establishing a larger intelligence agency such as ASIO was to become. It was the CPA link to the Soviet Union which had become a preoccupation of the CIS before the war. It was to interdict the assumed flow of money and literature from Moscow that passports were made difficult to obtain for CPA members, and baggage was searched for literature or money on their return. Literature was always found and seized, but no money was found. Foreign seamen were regarded as a clandestine means of avoiding this intelligence surveillance, and the actions of Latham in barring oil trade with the Soviet because of such fears has been discussed in Chapter 1. The establishment of the Soviet ministry in Canberra in 1943 led to a reorienting of intelligence assumptions. Intelligence authorities now viewed the Soviet ministry or embassy as the new source from which the CPA could obtain its money and literature. The CPA courier with his suitcase ceased to be the attraction for the intelligence authorities.

Discussions leading to the establishment of diplomatic relationships and the exchange of ambassadors was initiated by Dr Evatt, Australia's Foreign Minister, on 26 May 1942 when meeting Molotov in London.[11] With Australia facing the the threat of Japanese invasion, the establishment of closer relations with the USSR was a sensible and practical move. The Soviet Union also looked to Australia for raw materials and by September 1942 Australian lead, wool and sheepskins were being shipped in Soviet vessels via the Persian Gulf.[12] On 5 November Dr Evatt announced the composition of the Australian legation to Moscow and on 3 March 1943 the Soviet chief minister arrived in Australia with his staff.[13] Whereas the Australian staff totalled eight, the Soviet staff amounted to approximately 34, because they included cooks, drivers, book-keepers, clerks and doorkeepers, positions which the Australian ministry would have filled locally.[14]

The UK Ministry of Information was interested in knowing the personal details of all Russians in the legation. Certainly British intelligence had been keeping watch on Soviet delegations in the UK, as the pre-war raid on Arcos, the Soviet trade office in London, has shown. The British now sought in a letter of 21 June 1944 all details of these embassy officials, including the name, rank, age and positions held in the Soviet Union in both diplomatic and other life.[15] The External Affairs Department estimated the ages of the staff and on approaching the legation for the career information was told that it was never provided, except in the case of the ambassador. The Soviets were not about to help the British identify who their intelligence operatives were, if that was the purpose of collecting the information.

The legation occupied premises at Griffith House in Canberra Avenue and the Minister, in a nice point of irony that escaped most observers at the time, leased the house formerly occupied by H.E. Jones, the scourge of the Bolsheviks and Communists in pre-war years. Aerials were installed at the legation for use with AWA radio receivers provided by the Australian government at the request of the Russians in order that they might remain informed about events in the Soviet Union by short-wave radio news bulletins. The question of whether or when the legation installed a radio transmitter for communication with the Soviet Union cannot be answered positively. Because it is such an important question, directly related to the Venona decrypts and the Petrov affair, it will be analysed further in the next chapter. The legations in both countries were raised to embassies on 22 May 1948 after discussions between Dr Evatt and Molotov.

The opening of the embassy gave a great boost to the numbers of staff employed in local intelligence work. It became another of the unstated reasons for establishing ASIO. It was perceived as the terminating point of a long supply line from Moscow to enlarge the finances and propaganda power of the CPA. No longer would Australian intelligence sources have to wait on baggage searches at Customs clearing points to discover the latest directions from Moscow. Here in the leafy suburb of Griffith the long arm of international Communism could be observed in action. The enlarged numbers of intelligence operatives, armed with binoculars, became engaged in observing the functioning of this process from the upper-storey windows of Tobin's Funeral Parlours directly opposite the main gates of the Soviet embassy or from the upper-floor rooms of the Kingston Hotel opposite the visitors' entrance. Attempts were made to persuade the Soviet diplomats to defect (which succeeded with Petrov in 1954), their telephone calls were intercepted, they were followed when travelling outside Canberra, and, as we see from the Combe–Ivanov affair in 1983, their private residences were electronically bugged and recordings of conversations were thereby collected.

FOREIGN POLICY AND INTELLIGENCE

The connection between Australia's foreign policy and the establishment of ASIO may not appear to be very obvious on first inspection. Australia's foreign policy in the years of Dr Evatt and his departmental secretary, Dr Burton, however, was by the contemporary standards of London and Washington very controversial. Dr Evatt's policy quickly aroused the hostility of the British and the Americans, and he and Dr Burton became objects of suspicion in those centres. In hindsight their foreign policies can be seen to be rational and appropriate, but they were totally unwelcome. The establishment of ASIO and its incorporation into the Western intelligence community was offered as one means of demonstrating Australia's loyalty to the West.

Evatt was suspicious collectively of the three great powers, the UK, US and USSR. He criticized their tactics of arranging the structure of the new world behind closed doors and insisted that the smaller powers, who in some cases had contributed more on a proportional basis to fighting the war, should also be consulted about the settlement of post-war affairs. His firm commitment to the role of the United Nations sprang from his belief in the concept of liberal internationalism as much as it did from his conviction about the necessity for smaller countries to be heard in the world's council.[16]

Evatt kept reminding his critics that what was seen as the Soviet Union moving its boundaries westwards was the direct result of the wartime agreement between Marshal Stalin, President Roosevelt and Mr Churchill. Evatt ascribed the Soviets' apparent lack of co-operation and compromise to Russia's disenchantment with the behaviour of the Western Allies before the war in refusing to join together to contain Germany. The Soviet Union's attempt to build an alliance both inside and outside the League of Nations against militarized Germany and Italy was met with rebuffs from Britain and France, who adopted the foolhardy policy of appeasement. Nevertheless, the question had to be faced by Evatt of whether the Soviets intended aggression and to this he gave the following reply:

> Having no clear evidence to the contrary and having during the last four years come to know some of Russia's greatest statesmen, I take the view that the Soviet Union's policy is directed towards self-protection and security against future attack. In my opinion its desire is to develop its own economy and to improve the welfare of its peoples. That is my view; perhaps it is wrong. One must arrive at some conclusion in these matters or it is impossible to move ahead with any policy. That is the opinion on which I act.[17]

The External Affairs Department was also aware that the mood in the US administration had changed from one of some tolerance towards the Soviet Union, as represented by Henry A. Wallace, one-time Secretary of Commerce, to one of firm opposition to all things Soviet. External Affairs noted in September 1947 that anyone speaking in support of the Soviets would be 'branded a "fellow traveller", and if in any position of responsibility, investigated by the Committee on Un-American activities'. The Department noted that:

> The whole country is in the grips of an extremely dangerous and mounting Russophobia, not unlike in its nature the Red hysteria of the early 1920's. It manifests itself both in the present Administration's policy of containing Russia from

further expansion and at home by the present loyalty check of civil servants which is being carried out by the F.B.I. and by the Civil Service Commission.[18]

The appointment of George Kennan to be adviser to the Secretary of State on questions of long-term policy was noted by the External Affairs Department to be of significance. Kennan had not only served in Moscow, and had become a Russian expert, the Department noted, but he was also a confirmed pessimist about Russia's intentions and was undoubtedly behind the new drive in American foreign policy. The Department was also aware that the US was gravely concerned at the economic plight of France and Italy in particular, and the effects this had on attracting electoral and popular strength to their respective Communist Parties. The External Affairs Department judged that the administration was dramatizing the conflict behind the debates in the Security Council and elsewhere in order to impress Congress to support the proposals under the Marshall Plan, which was not so much an economic plan to restore prosperity as a political plan to win support away from the Communists. The Department quoted the statement by Averell Harriman, Secretary of Commerce, to illustrate this point: 'Famine conditions breed political chaos on which dictatorships have always thrived. We all know that the forces of Communism plan to seize power at the moment of chaos – and retain power permanently with the establishment of the police state'.[19]

As the world began to divide into the two hostile camps of East and West with the hardening of the Cold War postures, there was little tolerance in London or Washington for independence and objectivity in a minor country like Australia. Security and intelligence concerns come to the forefront of inter-governmental relationships and while Australia tried to maintain its independent foreign policy stance, the establishment of ASIO was one of the prices it had to pay.

POST-WAR REARMAMENT

Through a series of inter-related events Australia, the UK and the US, instead of totally disarming at the conclusion of the war, actually began to rearm. In Australia's case the government had decided to establish a permanent armed force, which, together with a more active regional foreign policy, would allow Australia to exert a greater influence in the South West Pacific. Australia was determined not to be caught unarmed and uninformed as it had been before the war. The rearmament programme of the US and the UK involved Australia in a complicated process, to be explained in the remainder of this chapter. These events also led directly to the establishment of ASIO.

Britain also re-thought its defence posture in the light of the war and the preceding years. The balance of power had swung greatly in Britain's favour leaving it as the single strong power in Europe facing a still standing, but badly damaged Soviet Union. British post-war defence and foreign policy thinking envisaged a powerful Britain dominating a new European alliance against possible Soviet expansionism, in which the US was to be firmly involved and also to which the members of the British Commonwealth would be loosely allied. Australia, for example, was again to guard the Middle East and hold the Southern Mediterranean and the Suez Canal against possible Soviet attack.

The US planners in defence and foreign affairs likewise looked to holding on to a large permanent defence force to dominate the Americas and avoid a recurrence of the late 1930s when the US military found itself in a parlous state. At the presidential level there was also support for the British plan to construct a Western Alliance of the European nations against a re-emergent Soviet. The US Air Force had been established as a third arm and the Defense Department was being reorganized. The post-war years were marked by a turning away from Roosevelt's New Deal philosophies towards nativism, fear of radicalism and dislike of foreign entanglements, particularly with the British. It was a mood favouring rearming for the Cold War and the rapid expansion of intelligence and security agencies of a size and sophistication never seen before.[20]

At the head of the British rearmament programme was the development of the two most effective weapons to evolve from the war – the atomic bomb and the guided missile. A combination of these two weapons, that is a nuclear armed missile, was then considered to be the ultimate and unbeatable weapon. The British were barred by Act of Congress from sharing in the secrets of atomic bomb production to which they had contributed during the war. The British government decided to produce its own atomic bomb, and when it sought to explode it on the Nevada testing site in the US it again faced obstructions which led it to test-fire the bomb on the Monte Bello Islands in Western Australia.[21]

The other high-technology weapon that Britain sought to develop was the liquid-fuelled missile that the Germans had displayed such prowess in producing. Appreciating the vast significance of this weapon in future wars, Britain and the US competed with each other during the invasion of Germany to be the first to reach the missile manufacturing sites and seize the laboratories and scientists responsible for this wonder weapon. The Americans won the race to the Hartz mountains, the centre of production, and carried away 100 V-2 missiles together with the scientists and testing equipment. These were re-established at the White Sands testing range in New Mexico, and thereafter the US rushed ahead with missile production to make it the world's leader within five years.[22]

In November 1948, President Truman authorized the expenditure of US$16,200,000 for the development of an air-to-air missile for the US Air Force. Several large US corporations were funded for research and production of these weapons. It was against this large US government-funded programme, which could call on the extensive military-industrial complex, that the UK government was competing in an effort to develop its own guided missile weapon.[23]

AUSTRALIA AND MISSILE RESEARCH

The UK Department of Supply had been conducting rocket research and development during the war and after collecting what was left of the V-2 rockets, scientists and equipment not seized by the US, it undertook missile design and development work at the Royal Aircraft Establishment (RAE). The testing of the early rockets and missiles had been conducted at a former artillery range at Aberporth, Wales, where firings were conducted out to sea.[24]

This arrangement was clearly impractical because the missile-firing experiments had to be photographed with cine-cameras to help detect the effects of any malfunction. A large testing site in a dry temperate climate which could provide a very long range for firing, security from detection by the Soviet and safety from damage to civilians was required. Lieutenant-General J.F. Evetts, Senior Military Adviser to the UK Minister of Supply, was sent to Australia in May 1946 to select such a site. In conjunction with the Australian government, a site was agreed upon in South Australia, which was to become the Woomera rocket range, and a former munitions factory at Salisbury, 30 kilometres north of Adelaide, was selected to become the laboratories and workshops for missile development.[25]

The Australian government was keen to be involved in this arrangement. It gave Australia access to new technology, it would provide substantial employment opportunities for skilled and semi-skilled people and, because the agreement also provided for the sharing of information between the two governments, it gave the potentiality for the Australian government to develop its own missile industry should this be required in a future war. The experience in the previous war, where Australia had the manpower but not the advanced weaponry because it could not be provided from overseas sources, was not one the government wished to see repeated.

In order to ensure the maximum use of Australian skills, the Agreement provided that the British government would recruit and train Australians for the Project and would employ UK specialists as required. On the assumption that the spin-offs from this development would be of considerable benefit, the government supported the cost of the scheme in Australia, which was estimated at $51 million for the five years from July 1947 to June 1955.[26]

US military officers visited Woomera and Salisbury and reported favourably on developments recommending that the US defence authorities consider using the testing range. The US Defense Department did study the question in December 1947 but rejected the proposal. US obsession about not allowing their technical secrets to be revealed, even to a former ally, would have been an important consideration. The reasons they gave, however, were that they would have difficulty recruiting qualified civilian technical personnel prepared to live in Australia. Another was that the test site in Australia would be too far from the centres, where the data would be analysed in the US, for the existing communication facilities to handle.[27]

The US began developing its own long-range testing site at this time. When the Australian government learned this it was concerned that the British might use that site and the Australian expenditure would be wasted. The US Joint Chiefs of Staff had decided on a testing range which involved firing out to sea from Banana River in Florida over the Bahamian Islands. This involved agreement with the British government, which sought to have the arrangement declared a United States–British project, although the British participation would be purely nominal and the US would have complete control. Negotiations continued until May 1949, but the US administration refused to be put in any position where an ally could have some advantage, particularly where defence technology was concerned. The British Foreign Office suggested giving way to the US pressure, the government acceded and the matter was confirmed in a Bill passed by Congress on 11 May 1949.[28] Chifley had already been assured by the British government in December 1948 that it would remain committed to the Australian testing range. The British government was aware that the US defence and political leaders would refuse to work jointly with the UK on sharing a missile-testing range.

INTELLIGENCE AND THE CHANGING US ALLIANCE

Australia was not consciously aware that it had become involved in the highly competitive and highly expensive arms technology race between the UK and the US. During the war, the US had shared some of its technical secrets with the UK. That open exchange had immediately ceased with the last shot of the war. The US was far ahead of Britain in this technology development, but instead of refusing point-blank to hand over information it raised excuses, such as accusing Britain's partner, Australia, of having lax security and of being unreliable. In response to this accusation, Australia had to establish ASIO under MI5's aegis to demonstrate its trustworthiness. Security was not the real reason for the US not sharing its technology. The exercise did not achieve its aim. Britain did not get the technical secrets; Australia was left with ASIO.

The obstructionism adopted by the US defence establishment towards sharing defence technology information sprang naturally from the attitude that US secrets were their own and should not be shared with a declining power such as Britain, or its Commonwealth of Nations members. Because the US Defense Department was so large and powerful there was little that the US Administration could do to counter this policy. Another excuse often resorted to by the Defense Department for refusing to exchange information with its allies was the excuse that copyright and patent rights applied to all their defence technology. Contrary to British-style countries where government defence science establishments produced most of the new defence technologies, it was the private defence corporations in America who developed these technologies, albeit with US taxpayers' funds. Defense Department officers were thereby able to claim that they were unable to share or exchange information protected by patents.[29]

The US defence establishment resorted to other subtle strategies of erecting bureaucratic fences to exclude British inquiries. Twenty-six copies of a form had to be completed for each request to visit a part of a defence factory. If ten factories were to be visited 260 forms had to be completed and a restriction by one of the sections to the acceptance of its form led to restrictions being imposed in other areas. In any case it took six weeks to distribute and obtain clearances for the multitude of forms, with the result that a visit to the US by a British defence official could be expensive and time-wasting.[30]

The Australian munitions industry was also to feel the impact of this US policy of not sharing its defence technology with Britain and the Commonwealth nations. It related to the production of the variable timed (VT) fused artillery shells in Australia. This was a wartime development over which the US claimed the right of ownership and consisted of an electronic device in the tip of the artillery shell which could measure the distance from its target and explode the shell at any pre-set distance, thus scattering its shrapnel to maximum effect. British and US scientists had developed it conjointly with one part, the reserve energizer, produced in the US. The US military attaché in Canberra had been allowed to visit the government's munition factory at Footscray early in 1949, and he reported with alarm that VT fused munitions were being produced there. The US

Defense Department, considering that Britain was sharing a jointly developed weapon containing an exclusively owned US part with a third country, that is Australia, made an issue out of the event. The Defense Department demanded that the British be informed that they should withhold all VT fuse information from Australia and if they did not obey, the US would terminate the transmission of all VT fuse information to Britain. The services of the State Department were thereupon pressed into service and it issued an *aide-mémoire* to the British ambassador on 10 June 1949 to this effect. The embassy replied on 25 July 1949 that the VT fuse was mainly a British design 'having only one component that is of United States or joint United States/United Kingdom origin, namely the reserve energizer'. Information about the energizer had been published in an American electronics journal and fuses containing the energizer had been left in considerable numbers on the battlefields of Europe after the war. The reply claimed that the British had not been given the production techniques for the US energizer and had developed their own to produce the British version of the energizer. By this stance the British indicated that they were not going to be bluffed by the US defence establishment into surrendering the rights to use technical information they believed to be rightly theirs.[31]

In order to monitor closely the divulging of information to foreign countries, the US administration established the State Army–Navy–Air Force Coordinating Committee (SANACC). In June 1949 this came under the control of the US National Security Council. It established from its membership a subcommittee to examine all applications for the release of defence technology and it was named the Subcommittee for Information Control. It was this SANACC committee which confronted the British over the Australian production of the VT fuse. It also imposed the embargo on transferring any classified information to Australia after Britain had asked it to consider divulging information to Australia for use in the Joint Project.[32]

The reasons for imposing the ban on the information flow to Australia will be discussed in the next chapter. It will be sufficient to note that the ban was applied as a result of military inter-service rivalry in the US and unfounded allegations about spying in Australia. Like many changes in the field of public administration, the explanation for the establishment of ASIO had direct and indirect causes. This chapter has attempted to outline the more important of these while emphasizing that the causes emerged from both past and present events. Fears of re-emergent communism, new directions in Australian foreign policy, new defence technology and even the collective US defence dislike of Britain and the British together with the US inter-service rivalry all had their origins in the previous decades. The new ASIO that was to emerge from the inter-relationship of these diverse events, while achieving a size and sophistication not seen before in Australian intelligence circles, also owed as much to the past as it did to the events of the early Cold War years.

NOTES

1. AA, CRS 472, Item W4452.
2. Jeffrey T. Richelson and Desmond Ball, *The Ties that Bind: Intelligence Cooperation Between UK/USA Countries* (Sydney, 1985), p. 137.
3. Ibid., p. 7.
4. Menzies papers, NLA, NIS4936, Series 20.
5. Tom Sheridan, *Industrial Relations in the Chifley Years 1945–1949* (Melbourne, 1989), Ch. 13.
6. AA, SP1714/1 Item, N43028.
7. AA, CRS A5954, Box 2081.
8. AA, 6119/28, Item 351, 21.
9. Melbourne, 1989, *passim*.
10. Ibid., Ch. 6.
11. AA, A981/1, Item 109, Consuls 249.
12. AA, A981/1, Item War 68A.
13. Documents provided by Mr Vladimir V. Sokolov, Deputy Head of the Historical Diplomatic Department, Ministry of Foreign Affairs of the USSR, on establishment of Soviet Australian diplomatic relationships, 1942, in possession of author; AA, A981/1, Item Australia 197.
14. AA, CRS 989, Item 45/845/8/1.
15. AA, CRS A989, Item 43/845/2.
16. Christopher Waters, 'Anglo-Australian Diplomacy 1945–1949, Labour Governments in Conflict', PhD thesis, UNSW, ADFA, 1990, *passim*.

THE AUSTRALIAN SECURITY INTELLIGENCE ORGANIZATION

17. AA, A3300/1, Item 584.

18. Ibid.

19. Ibid.

20. NARS, RG330, see memorandum for Director of Intelligence, 26 March 1948; 'Soviet Intentions, Report by Joint Intelligence Committee', 1 April 1948; 'Domestic Activities and Foreign Relations', Report by James Forrestal, Secretary of Defense, 26 June 1948.

21. CRS 6456, Item R84.061.

22. PRO, CAB 122/361, Rocket Firing Trials.

23. NARS, RG330, Background and Development of Guided Missiles.

24. PRO, DEFE 7/262.

25. Dedman Papers M987, NLA; PRO, DEFE 7/262; for a copy of Memorandum of Arrangements Between Australian and UK Governments to govern the operation of the Long Range Weapons Project, see RG 330, NARS.

26. NARS, RG330, Report by Sir Frederick Shedden to Secretary of Defense, 11 April 1949; NARS, RG330, US Naval Attaché Report, 30 March 1949, PRO, AVIA 54/1213; see also Peter Morton, *Fire Across the Desert, Woomera and the Anglo-Australian Project 1946–1980* (Canberra, 1989), Part 1.

27. NARS, RG330, Report on Long Range Proving Ground, 20 June 1947.

28. NARS, RG330, Minutes of Meeting of Secretary of State, Defense, Army, Navy, Air Force, 27 Oct. 1947; PRO, DEFE 7/268.

29. NARS, RG330, SANACC, Report on Disclosure of Classified Military Information to Foreign Governments, 15 June 1948; Report by Secretary of Navy to President's Air Policy Commission, 21 April 1948, RG330, NARS; Frank Cain, 'Missiles and Mistrust: US Intelligence Responses to British and Australian Missile Research', in *Intelligence and National Security*, Vol. 3, No. 4 (October 1988).

30. PRO, DEFE 7/291, report by DTS (Air).

31. NARS, RG330, Reports, Exchange of Classified Information, 20 July 1949.

32. NARS, RG330, SANACC Report 206/29, 15 June 1949.

3

Embargoes, Espionage and ASIO

The events which led to the US imposing the embargo on the
transfer of all classified information, and which in turn led to
the establishment of ASIO, began on 18 August 1947 when the
British Joint Services Mission in Washington approached the
Subcommittee for Information Control for information about
the operating techniques of long-range missile proving grounds
released to Australia along with complementary information
about the guided weapons themselves. The Joint Chiefs of Staff
approved this British request and recommended to SANACC that
the information be provided. But when on 17 February 1948 the
British made a further request for the release to Australia of all
guided missile information, the approval of the Subcommittee of
Military Information Control was questioned by the US Navy,
which proceeded to make an issue of the Australian involvement
in the Joint Project. It complained that when, in accordance with
the Subcommittee's recommendation of 18 August 1947, the navy
had approached the Australian government offering information
on proving grounds and associated missile information, it had
sought in return information from Australia about testing at the
range but, much to its chagrin, Australia had offered no reply.
The navy now saw little legitimate need for Australia to be given
advanced research and development data about the US guided
missile programme, and to reinforce its objections it provided
an unsolicited political judgement showing what it thought of
Australia's Labor Party government:

> Because of political immaturity, a leftist government greatly
> influenced by communistic infiltrated labor organizations,

and the fact that Australian governmental activities have violated the basic security principle that classified information should not be divulged to unauthorised persons Australia is a poor security risk.[1]

While the navy thus opposed the British request of 17 February 1948, the State Department, the army and air force did not, so a recommendation went to the SANACC meeting to allow the British to disclose the information to Australia. The navy played its last card, however, by producing at the SANACC meeting on 18 May 1948 an allegation of spying in Australia which, it claimed, revealed Australia as being a security risk. By association, Britain too stood condemned.

The basis of this anti-Australian allegation was a report to President Truman almost four months earlier, on 27 January 1948, by Rear Admiral R.H. Hillenkoetter, Director of Central Intelligence in the CIA. 'Indications have appeared', he said,

> that there is a leak in high government circles in Australia, to Russia. This may, in magnitude, approach that of the Canadian spy exposé of last year insofar as high Australian Government officials are concerned. The British Government is now engaged in extensive undercover investigations to determine just where, in the Australian government, the leak is.[2]

This final throw by the navy hit its target and in spite of the dated nature of the information, then four months old, SANACC deferred passing information to Australia pending investigation on the 'reported security breach by Australia' and also suspended the release of any other classified information. The navy was not prepared to let the matter rest there. It suggested that while 'recognizing the importance of collaboration with probable allies', it was evident that Britain was unable to deny guided weapons information to Australian scientists and that an interim restrictive policy towards the UK should be adopted until the entire disclosure policy of the US towards nations of the British Commonwealth was resolved. The British Joint Services Mission was informed of events and, aware that another friction point had been reached with the US, tactically withdrew by asking that action on their initial request be suspended.

This CIA report to President Truman begs two questions. The first is why was there no follow-up report to expand on this initial and alarmist warning? The matter had been referred to British intelligence, presumably because the CIA did not know how to contact the CIS, but four months later in May 1948, when the US Navy had seized upon this damaging report to stop all defence information flowing to Australia, some clarification would have been made to the initial report. The second question arises over the date of the CIA statement about the 'Canadian spy exposé of last year'. This would refer to the Gouzenko defection of 5 September 1945. The Canadian Prime Minister, Mackenzie King, refrained from announcing or acting on the defection, but the US administration knew of the event and leaked it to the news media in February 1946, whereupon Mackenzie King announced that a Royal Commission would be held on the affair and on the documents Gouzenko brought with him from the Soviet embassy. This began on 13 February 1946. The CIA comment about the 'spy exposé of last year' indicates that the alleged leak must have been detected some time in 1947, assuming that the CIA regarded the Gouzenko affair as occurring early in 1946 when Mackenzie King made the announcement about the Royal Commission. How long, then, had the CIA been aware of the alleged leak before notifying Truman on 27 January 1948? This is a question to which an answer may never be known.

This crucial if dated piece of information produced by the US Navy to thwart both British and also Australian defence programmes came from unknown sources. It is most likely that it was derived from decrypts of Soviet diplomatic traffic collected during and after the war principally by the US. This is an area of post-war history where fact and fantasy intermingle. During the Pacific War the Australian Army's Sigint operation detected military information being transmitted from the Soviet and Chinese embassies to their home governments. The Soviet transmissions were received in the Soviet's consular office in the Japanese-occupied city of Harbin in China. A Japanese spy was alleged to have stolen these messages, and when he was transmitting them to Tokyo they were detected by Australian Sigint operations. The Soviet Union and China were of course wartime allies. The Soviet Union and Japan were not at war, although Australia and its allies were eager for the USSR to join the Pacific War. The Australian Army was concerned that information (likely to persuade the USSR to attack Japan) was being transmitted from Australia, and it warned the government accordingly.[3] The decrypting operation by Australia's Defence Department continued after the war and is maintained to this day in conjunction with the US and Britain and others under the UKUSA alliance. It is not impossible that the US obtained its decrypted information from the Australian Army. It is likely that it was the Chinese material being intercepted because the Soviet embassy, being aware of those Sigint operations, did not use a transmitter. Certainly there was no transmitter in the Soviet embassy in 1951.[4]

The real truth of these decryption operations is difficult to estimate. We rely for the most current explanation of them on Peter Wright, and his colleague Paul Greengrass, in *Spy Catcher, the Candid Autobiography of a Senior Intelligence Officer*,[5] where the matter is discussed under the title of Operation 'Bride' or 'Venona'. On their version of events (and because their sources are not quoted their authenticity remains qualified) the US, UK and Swedish intelligence recorded all Soviet transmissions during the war, and probably well before then, including transmissions from Canberra to Moscow. The finding of a partly burned Soviet code book during the Finnish–Soviet war and the discovery that the Soviet had used their one-time pads more than once led to the deciphering, Wright alleges, of some of this recorded traffic. He puts the figure at one per cent of the 200,000 messages held, and 'many of these were broken only to the extent of a few words'. Nevertheless, claims Wright, this tiny amount of cracked code was sufficient to expose the so-called spies, Donald Maclean, Klaus Fuchs and the Rosenbergs, and it was also sufficient to indicate that Alger Hiss could have been a spy in the State Department.[6] It is not known whether it was these decrypts that the navy was producing, and because the alleged decrypting incident appears later in this chapter, further analysis will be left until then.

Given that the navy was acting on this dated intelligence information, the question arises of why its officers were so firmly opposed to the release of information to Australia when the other two military services supported its release. The navy's determination to remain independent of the other services has already been discussed, but it also now exhibited a deep suspicion of Britain which carried over to Australia. For example, it reported to the Military Intelligence Committee of SANACC in May 1948 that the British contribution to the US Navy's guided missile programme was 'minor to insignificant' and that 'Australia's contributions are insignificant to infintesimal'. The navy also claimed that Britain leaked US military information to European nations: 'In at least one instance British military authorities sanctioned a disclosure of US information to France' and had leaked 'US VT fuse information to a Swiss arms manufacturer'.[7]

One leak does not an embargo make, and we probably have to look wider for the navy's basic objections on this question. Leaving aside the matter of personality and the evidence that some of the navy's senior staff held strong views amounting almost to a fetish about the necessity for tight security, the navy was deeply concerned about the development of land-based missile-testing ranges. The US defence organization, as has been explained, was itself establishing a missile range in Florida known as the Banana River Range from where the missiles were flown out to sea and over the Bahamas. This range relied greatly on naval resources, and shipboard missile-monitoring equipment had been developed by the navy which could, of course, be used on land but not by the navy. The animosity of the navy towards Britain generally and Australia in particular cannot, therefore, be ascribed to any single factor and must be seen in terms of US inter-service rivalry and the navy's concern to establish its own individuality by refusing to allow its support for any inter-service project to be assumed.[8]

It was characteristic of US obstructionism, already remarked upon, that confrontation was always avoided in favour of indirectness. Regardless of the extent to which the Defense Department might wish to avoid sharing its technological information with Britain, it was positively unwilling, because of alliances in the past and those it might seek in the future, to issue an unqualified refusal to exchange information. By denying information to Australia, a close but not crucially important ally of Britain, the Defense Department could clearly signal that it was unprepared to assist in the development of a British missile industry while avoiding having to say as much to the British government. Coincidences of dates can mean a lot or a little in historical analysis, but it is worth noting that this ban on transferring all classified information to Australia occurred just eight days after the British government announced that it was about to develop its own atomic bomb after the denial of assistance by the US.

MYTHS AND SPIES

While much of the future of the exchange of missile information technology between the US and Britain hung in the balance over these CIA/US Navy revelations about Australia it is important to establish how much the Australian government was aware of events. A short answer seems to be that the Prime Minister, J.B. Chifley, was aware of the details of the alleged spying, but considered that the affair was not of any importance. The details seem to be as follows. In approximately March 1948 Sir Percy Sillitoe visited Australia to advise Chifley that MI5 had learned that a British Post-Hostilities Planning Paper on Security in the Western Mediterranean, probably prepared in 1945, had come into official Soviet hands. It was alleged that it had been obtained from an agent in Australia. There seemed to be little else that Sillitoe could add to this report. The paper was identified and the several copies of it sent to the Australian Defence Department were traced and totally accounted for. The mystery remained. Chifley had a report prepared on the incident which he sent to Prime Minister Attlee in London. He referred particularly to the vagueness of Sillitoe's report in the following comments.

> I must say that, in the absence of full particulars to enable me to study the specific information that came into the possession of the United Kingdom Government and to assess the credibility of the informant, we were placed at some disadvantage in dealing with the matter. For example, the Russians, in disclosing the source of information to the informed, may have doubted his reliability and have purposely mentioned Australia to cover up the true source. Nevertheless, we proceeded to make the most thorough investigation of the report.[9]

He closed by reporting that enquiries into the leakage of the report met with no success. It appears that the British authorities made no further effort to follow up the matter.

When the Chifley government decided to establish a new counter-espionage organization along MI5 lines, Roger Hollis, then in charge of counter-espionage in MI5, visited Australia and was reported some years later to have brought with him code names supposed to have been obtained from the Soviet Union and to apply to Australian officials. One was reported to have applied to a secretary working with Dr Evatt, then Minister for External Affairs and Attorney-General. Hollis met with Dr Burton, who was Secretary of the External Affairs Department and was also standing in for the Secretary of the Attorney-General's Department. Burton later recounted these events to the Royal Commission on Espionage in 1954. He added that he had instructed his staff to open dialogue with the officials of the Soviet embassy by inviting them to the Department of External Affairs to discuss Western diplomatic policy generally. Dr Burton believed that if the Soviet officials were made aware of the broad thrusts of policy they would be less reserved and antagonistic towards the West. It was possible, explained Dr Burton, that the names of his officers had become involved with the transmission of this information to Moscow and that is why one of them, Jim Hill, was detected by MI5 in these transmissions.[10]

In theory, though not in reality, there were two lines of information flow to the Soviet Union. One was the Burton–Hill flow revealed in 1954. The other was the post-hostilities planning documents which Sir Percy Sillitoe mentioned to Prime Minister Chifley in 1945. Chifley was not very impressed with Sir Percy's vague story about the leak. We know this from the report he gave to a visiting Foreign Office official when it was discussed. M.E. Dening, Assistant Under Secretary of the Foreign Office, was sent to Australia in May 1948 by the Foreign Minister, Ernest Bevin, in order to speak directly with Chifley about becoming involved in secret talks with the UK, US, New Zealand and Canada regarding Far Eastern questions. He was in Canberra early in May 1948 although he held little confidence that he would be able to win Australia away from the more independent line over the developing Cold War and its support for the nationalist forces in Asia. It was probably in an effort to win

Chifley's personal support for the UK–US proposals (Evatt, the Minister for External Affairs and John Burton, Secretary of that Department, were excluded from these discussions) that he re-introduced the matter of the security leak, as if to reinforce the argument that Soviet espionage and subversion could be the way of the future against which a Western pact could guard.

Chifley was sceptical about both the leak and the proposed Far Eastern Pact. Dening was put out by the rebuff on both counts and expressed his displeasure in the report which he wrote to his master, Sir Orme Sargent, Under Secretary of State for Foreign Affairs, on 10 May 1948. Dening's suspicion of many aspects of the Labor government, not the least of which was its liberal internationalist foreign policies, was reflected in his writing this letter to Sargent in longhand because he found no secure typist available to him in Canberra:

> The Prime Minister did not satisfy me that he has really taken adequate steps to preserve security. He said top secret communications made to him by High Commission went into a locked box, from which they were only taken to be burned. That is all very well, but there was no assurance that papers which go to the Department of External Affairs are really secure. Chifley went on to make a disparaging remark about sleuths who have to have something to show to earn their keep, and he seemed to have some doubt whether there was really any foundation to our story. So we are really rather on the spot.[11]

It can be deduced from this report that the alleged leak related to a British document which had possibly been supplied by the British High Commissioner in Canberra to the External Affairs Department. This means of distribution indicates that it would have been a routine type of correspondence. Urgent and top secret material would have been sent by safe-hand courier or by diplomatic telegraph cipher to the High Commissioner for delivery to the Prime Minister who would pass it to the Minister for External Affairs.

During the course of the Royal Commission into Espionage in 1954 it was revealed that a telegram of little importance from the Foreign Office was shown to a Soviet diplomat as part of the normal course of appraising a foreign diplomat of Commonwealth of Nations policy.[12] It was also revealed at the hearings that there was evidence, although no such evidence was produced at the hearing, nor since, that a document issued by the Post-Hostilities Section of the British government had found its way, in part or in whole, into Soviet hands.[13] It may have been that these were the nature of the leaks revealed to Chifley by the British officials. It may have been neither.

It is also worth observing that the Foreign Office seemed less concerned about the nature of the alleged leak than about Chifley's discounting of the importance of the event. From their general reaction it is evident that the British officials were aware that they had little control over this affair. It confirms that all information about the so-called leak was in American hands. Further evidence demonstrating this point is contained in a note attached by Sargent to Dening's letter before sending it on to Foreign Minister Bevin: 'As regards security, we are asking the Americans whether we may not tell the Australians the *real* [underlined] reason for our anxiety, since only by this means shall we convince Mr Chifley of the seriousness of the situation'.[14]

The US administration's response is not known, but circumstances indicate that the reply would have been a firm 'no'.

POST-WAR INTELLIGENCE STRUCTURING

It was not so much the pressure from the Foreign Office, more the initiative of the Australian Defence Department, that led to a deeper awareness of intelligence security matters in Canberra. The Australian government had considered the proposal on 23 July 1946 of establishing a Defence Security Intelligence Organization in conjunction with the formation of the Joint Intelligence Organization, which was to vet staff in the higher levels of the Defence Department and maintain the security of all defence matters. The government saw little need for such an organization because it would simply duplicate the work of the CIS, but the question was referred to the Attorney-General's Department for consideration. The Department of Supply, which was responsible for the Joint Project, had already established its own security body, but the British complaints over how the embargo was affecting the flow of technical information to the project led the Defence Department on 7 June 1948 to look again at guarding defence documents that could be seen by people in other departments. The Minister of Defence, J.J. Dedman, called on those departments who handled Defence Department information, such as the Treasury, Prime Minister's Department, and External Affairs Department to join with the Defence Committee (consisting of heads of Services plus the civilian Secretary of the Defence Department) to plan for maintaining the security of defence information.[15]

The outcome of these discussions was the four-point agreement made between the departments that the CIS should vet all officers, service and civilian, who handled Defence Department documents of secret and high classifications; that all departments should appoint full-time or part-time security officers; that security of buildings be attended to; and that each department consider internal security measures to safeguard all defence documents. In spite of this agreement some departments – the army, air force, Treasury, Public Service Board and Council for Scientific and Industrial Research (CSIRO) – were slow to reply to all these recommendations, and on 22 December Dedman wrote to the Prime Minister to request these departments to expedite their replies. Dedman put the proposal also that the vetting of persons should be extended to include those handling not only defence information of a secret level and above, but all documents bearing such categories.[16] The widening of the vetting procedures may possibly have been in response to suggestions from MI5 because this proposal of Dedman was approved by Roger Hollis and Robert Hemblys-Scales in February 1949 on their visit to Australia.

Prime Minister Chifley was committed to visit the UK in July 1948 to discuss economic and British Commonwealth defence matters and he took the opportunity to discuss the question of security measures in a conference with the British Minister of Defence, A.V. Alexander, on 12 July 1948. The question of the role of the CSIRO had become of some concern to both the UK and US governments, mainly because of connections between CSIRO scientists and other scientists working on nuclear energy at the physics laboratories at Harwell. Australian scientists naturally wished to keep abreast of the developments in this new area of physics for intellectual reasons. The chairman of CSIRO, Sir David Rivett, had publicly declared that he did not wish the CSIRO to become involved in defence science projects and was willing to have its aerodynamics laboratories transferred to the Department of Supply so that the CSIRO could continue with open and publishable research. The Opposition decided to attack the government on this point alleging that there were Communists active in the CSIRO and on its management board as well. The US and UK officials were concerned at these attacks because they had become suspicious of scientists and their long-established principles of sharing the results of their researches among fellow scientists and saw this as a means by which the Soviet would gain nuclear secrets. This was quite impossible in the case of the CSIRO scientists because they received no secret information to pass on. There seemed to be, however, a determination in the UK and US to believe much of the partisan attacks on the Labor government. Even so Chifley was interested in exchanging information on nuclear energy questions, but the UK government was reluctant to join with Australia and a paper sent to Sir Norman Brooks, Secretary to Attlee, urged that Chifley not be led to expect too much in this field even if adequate security measures were established in Australia.[17]

TRACING ALLEGATIONS AND ACCUSATIONS

Chifley dealt with both attacks (the CSIRO and the leak) in the conference with the British Minister of Defence by pointing out that the US obstructionism towards exchanging defence information with Britain lay at the base of both allegations. He said that he would explore having the missile development work being made a secret branch within the Supply Department to convince the US that secrets would be safe. He knew that he did not have to convince the British of Australia's tight security measures. Sir Ben Lockspeiser, chief scientist of the UK Ministry of Supply, visited Australia late in July 1948 and reported very favourably on the development of the missile range and the quality of the security measures taken to guard the Project.[18] Alexander acknowledged this when he replied to Chifley: 'While the United States had a close link with Canada they were not at present prepared to go further and the Minister thought that any steps which Australia could take to tighten up security would be a help'.[19]

On the question of scientific security measures Chifley, at Alexander's invitation, discussed affairs with Sir Henry Tizard, the leading British defence scientist and Chairman of the Defence Research Committee. He also met Sir Percy Sillitoe, Director-General of MI5, for the second time in recent months. No records are available of what transpired at this meeting at Chequers, which Bevin also attended, but it is possible that it was agreed that Roger Hollis would visit Australia. The main preoccupation in this meeting with the Australian Prime Minister was to incorporate Australia into the British proposal of the five-power defence structure while acknowledging the Australian initiative in taking a higher defence posture in the Pacific. In a briefing paper of 3 July 1948, for Alexander's use in the Chifley discussions, the UK Defence Department sought to incorporate the Commonwealth into the five-power structure:

> The connecting pin between European and American co-operation is the United Kingdom. With all the planning now proceeding with both America and the French and the Benelux powers, we wish to associate the Commonwealth countries as urgently as possible.[20]

With the defence planners attempting to promote Britain and its Commonwealth as a leading force in European defence against a possible Soviet attack by 1957 (by which time it was estimated it would be a nuclear power) Australian intelligence security interests seemed to assume a very minor role in these much wider defence discussions.

But the Australian government still did not know why the US had imposed its embargo on transmitting classified information. The Australian ministers seemed to be aware that the secret clue was held in the US administration, not with the British authorities. The Australian ministers went to some lengths to discover the reason. They seemed to be unaware of the complex manner in which the US Defense and State Departments arrived at the policy decisions which may have been small in themselves but had extensive ramifications such as this one that seriously affected Australia. The ministers also seemed unaware of the deep inter-service rivalry in the US and of the power that the navy, for example, could exercise in this area. J.A. Armstrong, Minister for Supply and Development, attempted to prise out the reasons from the US Defense Secretary, J.V. Forrestal. Together with the Australian ambassador in Washington, Norman Makin, Armstrong interviewed Forrestal on the question on 3 September 1948. Armstrong and Makin had carefully prepared the ground. They arranged for two important American businessmen, who knew Forrestal, and were sympathetic towards Australia, to speak to the Secretary of Defense before they visited him. These two were Floyd Blair, a director of the National City Bank of New York, and Bernard M. Baruch, a prosperous financier who was pressed into service by W.S. Robinson, a friend of Australian prime ministers, a wealthy mining magnate and a kind of Australian roving ambassador-at-large. The meeting was conducted in the company of others and, after they had withdrawn, Armstrong spoke to Forrestal privately, making a personal plea to be told the reason for the embargo with the promise that he would pass the information to no one but the Prime Minister. Forrestal replied that he had no first-hand knowledge of the matters. Forrestal was highly experienced in ways of the Defense Department and it was unfortunate that he was not prepared to confide in Armstrong by indicating something of the convoluted nature of decision-making in his department. Nor do the records indicate that he kept his promise to Armstrong to look into the question and communicate with him before he returned to Australia.[21]

Dr Evatt also pursued the matter of the embargo when he spoke to Forrestal on 12 November 1948 when they were both in France. Evatt knew that he would not obtain a direct answer from Forrestal, but he wished to let the Secretary know that he was aware that the allegations against Australia had US origins. He simply announced to Forrestal that he was 'embarrassed by the fact that communication of some apparent security breaches had not been made directly to the Australian government, but had been communicated through the British'. He said that the Opposition had exploited the event, but that measures had been taken to establish counter-espionage activities using British experience and practices. He said (somewhat optimistically) that he felt the matter was now a 'dead issue'. Unfortunately for Australian political life, the affair failed to die but went on to enjoy a great longevity.[22]

PLANNING FOR THE NEW ASIO

Other events seemed to conspire to prevent a solution being reached on the affair. The US presidential election was close at hand by late in 1948 with Truman likely to lose office; Forrestal was to commit suicide early the next year; and one of the leading opinion-makers in Australia, Sir Keith Murdoch, chief of the Melbourne *Herald* newspaper consortium in Australia, declared confidently that R.G. Menzies would defeat the Chifley government at the election to be held in twelve months' time. He visited Forrestal on 11 October 1948 to inform him that the 'Labor government would unquestionably be defeated in the elections next September'. The reason, he claimed, was that Chifley 'had made a mistake in advocating the nationalization of all banks

Roger Hollis of MI5 who helped establish ASIO. The question of his being a Soviet mole is still being debated in intelligence history circles. (*Age*, Melbourne)

ASIO was established in response to the US embargo on sending US information to Australia. Sir Frederick Shedden, Secretary of the Defence Department, went to Washington in an unsuccessful attempt to get the embargo lifted. (Australian Archives)

and that the Australian people reacted very strongly against this idea'.[23]

Information about Chifley's visit to the UK to patch over the alleged leak in diplomatic circles was passed to the Opposition and used by Arthur Fadden, leader of the Country Party, to embarrass the government. The documents he quoted were copies of British government papers sent via the British High Commission to Chifley before his visit to London. The British Prime Minister's office was concerned that there could have been a leak, and although Chifley ordered an inquiry it was never established whether Fadden obtained the documents from British or Australian sources.[24]

Events were now moving early in 1949 towards the establishment of ASIO when Roger Hollis, head of the Soviet counter-intelligence of MI5 (later to become Director-General), arrived with Robert Hemblys-Scales. Hollis had visited Washington before coming to Australia, perhaps in the hope of persuading the US authorities to divulge more of their case against Australia or at least to brief them on the intelligence service the British were proposing for Australia. By late March Hemblys-Scales had been transferred to Egypt, to be replaced by Courtney Young who later went to Singapore. February and March were busy months for intelligence planning in Australia. A proposal had been prepared, probably by Hollis, and presented to the government on 7 February 1949 arguing that there must be one security authority only in Australia. It was this plan that became the blueprint for the new ASIO. At the same time President Truman and Prime Minister Attlee had been in communication over the exchange of classified information in general and the Australian situation in particular. Truman had written to Attlee on 28 January 1949 saying that his Defense Secretary wished to invite the Australian Secretary for Defence, Sir Frederick Shedden, to visit Washington on his way to London in May and 'have a full and frank discussion with him' on the problems that had arisen. Attlee replied to Truman on 6 February 1949 thanking him for taking a personal interest in 'our problem with the security position in Australia' and announcing that he was

happy to be able to assure you that the appropriate authorities in this country are in constant and fruitful touch with the Australian Government and that satisfactory progress has been reported to me in improving Australian security and maintaining a higher standard.[25]

The visit by Shedden will be discussed in the following chapter; it remains here to discuss how the planned security service came into being. In the proposal, ascribable to Hollis, the existing intelligence arrangement was strongly criticized. Because the CIS and the army covered the same field, security measures were 'not being done comprehensively and thoroughly'. The recommendation proposed that the new body should be represented on the Australian Joint Intelligence Committee, it should be responsible to the army for internal security during a war and it should co-operate with the police forces and their special branches. It was to have five objectives: the investigation of subversive organizations and activities; maintenance of central records by absorbing the CIS records; security checking of individuals; security checking of immigrants; and acting as the sole channel of liaison for security matters with the overseas organizations, the state authorities, and the defence military services. It proposed that the CIS should become a general investigatory body like a police force, conduct prosecutions on behalf of this intelligence body and control the Peace Officers (the successors to the Commonwealth police force).[26]

This outline appears to have become the plan on which ASIO was structured. When the memorandum was produced by Prime Minister Chifley authorizing the first Director-General of ASIO to establish this security intelligence body on 16 March 1949, it incorporated many of these recommendations. It added other clauses directing that the organization be free of any political bias, that its inquiries be conducted solely in the interests of the public and the national defence, and that ministers were not to concern themselves with the detailed information, but only as much as to determine an issue.

The search for a Director-General produced a justice of the South Australian Supreme Court, Geoffrey Sandalford Reed, who, Prime Minister Chifley announced in Parliament on 2 March 1949, would take up his duties in one week's time. The future role of the CIS was not discussed publicly at this time, and it continued with its vetting and security intelligence-collecting as usual. The question of duplication and overlapping of work between these two intelligence bodies was a question yet to be settled. But that occurred after the Chifley government was replaced in December 1949 by the Menzies-led coalition government.

Mr Justice Reed was then aged 56, a supporter of the non-Labor forces and a judge since 1935. He had been Chairman of the South Australian National Security Advisory Committee since 1941. Contrary to what the name implied, this Committee had been constituted under wartime National Security Regulations to deal with objections to internment. He had also taught at the University of Adelaide in private international law and law of evidence and procedure. It is not known why he was selected for this position, but many of the decisions relating to the early months of ASIO remain unexplained.[27] The timing of its establishment seemed to be linked to the Attlee–Truman negotiations which in turn, may have evolved from an offer by Forrestal to help settle this new question on the exchange of technical information with Britain and the Commonwealth nations such as would attract support from the US Joint Chiefs of Staff Committee and the three military services.

By appointing a judge as Director-General the Labor Party expected that this new and secret intelligence body, which was to function in only a loose subordination to the ministry, would work within the law and observe the principles of a liberal parliamentary democratic society. The party was prepared to extend a large amount of autonomy to the new organization. Chifley informed Parliament on 10 March 1949 that he would not discuss the details of the activities of ASIO 'unless they involved matters of great public interest'.[28] Dr Evatt told Parliament six months later that 'to all intents and purposes the Director-General of Security is free from ministerial direction' in order to maintain maximum internal security. He added one significant point, however, that 'in principle everything is left to the discretion, good sense and sense of justice of Mr Justice Reed who for many years has been a distinguished justice of the Supreme Court of South Australia'. He added that ASIO's charter was 'as ample as that possessed by the corresponding authority in Great Britain'.[29] Upon these basic principles enunciated by the Prime Minister, that he would not interfere in ASIO unless 'great public interest' was involved, and from the Attorney-General that its administration relied on the sense of justice of an experienced judge, this new and startlingly different administrative institution, modelled on its British counterpart, began operations.

WHY A NEW SECURITY INTELLIGENCE BODY?

How much ASIO was established in the form it was to meet US administration objections about secret security weaknesses in Australia and how much in response to the wielding of British government influence will be analysed in the following chapter. The question to be answered at this point is what persuaded the government to establish a new intelligence body that would supplant the CIS – what were the faults in the CIS that prevented it continuing as the principal intelligence security body? Some of the answers to this question are to be found in the report given by Shedden to the US Defense Department in June 1949. In this presentation he discussed the role of the CIS as follows:

> It has maintained dossiers on persons and organisations of doubtful loyalty and undertakes security checking of government employees when required. However, it has never been staffed or organised to provide a counter-espionage section.[30]

The main justification for establishing ASIO appears, therefore, to have been the necessity to watch the Soviet spies supposedly operating in Australia or those about to operate in the future. This declared weakness in the CIS was perhaps overstated. The CIS and its predecessor, the Investigation Branch, as demonstrated in the previous chapter, had been watching and reporting on the Bolsheviks, Russians and the Soviet embassy as each one of them became a prominent element in Australia. As the Australian representative of MI5, the Investigation Branch had regularly reported information about Soviet trading and diplomatic activities to London. The significant change from the past was the establishment of the Joint Project which, it was thought, might become a target for Soviet spies. Here again

Soviet subversion had been anticipated and a separate intelligence body established to guard the missile secrets. Shedden referred also to this organization in his report to the Defense Department:

> A special security organisation was set up in 1947 to cover the Project. The general direction is vested in a Security Committee of which the three Service Directors of Intelligence and the Director of the Commonwealth Investigation Branch are members . . . A general measure of co-ordination with Defence is achieved by virtue of the fact that the Services Directors of Intelligence are members both of the Long Range Security Committee and the Joint Intelligence Committee.[31]

This new emphasis on the defence aspect of the role of security intelligence implies that ASIO was established for national defence requirements. Added weight is given to this assessment when it is observed that Shedden described ASIO as the fourth arm in the defence of Australia. Having this defence connotation would mean that the proposed ASIO would be tied to the Defence Department and the military services. In this regard the establishment of ASIO can be seen as the continuation of the struggle in the intelligence field in Australia, going back to the years of the First World War when the army sought to be the dominant factor in the Australian intelligence field. The army was the strongest element in the Defence Department, and it will be seen in the following chapters how the army re-emerged as an important force in the post-war intelligence world.

Another administrative struggle was ensuing in these years which must be taken into account when understanding why the CIS was displaced by the new ASIO. This tussle was between the Defence Department, under the redoubtable Sir Frederick Shedden, and the External Affairs Department, under the highly capable John Burton, and it reflected the impact of the independent post-war defence and foreign policy stance by the Chifley government. Under Burton's management and with Dr Evatt's inspirational drive, External Affairs was expanding in influence to rival and surpass the Defence Department in the making of high government policy. Rather than follow the British and US policies of anti-Sovietism and rearmament, Evatt and Burton, with Chifley's support, adopted policies of settling disputes by diplomatic processes, expanding the strength of the UN, maintaining a policy of open dialogue with the Soviet Union and recognizing the importance of Asian nationalism, as analysed in the earlier part of this chapter. Such policies did not harmonize with the concept of establishing a counter-espionage organization and Burton clearly expressed his opposition to its creation.[32]

Why then did Evatt support the establishment of ASIO? The direct answer is that he could see that the forces in Washington and London would settle for nothing less. Indeed he had given a commitment to Dean Acheson, Secretary of State, during a meeting with him and President Truman in the middle of April 1949. Acheson at that meeting asked Evatt to give the establishment of ASIO his fullest support, to which Evatt replied that he would do so.[33] Evatt could be excused for thinking that the Acheson wink was as good as a nod and for believing that the establishment of ASIO would thereby lead to the lifting of the US embargo. Other factors inducing Evatt to support ASIO's founding were that civil liberties would be sufficiently preserved by the Organization being in his Attorney-General's Department, that it would be directed by a Supreme Court judge and that the CIS would be retained if only in a slightly inferior role.

Administratively speaking, ASIO in its early stage was seen as filling the role of the 'D Branch' of Australia's intelligence machinery. The CIS then consisted of 74 staff distributed over all Australian states and led by Eric Longfield Lloyd, whose intelligence experience dated back to the First World War. But it did not have a functioning 'D Branch' which, following the MI5 model, assumed the role of counter-espionage activity against the Soviet Union. The CIS was never large enough to have the specialized branches of MI5 such as a 'C Branch', which vetted public servants, or an 'E Branch', which watched the local Communist Party. That the CIS operatives were all-rounders in the arcane world of intelligence did not seem to be acceptable to the likes of Sir Percy Sillitoe and Roger Hollis. They believed that Soviet counter-espionage work was a job for specialized experts and that a new intelligence body should be established to undertake that work in Australia.

In summary, then, ASIO was established for two reasons. The first was that it was to be the means of persuading the US defence organization to reverse its post-war policy of refusing to share its high-technology defence information with Britain, and to lift its ban on the transfer of information to Australia. Another reason was to provide a specialized intelligence-gathering unit which would concentrate on possible Soviet espionage. The government, however, was properly aware that a new and secret surveillance body would require a specialized system of administration to make it accountable not only to the Prime Minister but also to the Attorney-General and thereby to Parliament as well. How all these basic conditions were to be expertly circumvented and how they were instituted 30 years later by political forces will be the topic of the following chapters.

ASIO OPENS FOR BUSINESS

ASIO opened its head office in Sydney soon after Mr Justice Reed took up his appointment. By 1 June 1949 he was reporting steady progress in building up the staff to its maximum provisional establishment of 105. By then 15 officers had been appointed, six were in the process of transfer and negotiations were in progress with 38 people. Among the transferees was R.F.B. Wake, Deputy Director of the CIS in Brisbane, Queensland, against whose appointment the army objected very strongly. This indicated that ASIO was perhaps more a creature of the military than the Attorney-General's Department.[34] Reed faced legal difficulties in appointing staff under the terms of his charter which, he said, could be remedied by legislation. He was informed that this was regarded as politically impossible, indicating that the government did not wish to give ASIO legislative status. The problem was solved by delegating to Reed authority to appoint staff under Section 67 of the Constitution by Governor-General in Council.

Not unexpectedly, the CIS was reluctant to transfer its very heart and soul – that is its valuable record system – to ASIO and Longfield Lloyd had to be ordered to do so. The 'D' files which the CIS already held were the most important in this regard because they related to subversives and espionage. Reed was also eager to assume the duties of public service vetting that were being conducted by the CIS except that shortage of staff prevented him doing so. In the long run, he had to find

The first Director-General of ASIO, Mr Justice Reed. (South Australian Law Institute)

employment for the potential force of his 105 officers and vetting was the prime occupation offering. Reed's other principal task of exposing the Soviet spy-ring alleged to be operating in Australia was being undertaken by his Director in Sydney, Wake, assisted by the MI5 liaison officer, then Courtney Young, and possibly by Roger Hollis who could have still been in Australia. But little progress had been made, Reed reported, other than 'narrowing down the field of suspects'.[35] By the end of July, however, Reed was announcing that the spy-master had been tentatively identified and that one of the leaders of the spy network had been positively identified, but that he had left the country.

Meanwhile the CIS continued its vetting of the staff who handled secret Defence Department material in the various departments, such as Treasury or External Affairs or the CSIRO. By 1 July 1949 the External Affairs Department had completed the security checking of all officers in its External Communications Branch and in the Political Division. Much of this vetting procedure was done on the initiative of the Defence Department who had produced a booklet on security; External Affairs sought copies of this to distribute to its officers and overseas embassies. The CIS became bogged down in vetting not only the senior public service staff but now all staff including recent recruits. It was faced also with checking all nominated migrants in the post-war immigration programme. The CIS was in a state of despair because many of its records had been lost to ASIO as well as some of its staff, who were attracted by the higher salaries. Longfield Lloyd estimated that under these conditions the vetting work would take two or three years to complete. That was not what the Defence Department, or Sir Frederick Shedden, wished to hear. Shedden was then in Washington attempting to convince the US administration that Australian intelligence was quickly and thoroughly vetting all its public servants and rooting out the Communists.[36] The slowness of the CIS vetting operation and Longfield Lloyd's continued excuses for the delays hastened the transfer of this work from the CIS to ASIO.

Reed continued to expand his staff and by August 1949 he had confirmed R.F.B. Wake as Director in Sydney, Bernard Tuck as Director in Canberra, and Commander Harley Wright as Director in Melbourne. He also allocated more resources to tracing the alleged Soviet spy-ring in conjunction with MI5, because he believed that, rather than building up ASIO's staff, this would impress the American authorities more and be likely to hasten the restoration of relations. Other Directors were being selected for Adelaide, Perth and Brisbane and representatives for Darwin and Papua New Guinea. The term Australian Security Intelligence Organization was also announced by Chifley to be the official name for this new intelligence body.

The tensions that had always existed in Australian intelligence circles between military intelligence and the civilian intelligence bodies continued during these formative years of ASIO when it appeared that the army was again wishing to exercise direction in its establishment and manning. Wake seemed to be a friend of Prime Minister Chifley and kept him apprised of events. He discussed the establishment of ASIO with Chifley and the progress of 'the case' in August 1949. Wake was concerned that he was under some personal attack from military intelligence and that the momentum of the attacks was maintained by Jack Lang in the Australian Parliament. Lang, a former Premier of New South Wales, was by then the leader of a one-man Lang Labor party. Arthur Calwell, then Minister for Immigration, and some of 'his Melbourne cronies' were also seen by Wake as wishing to depose him, but behind much of this, he reported, was Colonel Spry, Director of Military Intelligence. 'He had an intense dislike for me,' Wake told Chifley, 'and was friendly with Liberal right-wing politicians [which] did not foreshadow a very comfortable appointment' as Director in Sydney.[37] Certainly these confessions of Wake seemed to be supported by the opposition from the army against his appointment to ASIO, as we have already seen.

Wake was able to cast only a very small light for the Prime Minister on the nature of the security breach about which the US authorities held all the details. He told Chifley that the amount of MI5 material that ASIO had was 'very meagre' and that he did not know from where it came. He said that, from the information supplied by MI5, the person identified was not a spy 'but could be classified according to MI5 standards as either a "talent scout" or a liaison officer between the Communist Party and some Russian official'. Wake acknowledged to Chifley that the two MI5 men were influenced neither by Colonel Spry's opinions nor by 'the right-wing politicians' and that they regarded the investigation objectively and were 'non-political' in their outlook.[38] Chifley may have been cheered to know that the visiting MI5 agents, Roger Hollis and Courtney Young, were non-political in their conduct in Australia. It would have given him little consolation, however, to know that all the details about the now notorious intelligence leak that was having such a significant political effect on his government, were being denied to him and hidden behind the veil of US and UK intelligence secrecy.

NOTES

1. NARA, RG353, Report to meeting of SANACC-MIC 206/57, 18 May 1948. Underlining in original.
2. Memorandum for the President from Rear Admiral R.H. Hillenkoetter, USN, Director of CIA, Washington, 27 Jan. 1948, Truman Papers, Harry S. Truman Library, Independence, MO, USA.
3. General Blamey to Senator J.M. Fraser, acting Minister for the Army, 6 Jan. 1945, Blamey Papers, Australian War Memorial.
4. Royal Commission on Espionage, Official Transcript of Proceedings, p. 130, paras 385 to 393.
5. Dell Publishing, New York, 1988, Ch. 13.
6. Ibid, p. 203.
7. NARA, RG 330, Letter Chief of Naval Operations, 23 Dec. 1948.
8. NARA, RG 330, SANACC Report 206/57.
9. Letter Shedden to Burton, 7 April 1948, A669/1, Item 33/1.
10. Evidence given in camera to RCE by Dr John Burton, 2 Nov. 1954, CRS A6213, Item Z/9.
11. PRO, FO 800/277, Dening to Sargent, 12 May 1948. I thank Chris Waters for bringing these documents to my attention.
12. AA, CRS A6213, Item Z/9.
13. Robert Manne, *The Petrov Affair: Politics and Espionage* (Sydney, 1981), pp. 180, 181.
14. PRO, FO 800/277, Sargent to Bevin, 24 May 1948.
15. AA, CRS A816, Item 25/301/492.
16. 987/6/98–104, Dedman Papers, NLA.
17. PRO, CAB 21/1793, Report 8/7/48.
18. Report 13 August 1948, Dedman Papers, 987/9/301, NLA.
19. PRO, DEFE 7/712.
20. PRO, CAB 21/1794.
21. Forrestal papers, p. 2465, Princeton University Library.

22. Ibid., p. 2640.
23. Ibid., p. 2565.
24. PRO, PREM 8/720, report 1 Oct. 1948.
25. NARA, RE330, letter 6 Feb. 1949.
26. 987/9/2627, Dedman Papers, NLA.
27. NARA, RG330, despatch to State Department 24 March 1949. Mrs R.F.B. Wake, widow of Colonel Wake, first Director of NSW Branch of ASIO, informed the author in an interview in Sydney in February 1990 that Colonel Wake had been responsible for suggesting the appointment of Mr Justice Reed to the Attorney-General, Dr H.V. Evatt.
28. CPD, 10 March 1949, p. 1253.
29. CPD, 20 Sept. 1949, p. 347.
30. NARA, RG 330, 'Brief of Aspects of Security in Australia, submitted by F. Shedden to Defense Department'.
31. Ibid.
32. AA, CRS A6213, Item Z/9; Evatt Papers, Flinders University, Report by Dr Burton 15 Sept. 1955.
33. AA CRS A5954, Box 1795, letter 10 May 1949.
34. AA A5954, Box 1795 [1], letter 13 June 1949.
35. AA, CRS A5954, Box 1795 [1].
36. Ibid.
37. Evatt Papers, Flinders University, Report on the 'Net', August 1948.
38. Ibid.

4

The Acceptance of ASIO in the USA

The establishment of ASIO was expected to solve three points of tension in the post-war alliance between Australia, the UK and the USA. With a functioning ASIO, Australia would become the recipient of US missile-range technology; the UK would receive US missile design material; and the CIA report of 'the leak in high government circles in Australia', reputedly akin to the Gouzenko affair in Canada of 1945, would be investigated and the spies uncovered. However, in the short run none of those expectations was met. This lack of outcome confirmed the fact that the establishment of a new civilian intelligence body in Australia was not the real issue for the US. The US was seeking a simple excuse to deny technical secrets to the UK and Australia while retaining their friendship and support in the Western alliance. Thwarting the British development in military high technology and slowing the US sales of new British jet-engined aircraft was also an important motive in raising an intelligence scare.

MISREPRESENTATION OF AUSTRALIA IN THE US

Although Australia had been a close wartime ally of the US and Australia had been the point of assembling and launching a one-million-man US Army against the Japanese invasion of the Pacific, little was known about Australia in the US administration. It was a typical relationship of a superpower to a minor country. The larger power reacted to events in the small only if it suited their interests. Unfortunately for Australia, the little that was known about it in Washington was distorted through the prism of anti-Britishness and, more significantly, anti-Communism – both strong influences in the US government hierarchy. The State and Defense Departments relied for their information about Australia on the US ambassador, Myron M. Cowen, and the office of the US naval attaché, then under the control of Commander Stephen Jurika junior. These reports were characterized by distortions and misleading comments about the radical nature of the Labor government and the CPA influence in Australian political life.

These biases were reinforced by the nature of the informants used. The naval attaché who collected his information from such limited sources as the Director of Australian Naval Intelligence, Lieutenant Commander Mackenzie, who was Staff Officer, Naval Intelligence Sydney, an unnamed feature writer on the Melbourne *Herald* (then directed by Sir Keith Murdoch), the Papal Nuncio to Australia, Monsignor Pannuci, an active anti-Communist priest, Father Ryan, and the resident Dutch intelligence officer, Jenkeer John de Serriere. Dutch intelligence operated with a staff of six out of the Dutch Consulate-General's office in Sydney collecting information about supporters of the Indonesian nationalists whom they were then fighting in Java.[1] These agents were watching the Waterside Workers' Federation of Australia (WWF) which was refusing to load those Dutch ships carrying supplies to its forces in the Netherlands East Indies. The secretary of the Federation, Jim Healey, was a member of the CPA and this, together with the CPA's support for the Indonesian nationalists, ensured the establishment of a close bond between the Dutch and US intelligence officers against what they believed to be their mutual enemy. The US attaché was amazed that the WWF was siding with the nationalists, who he was firmly convinced were Communists, and that the Australian government took no action in this matter. He seemed to be unaware that Dr Evatt, as Foreign Minister, was attempting to establish a settlement between the nationalists and the Dutch colonial authorities. The attaché enjoyed the entrée to Naval Intelligence circles and attended a conference on 'Communism in the Trade Unions of Australia' arranged by Naval Intelligence in Sydney in February 1948 at which representatives of the CIS and the Security Service at the Long Range Weapons Establishment were present.

Many of these reports about the CPA exaggerated its strength and authority. For example, the report of 6 August 1948 claimed that the CPA maintained a type of para-military organization that included a supply branch containing a transport section 'able to provide trucks to take 200 men (and equipment) anywhere in Sydney on ten minutes' notice: it could on 24 hours' notice transport 3,000 men by road anywhere within the state of New South Wales'. This, the report calculated, would require two hundred vehicles which represented twice as many trucks as the army had available in New South Wales. At a time of petrol rationing and when the effect of the suspension of all civilian truck production during the war was still being felt, the attaché reported this impossible mustering of transport as a fact.[2] Other reports provided thorough analyses of the trade unions supposedly dominated by the CPA and other groups belonging to that party such as the Eureka Youth League and the Australian–Russian Society.

The naval attaché held the Labor Party leaders responsible for much of what he saw as the drift to left extremism in Australia. Senior members of the government such as Eddie Ward and Arthur Calwell were described as being CPA members and others such as John Dedman and the Speaker, John Rosevear, were reported as active supporters. Chifley was accused of closing his eyes to CPA subversion; prosecutions of the party under the provisions of the Commonwealth Crimes Act were reported as always being avoided and the despised Dr Evatt was, by association, firmly implicated in this toleration of subversion. The attaché concluded one of his reports with this sweeping indictment of the Australian political, administrative and security arena:

To be terse and to the point, Australia, its life and industry, are dominated by the Communist controlled unions and a Commonwealth Government which condones the actions of these unions, even when those actions are in defiance of law and the Australian Constitution. The Public Service is riddled with Communists on all levels, and there is nothing, of possible interest to the USSR, that cannot be obtained by its agents or sympathizers. Only in a direct service level can classified information retain its secrecy.

Until the Parliamentary Labor Party is removed from office there is not one chance in ten million that any effective action against Communism can or will be taken. A minority of the Australian people are actively concerned with the encroachment of Communists on their civil liberties. They are gaining strength, slowly but inevitably, as the toll of stupid general strikes and curtailed utilities increases daily. On a Government to Government level, particularly through the department of external affairs, I would consider any information given the Commonwealth Government to be almost immediately available to the USSR.[3]

BRITISH REACTIONS

Senior US naval officers wanted the embargo on Australia extended to include Britain as well. Rear Admiral Thomas B. Inglis, Chief of Naval Intelligence, initiated such a move early in 1949. He instructed the British defence representative in Washington that 'in view of the absence of a written undertaking that no United States information on guided missiles will be seen by any Australian, the flow of information to the United Kingdom must cease'. He 'requested that all papers theretofore furnished be returned'. Other officials in the Defense Department were quietly alarmed at Inglis's apparent unilateral action. They implemented a local form of damage control leading to Admiral Denfield of the US Navy suggesting that the British military staff should ignore Inglis's instruction and that Denfield would 'probably have Admiral Inglis withdraw his memorandum'.[4]

This new US tactic of widening the embargo was taken very seriously in the British Defence Ministry. The Minister for Defence, A.V. Alexander, complained to James Forrestal on 24 March 1949 that Britain was 'most dissatisfied with the way in which present arrangements are working' in regard to the 'general problem of disclosure of information between our two countries'. He devoted almost one page of the letter to discussing the Australian embargo and he emphasized that guided missile and other technological secrets were totally secure in Australia.

The British seemed confident that the US would not curtail too drastically the information flow in the face of the claim that Britain was a strategic centre for the developing European defence alliance and the centre point of the British Commonwealth defence arrangement. Some elements in US defence circles were, however, quite uncompromising about assisting Britain with information and the US Joint Chiefs of Staff informed the Secretary of Defense on 1 April in no uncertain terms about their stance on this question as follows:

> That the British be informed that the rigid position of the British Government, as stated by Mr Alexander . . . leaves the US no apparent alternative than to cease the flow of such information to the UK, in the absence of specific assurances that such information can be withheld from elements that constitute unacceptable security risks, specifically Australia. It is believed that the UK should be requested to furnish the US with such specific assurance for our consideration.[5]

With a recommendation of this nature lying on the desk of the new Secretary of Defense, Louis Johnson, when Shedden visited him later in the month, it was unlikely that he would be prepared to have the embargo lifted quickly.

SHEDDEN SENT TO THE US

These US scares and alarms about Soviet spying in Australia and the alleged dominance of the CPA were perceived by the British government as a further tactic adopted by the US officials to destabilize the information exchange arrangements. The British officials were confident that such allegations were baseless, an opinion bolstered perhaps by their knowledge that the Venona decrypts contained little information that could be regarded as damaging to Australia's intelligence and security arrangements. Determined to prevent these harmful allegations corroding the US relationship any further, British officials asked Prime Minister Attlee to raise the matter directly with President Truman and arrange for Sir Frederick Shedden, Secretary of the Australian Defence Department, to visit Washington on his way to Britain in order to give a direct and convincing rebuttal of these allegations to the US officials concerned. The resulting invitation was issued by James Forrestal to the Australian ambassador in Washington, Norman Makin, on 11 February 1949. The Australian Minister of Defence, J.J. Dedman, formally accepted the invitation on 28 February and arrangements were made for the visit to start on 7 April.

Shedden sailed for Washington with a small entourage of an official secretary, a typist, and his wife. His briefcase was full of documents selected for the purpose of bringing US officials completely up to date with the defence and intelligence issues in Australia. These dealt with three areas: intelligence and security in Australia, the co-operation in defence planning between Australia and the US and Australia's co-operation in British Commonwealth defence arrangements. Shedden expected to swamp the US officials with detail, but his plan backfired. They read little of it. Shedden's deathless prose would not have helped hold a reader's attention.

The removal of Forrestal from the scene seriously disadvantaged the chances of obtaining a quick lifting of the embargo. It was he who issued the invitation to Shedden after discussion with President Truman, but he later became ill with a type of mental depression and Truman forced him to resign. His behaviour had become erratic: according to one account, while being cared for by a friend in New York, he wildly jumped out of bed after hearing a fire siren, and ran into the street in his pyjamas shouting that the Russians were attacking. He had previously been telephoning the Attorney-General, Tom Clark, alleging that his house was being watched and his telephone tapped by Clark's FBI agents under J. Edgar Hoover. 'What are you trying to crucify me for?' he was said to have demanded of Clark. Following his admission to the Bethesda naval hospital soon after Truman replaced him with Louis Johnson on 28 March 1949, he committed suicide by leaping from the window of his guarded room on the fourteenth floor.[6]

It was not just Forrestal's removal from the scene that made Shedden's visit so ill-starred. There was an added series of events that hindered the prospect of a positive result. The navy feared that it would lose much of its air-power strength to the newly established US Air Force. The construction of a new aircraft carrier (the keel for which had recently been laid) was cancelled. It was believed that this would lead to the abolition of the Marine

The three US administration figures involved in the US security embargo on Australia. From left, James Forrestal, Secretary of Defense who resigned in the middle of the embargo and later committed suicide, President Truman, who seemed to know nothing of the embargo, and the new Secretary of Defense, Louis A. Johnson, who showed no eagerness to lift it. (Harry S. Truman Library)

Corps air force and much of the Marine Corps itself. The decision on the carrier had been made by the Joint Chiefs of Staff and had led to the resignation of the secretaries of the navy and the army. Johnson had quickly announced the appointment of Curtis Calder, a large investor and significant contributor to Truman's re-election campaign, as the new secretary of the army. But Calder, aware of the problems and personal financial loss that such an appointment would have incurred, publicly refused it.[7]

Another factor ensuring the lack of a positive conclusion to the Shedden visit was the appointment by Johnson of Gordon Gray, then assistant secretary for the army, to be in charge of the visit. Gray was an official of some status but lacked the power and seniority to impose a successful conclusion on the visit. His administrative tactic was to leave the resolution of affairs to committees. The committee members, however, being aware that an intelligence issue of unstated dimension about a country of which only the barest detail was known was at stake, steered clear of any quick settlement of events.

AMBASSADOR COWEN'S ANTI-AUSTRALIAN ATTITUDE

The most vocal opponent to the acceptance of ASIO and the lifting of the US embargo was the US ambassador, Myron M. Cowen. He had been a New York lawyer who was alleged to have been involved in a bribery scandal to obtain a liquor store licence in New York City. His Australian information was collected from higher-level informants than that of the naval attaché, but it was characterized by similarly intolerant views of the Chifley government. Sir Owen Dixon, a High Court judge, was one of Cowen's informants, but he also retailed Cowen's comments back to Australian officials. One snippet relevant to this study was that the US would work with Menzies and Casey if the government changed, but would refuse to co-operate with the Chifley government until after the election.[8]

Cowen was particularly annoyed at the policy of the Australian government for not agreeing to the economic and diplomatic requests of the US government. He saw Australia as being totally obstructive in opposing US policy 'against the USSR and in UN, in Berlin, Greece and Korea; in ERP [European Recovery

Programme] and ITO [International Trade Organisation]; in Fulbright, friendship and double tax agreements; and in attitude towards American industrial and transportation companies doing business here'.[9] The ambassador believed that he had the means of getting even with the Chifley government, and of stopping it being re-elected. Cowen was greatly annoyed that Chifley was using Forrestal's invitation to counter the accusation of Menzies, the Opposition leader, that the government no longer had the confidence of the US government. Cowen sought the permission of the State Department to inform Chifley that he was not to use the invitation in this political fashion. The State Department supported Cowen's stand. In a cable over the name of the Secretary of State, Dean Acheson, Cowen was authorized to announce that Shedden had merely been invited to visit Forrestal on his way from Australia to London. Chifley should not be allowed, Cowen was told, to 'over-emphasize US initiative and eagerness to invite Shedden' and that the 'SECDEF [Secretary of Defense] concurs this view'.[10]

The naval attaché weighed in with a cable of support objecting to Chifley's interpretation of the Forrestal invitation in the following terms:

> Burton of Ex Affairs [External Affairs] says Sir Fred Sheddon [sic] of Defense Dept was invited by Forrestal talk over mutual problems. Primin [Prime Minister] now asks embassy get OK from US to say visit Sheddon to Washn [Washington] enroute UK is at invitation US. Can see no reason to pull Labor chestnuts out of fire for PRIMIN [Prime Minister] especially after long list of anti-American moves, Sheddon will say that new security set up is working which is not correct . . . Sheddon is cold fish, hard bargainer, tireless worker.[11]

Cowen launched a three-point attack on ASIO itself. He declared to Washington that it was too new to judge its efficiency and that Mr Justice Reed was 'inexperienced in this field, not noted as an administrator and perhaps lacks "ruthlessness" required'. More importantly, Cowen warned, ASIO was to come administratively under the Prime Minister, but in practice it was nominally under the dreaded Dr Evatt. Cowen had been

This photograph was taken at the presentation by Ambassador Myron Cowen of his credentials to the Australian Governor-General, W.J. McKell, in July 1948. Those involved in maintaining the US security embargo in Australia were Myron Cowen (first from left, front row), Prime Minister Ben Chifley (third from left, front row), Dr John Burton, Secretary Department of External Affairs (fifth from left, second row) and Commander S. Jurika, head of US naval attaché's office, Melbourne (first from right, back row). (Harry S. Truman Library)

praised by Evatt during the Minister's visit to Washington, but this was not reciprocated by Cowen. 'During his month's visit here,' cabled Cowen, reflecting on Evatt's frequent absences abroad, 'I can confirm, if confirmation happens to be needed, that despite his endorsement of me he is completely unscrupulous and untrustworthy egomaniac.' Cowen concluded with a warning about ASIO:

> It is obviously much too soon [to] know whether establishment [of] new Australian service will tighten security here to degree that would justify us reconsidering our present policy. In strictest confidence Williams, UK High Commissioner here, concurs. I therefore strongly recommend Evatt and Shedden be told we are glad see Australia taking step right direction but must wait for new service demonstrate results.[12]

Cowen seemed unable to appreciate that Evatt was not involved in the Shedden visit.

THE CIA AND AUSTRALIA

Events continued to conspire against the Labor government in having the embargo lifted. Shedden's visit coincided with the publication by the Central Intelligence Agency of a monograph titled *Communist Influence in Australia*. It declared that the 'intelligence organizations of the State Army, Navy and Air Force have concurred in this report'. But the naval attaché's tendency to exaggerate the powers of the CPA shone through it. While admitting that the CPA had an estimated membership of no more than 15,000, its influence was far greater and 'the small membership' was:

> counterbalanced by the strategic position occupied by Communists in Labor unions where the ACP is reported to hold fairly effective control of 275,000 trade unionists and by interlocking relationships between the trade unions and the Labor Party. In recent months, energetic opposition by moderates had resulted in a decline of Communist strength

75

in several key unions, but ACP influence in the movement is still out of all proportion to its size. The ACP exerts pressure upon the federal and state governments, through Labor Party posts held by trade union officials and through federal cabinet members who represent the militant trade unions.[13]

The naval attaché's fixation on the military-style and mobilizing powers of the CPA was echoed in the following section of the report:

The Australian Communist Party has an operations branch which plans infiltration and political strategy, and exercises control over 'front' youth organizations. It has well-organized, personnel, transport and supply sections. Its intelligence branch maintains prodigious files on the life history, ambitions, background and activities of every prominent member of important political groups in Australia. In addition, this branch reportedly furnishes political estimates and is said to be in charge of a local Communist Party counter-intelligence system. All these activities are reported to be centred in 'Marx House' in Sydney.[14]

The report concluded with the somewhat ominous comment that 'The extent of direct Communist influence within the Australian Government (including the armed forces) however, cannot adequately be assessed on the basis of information now available to CIA'. The CIA was involved in the Shedden visit, but because it was then a comparatively new body it played a secondary role to the intelligence branches of the three military services in this affair. A full report was sent to the CIA after Shedden's visit had concluded.

THE SHEDDEN BRIEFING

The final factor to ensure the frustration of a quick conclusion to this intelligence problem was the arrival in Washington of Myron M. Cowen from Canberra. Evatt believed this to be a very bad omen and told Shedden that Johnson was to some extent under Cowen's influence and 'would therefore be guided by his views on any matter affecting Australia'. This judgement was supported by General Sir William Morgan, head of the British Joint Services Mission in Washington, who confirmed for Shedden that Cowen did indeed exert influence over the new Secretary of Defense. Cowen thoroughly immersed himself in the details of the visit (too much for Shedden's liking) and he met Shedden on several occasions and hosted a State Department dinner for the visitor. Shedden was surprised if not alarmed by finding Cowen waiting to speak to Truman as Shedden was leaving the President's office.

Cowen brought from Canberra his baggage full of resentments against Australia. American companies, he said, would not invest in Australia. 'Not one American company,' he warned Shedden, 'intended to put another dollar into Australia under present circumstances.' He quoted the statements of leading Australian businessmen such as Essington Lewis and Charles Lloyd Jones to prove his point and then stated that Thomas Playford, Premier of South Australia, had objected to Mr Justice Reed's services being used 'unless he was given a free hand in security matters'. He lobbied the general staff of the US Army with press clippings from Australia to illustrate how Chifley was distorting the visit by using it to demonstrate the cordiality of the US friendship. In a phrase which Shedden was soon to hear echoed from Johnson, Cowen said that the visit would not achieve any success because it was 'too premature'.[15]

Following his arrival, Shedden sought out the opinions of the friendly sources of information in Washington such as the British defence representatives and the two leading British defence scientists, Sir Henry Tizard and Sir Alwyn Crow, who were also visiting Washington at that time, the Australian ambassador, Norman Makin, and Dr Evatt, who visited Washington while in New York attending sessions of the United Nations. They provided him with the insights about the firm anti-Communist hysteria within the administration and about the prickly nature of Johnson and his programme of asserting his authority over the defence establishment.

Shedden's all-important briefing on 11 April to the *ad hoc* intelligence committee which Gordon Gray had established to handle the Shedden visit lasted for two hours. He traced the

77

history of security in Australia, the establishment of ASIO and how secrets in the Joint Project were preserved.[16] It became apparent that there was no specific reason for the imposition of the embargo based on allegations about intelligence leaks.[17] The intelligence representatives of the three military services who reviewed Shedden's material did not know what they were looking for. They were simple souls fixated on the Communist menace. They wanted to know the 'extent and manner of prosecuting CPA members' and how far the vetting of officials had proceeded. The Evatt phobia continued to inform some of the questioners. Major General A. Bolling, Deputy Director of Intelligence of the Army General Staff, raised his own question and answered it; 'why emphasis on access of Reed to PM – [answer] by pass [sic] man who is responsible'. ASIO, though responsible to the Attorney-General, Dr Evatt, was to have direct access to J.B. Chifley, the Prime Minister.[18] Shedden took the opportunity to press home two points that were basic to the embargo question. These were that there had been 'no evidence so far advanced of leaks from the military or higher defence' and that the 'security setup' for missile testing was totally secure. Both assertions were confirmed by the military intelligence as being correct. Major General Bolling said that he knew of 'no instance of such a leak' and the navy representative confirmed the positive report of its attaché about the firm security of Salisbury and Woomera. The attaché had been taken on a tour of Salisbury and Woomera to which he gave grudging praise.[19]

Australia was very small beer for these intelligence chiefs. They probably knew that there was no case of intelligence leaks in Australia, but they did not have the courage to speak up. They simply agreed with Gray's gratuitous summary that 'there was nothing inherently incurable in the political structure and that over a period of time, perhaps a year or so, a security organization could be developed which met our requirements'. They had probably been informed that Chifley and Dr Evatt would soon be removed from power. No one in Washington was brave enough to admit that there was no real evidence of espionage in Australia. President Truman and the Secretary of State, Dean Acheson, said nothing. They simply showed Shedden the door when he called on them with soothing words and invitations to keep in contact. Shedden realized that Johnson would offer no more. He told Johnson that he was 'extremely disappointed' that Gray would not tell him when the embargo would be lifted. He again pointed out that 'there had been no indication of what is precisely held against Australia, nor had there been any indication of leakage from the Departments which handle the information sought'. Johnson, like his senior officials, was not interested in confronting the truth and blandly told Shedden that the 'visit had been premature'. Shedden was shown the door for the last time with the repeated invitation to keep in contact.[20]

SHEDDEN IN RETROSPECT

Although the Australian government was aware of the anti-Labor bias in the US, it was probably a surprise to Shedden to find how deeply and strongly it was held in official circles. The intensity of this mood was probably not fully appreciated by him until he arrived in Britain and discussed the matter of the embargo with British officials. The Permanent Under Secretary of the Ministry of Supply, Sir Archibald Rowland, gave Shedden some insight into the feverish mind of the Washington officials and political figures when he made the following remarks to him on 18 July 1949:

> In regard to the restriction of classified information, the main difficulty from the American viewpoint was Dr Evatt and Australian External Affairs Policy, which was so often in alignment with Soviet Policy. The Americans feared, in view of this, that there was contact somewhere with the Russians and that classified information might be disclosed to them.[21]

Similar views were provided by none other than the Director-General of MI5, Sir Percy Sillitoe:

> Sir Percy said on 26th August that, when he had discussed the Australian security position with S.A.N.A.C.C. Committee in Washington some time ago, Rear Admiral Inglis (whom he described as Anglophile) and some of the other members said that there could be no settlement while the

Australian Labour [*sic*] Government was in power, as they considered the members pro-communist, and they looked to its replacment at the next election.[22]

Shedden passed these views to Chifley along with the report from members of the Australian Joint Service Staff, under Major-General Chapman, in Washington. The Australian military staff found that a 'recurrent question within United States Service Officers was whether such and such a Minister in Australia was a Communist'. The Australian military officers were being too diplomatic. If they had been pressed into putting a name to 'such and such' it would have been that of Dr Herbert Vere Evatt.[23] It was clear that these officials in Washington had been brainwashed into accepting that the Chifley government in general and Dr Evatt in particular were puppets of the Kremlin. And this distorted view of Australia was largely derived from two sources in the US government. These were the US naval attaché's office which relied on biased sources and an ambassador, of doubtful probity, who matched the naval informant in his exaggerations.

The exercise did not help in the speedier acceptance of ASIO. But it did provide an object lesson for future Australian governments – particularly Labor ones. This was that the changing moods of the US government had to be monitored at all times. Exaggerated reports from its officials in Canberra had to be countered immediately in Washington whenever possible. The US administration wielded too much power in all areas of relationships to be taken lightly. The Australians saw these events as an illustration of the oriental maxim that when the elephant sits down the ants get crushed.

Gordon Gray's original *ad hoc* committee continued to review Shedden's material about ASIO and the surveillance of the CPA as it arrived in Washington, but it saw no reason to lift the embargo. It reported on 20 September 1949 to the military intelligence chiefs and the senior State Department officials that a report had been sought from the US embassy in Canberra which was still pending, but that it was 'of the opinion that considerable time must still elapse before consideration should be given to any possible change in present US security policy with respect to Australia'. The Director of Air Force Intelligence, Major-General C.P. Cabell, commenting on this committee's report on 13 October, raised some hope for the lifting of the embargo. He suggested that if Shedden's future reports and the Canberra embassy report, plus the visit to Washington of the UK official, all proved positive and successful, the embargo be lifted, in his phraseology, 'piecemeal'.[24] The truth was beginning to dawn in some quarters in Washington that Australia had no case to answer. But the Chifley Labor government would be electorally defeated before Washington's officialdom would accept the reality of that truth.

Further reports from Shedden were reviewed, but the US officials saw little virtue in them. 'Australian contributions to the US military effort are generally considered of negligible value' stated one summary, adding that 'US interests in the Long Range Weapons Establishment is alone of insufficient magnitude to justify relaxation' and that:

> A possible weakness in security measures taken is the failure by the Australian Government to list the Communist Party as a subversive element. The implication of this failure is that the Communist Party can continue to be used to advantage by other minority parties in attempting to achieve political goals.

US officialdom could not understand why the Australian Crimes Act provided that the Attorney-General had to approve of prosecutions and suggested that an 'unscrupulous individual motivated by political opportunism could employ that provision to the detriment of society'.[25] The name Evatt was not mentioned in this context, but it was strongly implied in the comment.

EMBARGO PARTLY LIFTED

The long-awaited report from the Canberra embassy arrived in Washington by the middle of October. It was prepared by the three military attachés and the State Department officials who were given copies of Shedden's initial and progress reports. Again the size and activity of the CPA was to the fore in the discussion. Shedden had frankly reported that there were 100 known Communists in the Australian public service, but that none was in a security position. His honesty was not rewarded. The US officials declared that proof of this small number was lacking and that those who were in the post office, telecommunications department or the CSIRO could perform sabotage.

The report said that ASIO was too new to be judged properly. However, while recommending that a skilled US intelligence agent be sent to Australia to assess ASIO, the report did make the significant recommendation that the embargo be partly lifted to allow the exchange of information of a 'restricted' and 'confidential' nature. This was not a major concession because little of importance could be subsumed under these two classifications. What was significant in this report was that Soviet spying and leaks from the Department of External Affairs were not mentioned. The spying allegations that initially led to the imposition of the embargo seemed to have faded from the Administration's collective memory. The intelligence problem that allegedly lay behind it was now loosely alluded to as 'Australia's security problem'.[26]

The Canberra embassy report arrived in Washington and was considered by Gray's *ad hoc* committee. With the ALP government facing defeat, the embassy recommended that Australia be given access to 'confidential' and 'secret' information. However, Gray's committee recommended to the Secretaries of Defence and State on 15 December that access be given only to confidential material. This was approved, and the Canberra embassy was informed on 23 December.[27] The Chifley government had been defeated on 10 December. The State Department was aware that the Labor Party could claim that the change of heart in the US administration was the result of its electoral defeat. As a defence, it instructed the Canberra embassy to say that if such an interpretation was drawn it would be 'undesirable and embarrassing to US-AUSTRAL relationships'.[28] The new US ambassador, Peter Jarman, who had replaced Cowen, passed the news to Prime Minister Menzies on 6 January 1950 and asked that it be kept confidential. The new Australian government thanked the US government profusely in a Note Verbale on 18 January expressing the hope that the restricted classifications would soon be lifted beyond the confidential category. The change made little difference to the flow of information. But it did indicate that the fears of US officials about the Australian government being manipulated by Moscow were receding to a great extent.

ASIO AND THE EMBARGO SEQUEL

The partial lifting of the embargo on 14 March 1950 was probably directly related to the signing of the Burns–Templer agreement on 26 January 1950. Major General J.H. Burns was appointed Special Consultant to the Secretary of Defense on Political Military Affairs early in October 1949. He seemed to take over from Gray the settlement of the Australian embargo question and to become responsible for exchanging US technical information with other countries. General Sir Gerald Templer, Chief of the British Army, signed this agreement to exchange information between the two countries. Little was exchanged, however, because the US would only provide information for what it termed 'releasable projects'. This required the British and Australians to provide the US defence officials with all information about their defence technology developments in order that the US officials could judge whether the release of US technological information would aid that programme. It provided the opportunity for the US to become totally familiar with its competitors' programmes without divulging its own technical information. Given that the US was well ahead in missile development and that there were large profits to be had from the investments made by the government in this technology, such a policy had much to recommend it to the Defense Department.

The US did agree that Australia would be provided with information about operating techniques for long-range proving grounds and, subject to 'satisfactory arrangements', information about guided missiles sufficient for the requirements of the Joint Project. Actually the US provided little technical information until 1957 and the Joint Project went ahead using technology of British or British–German origin. Two agreements were discussed between the US and Australia on 14 March 1950 which the Australians believed would open a new era in US–Australian technological exchanges. In fact they provided for little more than that Australia must store US documents in three-position

83

dial-type combination safes, that London must first obtain US clearance for any information with US content that it sought to give to any Commonwealth nation and US patent rights must always be protected.

In conformity with the Burns–Templer agreement, the British submitted an outline of their programme as a requisite for their sharing the US material with Australia, but the US officials were slow to respond in spite of Australia joining the US in the Korean War and the warm reception and honours given to Prime Minister Menzies when he visited the US in July and August 1950. This US tardiness led Lord Tedder, Marshal of the Royal Air Force, to write to George Marshall, Secretary for Defense, complaining of the delaying tactics of the Military Information Control Committee. Marshall referred the complaint to General Bradley of the Joint Chiefs of Staff who replied on 21 February 1951 that while the Committee was responsible for the disclosure policy it was 'the Military Departments whose information that was involved' who had the final say. This reply confirmed that the importance of the military chiefs and their intelligence advisers in the exchange of information had, if anything, increased since Sir Frederick Shedden's unsuccessful visit in April 1949.[29]

The British kept probing the US defence organization to identify where the heart of the resistance to sharing information with Britain and Australia lay. The British Chief of Air Staff Sir John Slessor, in May 1951 (in the same month that Guy Burgess and Donald Maclean defected to the Soviet Union) reported on where he found the greatest opposition to the UK to be:

> I think it is clear that the Navy is really the nigger in the woodpile. Felix Johnston the new D.N.I. is much better than his predecessor, but the influence of the latter still remains in the lower echelons. It is a regrettable but well-known fact that the troglodyte level in the Pentagon can and frequently does obstruct and nullify agreements made by their seniors.[30]

By May 1953 the controls on the release of information by America were tightened further. President Eisenhower himself issued an edict, on the recommendation of the National Security Council, that he would hold the head of each department or agency responsible for ensuring that US classified information was given to foreign nationals only on a need-to-know basis or after it had been determined that it was to the best advantage of the US. In addition, Eisenhower instructed that each foreigner who was a 'prospective recipient' of security information classified secret or higher would, 'to the extent feasible', need to have security checks made on them. The President did not indicate how security checks would be made on foreign nations by US agencies. It is possible that this security measure marked the beginnings of a partial acceptance of foreign national intelligence and security organizations such as ASIO, by the FBI and other agencies who had to collect overseas information to implement this presidential edict.[31]

IMPLICATIONS FOR ASIO

This chapter demonstrates that the establishing of ASIO by itself did not lead to the lifting of the US embargo on the transmission of classified information to Australia. The US authorities were seeking assurances that the security of the Joint Project was intact and that Australian political figures would not have access to their technical information. The structure of ASIO, even with the MI5 imprimatur, did not impress them. It could be argued, in retrospect, that Chifley need not have established ASIO. He could have retained the CIS for the vetting work and expanded the security service that was guarding the secrets of the Joint Project at Salisbury and Woomera.

The allegations about the existence of a Soviet spy ring in Australia after the war received no confirmation from the details explored in this chapter. The Soviet spying story seemed to be a construct. It is worthwhile noting that the stale news about Soviet spying in Australia, as revealed by the CIA to President Truman and taken up by the US Navy, faded from sight after its initial disclosure. The allegations about Soviet spying in Australia were not the real reasons used by US officialdom to withhold information from Australia. Their excuse for denial was that they considered Australia too technically underdeveloped to justify providing it with missile technology or missile range-measuring equipment. The Australian spying allegations may have faded in

85

US circles but they remained dormant in Australia, to be revived in 1953 and 1954 during the Petrov affair.

The establishment of ASIO was not the only outcome of the fervid events surrounding the imposition and lifting of the US embargo on Australia. The question underlying that embargo – that is, how the US was to handle requests for information from its allies in the burgeoning Cold War – had to be resolved. The technique used by the military chiefs against Australia's and Britain's requests for information – that is raising the spectre of Soviet spying in one of the countries concerned – was no longer appropriate. The solution for the US administration was found in the notion of the 'releasable projects'. US officialdom realized that the essential factors in providing information to their allies were contained in three points: the US must know why the allies wanted it; royalties must be collected from the allied user; and any leakage to the Soviet Union must be prevented.

It was probably of little consolation to Chifley, Dr Evatt, Shedden and other Australian officials that they spent exhausting days and had their reputations impugned in the process of helping US officialdom to reach these more rational measures of deciding who would get what from its rich store of defence technology secrets.

NOTES

1. Federal Bureau of Investigation (FBI) Archives, Washington, DC, USN Attaché's Report, 21 June 1948, file no. 64–200–303–46.
2. FBI Archives, USN Attaché's report, 10 Feb. 1948, file no. 64–200–303–44.
3. FBI Archives, USN Attaché's report, 6 Aug. 1948, file no. 64–200–303–47.
4. NARA RG 330, Johnson to Gray, 29 March 1949.
5. NARA, SANACC, 206/66, Appendix 'A'.
6. Tyler Abell (ed.), *Drew Pearson Diaries, 1949–1959* (New York, 1974), pp. 39, 250.
7. AA, CRS A5954, box 1795, Shedden to Prime Minister, 10 May 1949.
8. AA, CRS A5954, box 1795, Supplementary Notes, April 1949.
9. NARA, RG 330, Cowen to State Department 14 Feb. 1949.

10. NARA, RG 330, Cable 22 March 1949.
11. NARA, RG 330, Cable 22 March 1949.
12. NARA, RG 330, Cable 15 March 1949.
13. Harry S. Truman Library, Papers of Harry S. Truman, Independence, MO, USA.
14. Ibid.
15. AA, CRS A5954 box 1795, Notes of Private Discussions, April 1949.
16. NARA, RG 330, Sir Frederick Shedden's Presentation, 11 April 1949; AA, CRS A5954, box 1795, Outline of notes, 11 April 1949.
17. NARA, RG 330, Review of Sir Frederick's Documentation, 20 April 1949.
18. NARA, RG 330, Department of the Army, Examination of Documentation submitted by Sir Frederick Shedden, 21 April 1949.
19. AA, CRS A5954, box 1795, Summary of Questions Raised and Conclusions Expressed by the Hon. Gordon Gray, 28 April 1949; NARA, RG 330, Australian Security: Memorandum for Record, 22 April 1949; Basis For Statement to Sir Frederick Shedden, 26 April 1949.
20. NARA, RG 330, Stoppage of Classified Information to Australia. Summary of Conclusions Expressed by the Hon. Louis A. Johnson, Secretary of Defense, at a Meeting on 28 April 1949.
21. AA, CRS A5954, Private Reports from Washington and London on Secretary's Visit to Washington, n.d.
22. AA, CRS A5954, Appendix.
23. AA CRS A5954, Notes of Private Discussions, April 1949.
24. NARA, RG 330, Study of Sir Frederick Shedden's Progress Report, 20 September 1949; Department of Air Force, Report by Major General C.P. Cabell, 13 Oct. 1949.
25. NARA RG 330, Report of Australian Security Situation, 7 Oct. 1949.
26. NARA, RG 330, Report, Release of Classified Military Information to Australia, 7 Oct. 1949.
27. NARA, RG 330, Revision Policy on Disclosure Classified United States Military Information to Australia, 19 Dec. 1949.
28. NARA, RG 330, State Department Cable, Washington to Canberra, 23 Dec. 1949.
29. NARA, RG 330, Tedder to Marshall, 15 Feb. 1951.
30. Ibid.
31. NARA, RG 330, Memorandum for Secretaries of Army, Navy, Air Force 7 Aug. 1953.

5

Anti-Communism and ASIO

The early 1950s witnessed an extensive growth in the size and power of ASIO. The new Menzies government contained many men who had perceived the CPA and its forebear, Bolshevism, as the most serious threat to the world in those post-war years. These were men whose political values and ideas had been formed after the First World War when middle-class attitudes towards Socialism and Communism were firmly equated with the horrors of mob rule and the devastations of the Bolshevik revolution. The minds of Menzies and his ministers were firmly set in the direction of suppressing the CPA, jailing its continuing adherents and expanding and strengthening ASIO as a measure against possible subversion or espionage. Two other reasons prevailed. One was that the US administration (as the previous chapter demonstrated) looked unfavourably on those countries where the local Communist Party was not assaulted with all the armoury of the state. The second was that attacking the CPA was popular with the Australian news media and thereby the public. There were definitely votes in it. As large as ASIO's staff then was, with 114 people, and as large as its financial resources were, none of its leaders could have predicted how quickly and extensively it was to grow in the succeeding Cold War years. It is the study of this administrative phenomenon (a study which has attracted the attention of historians in other Western countries where similar extensive expansions in their intelligence organizations have occurred) that this chapter sets out to undertake.

A photograph of Colonel Charles Spry, head of ASIO, taken when he was an army cadet. (Royal Military College, Duntroon)

R.G. Casey, Australia's intelligence supremo. As a senior cabinet minister he helped build up ASIO and later ASIS. (National Library)

POLICE TECHNIQUES AND ASIO

When Mr Justice Reed established ASIO, he looked to the State police forces as a source for recruitment. This tendency was understandable given that he had been a lawyer and was then a judge significantly involved in criminal work. South Australia did not possess a large commercial sector and the central preoccupation of its legal fraternity was mainly confined to criminal matters. Employing former policemen to maintain surveillance on Communist Party members, radicals, militant trade union leaders, and other 'disrupters' had a firm logic to it. The association in the public's mind of radicalism with criminality had become firmly established as a result of the police being used to suppress dissenters and radicals.[1]

Mr Justice Reed established ASIO's headquarters in Sydney and while he engaged Ray Whitrod from the South Australian police force, whom he appointed as Assistant Director to the NSW Director, R.F.B. Wake, his other police appointees such as the former detective sergeant, Devro McDermott, Richard Gamble and Leo Carter were recruited from the NSW police force.[2] Such policemen brought with them to ASIO the trade skills they had learnt and automatically applied in their previous occupation. These included such tactics as employing informers whom they remunerated with secret payments, placing incriminating evidence on suspects in order to obtain convictions, planting double agents in the midst of the target groups to bring out information and to place disinformation. Other trade skills included tapping telephones with the connivance of friendly telecommunications officials and opening letters while passing through the mail with covert approval from postal officials. Corruption and bribe-taking, also characteristic of policing activity, seemed, fortunately, not to have been carried over into this new field of political surveillance. While those in intelligence circles with more lofty scruples may have raised an eyebrow at these common police practices, their effectiveness in collecting useful information about ASIO's target groups was quickly proven. Another policing technique, that of artfully marshalling evidence to obtain a plausible prosecution in an otherwise questionable case, was to be of the utmost importance, as we shall see, in ASIO's involvement in the conduct of the Royal Commission into the Petrov affair.

Reed perceived two inter-related administrative goals for ASIO. The first was to expand ASIO'S manpower to handle the suppression of the CPA. The second was to solve the question of what to do with the CIS. Under the government's proposals the property of the Communist Party was to be seized and details on all Party members tabulated. But ASIO did not have the manpower resources to break up and suppress the Party. And because ASIO was to be a secret organization Reed did not wish to have ASIO agents called upon to give evidence in court where Party members were being prosecuted. Nor did Reed consider the Subversive Organizations Investigation Branches (SOIB) – these were extensions of the special branches of the State police forces – to be reliable. State Labor governments, he maintained, could withhold their employment in these Communist-suppression operations. Reed recommended to the Attorney-General that the CIS be incorporated into an enlarged Australian police force. It could help ASIO suppress the CPA by working with the State police forces. It could have its officers appear in court to conduct prosecutions thereby sparing ASIO agents having to reveal their identities.[3]

Reed returned to his judge's duties in South Australia in July 1950 and his replacement, Colonel Spry, implemented the proposal of Reed to make the CIS a type of police arm of ASIO by an easy administrative device. He simply appointed the senior ASIO agent, Ray Whitrod, to be the new head of CIS after E.E. Longfield Lloyd, an intelligence agent whose experience stretched back to the First World War, retired. The understandable friction and jealousy that had emerged between these two intelligence bodies (discussed in Chapter 2), as they competed for the small amount of political surveillance work then available in Australia, subsequently disappeared. The CIS was incorporated into a newly enlarged Australian Federal Police Force in the succeeding years.[4]

The arrival of Colonel (later Sir Charles) Spry as the new Director-General of ASIO on 17 July 1950 heralded other innovations in the management and philosophy of the Organization. He was seconded from his position as Director of Military Intelligence and given a large salary increase while maintaining the right to return to the army if he so desired. This secondment from the army ceased on 20 August 1954. Reed had been due to retire from ASIO in February 1950, but the new Menzies government extended his appointment, presumably to give it time to find a replacement who was closer to its own ideological convictions about the subversive nature of the CPA and the Soviet embassy in Australia.

Charles Spry had been born in Brisbane on 26 June 1910 where his father worked as an apiarist in the outer suburb of Eagle Junction. He was educated at the local state schools and Brisbane Grammar school and entered Royal Military College, Duntroon, at 18 years of age to undertake training as a military officer. He completed the course there at the end of 1931 when the Great Depression was making 30 per cent of the Australian work-force unemployed. He was judged in his final report as 'being slow to grasp essentials, a fair horseman, boxes well, a good cricket and tennis player' which was probably a fair commentary on the essential skills required for a military officer at that time. He served as an infantry officer in Hobart and Sydney and from 1935 served for a year in the Duke of Wellington's Regiment with the British Army in India where he joined in operations on the Northwest Frontier.[5] He served in

91

Papua New Guinea and was awarded the DSO for maintaining the flow of supplies there, and he also worked in military intelligence. Unlike many of his contemporaries who pursued other careers in civilian life after the war, he remained in the army.

RICHARD CASEY, THE INTELLIGENCE SUPREMO

The selection of Colonel Spry as the new Director-General of ASIO owed much to the influence of Richard Casey. Casey was a senior minister in the government, a leading Liberal Party official and a man of extensive intelligence experience stretching back to the First World War. He inherited much of his father's estate founded on the ownership of a large copper mine in Queensland. He would have been Prime Minister except that he was not in the appropriate place at the right time when he could have taken hold of the leadership of the Liberal Party. His wife also inherited wealth and together they lived in a grand mansion on a thousand-acre property near the town of Berwick, 30 miles from Melbourne. Casey established his own airfield there and with a fleet of two aircraft commuted to Canberra where he served initially in the Menzies government as Minister for National Development. Later he became Minister for External Affairs. Because of his father's wealth and British mining contacts Casey grew up as a man of both the British and Australian worlds. He was initially educated in Melbourne but decided to attend Trinity College, Cambridge, for his university education and thereafter mingled with British political and social leaders. Few in Australia were surprised that after retiring from politics in 1960 he accepted a British peerage and sat in the House of Lords as Baron Casey of Berwick and the City of Westminster. In 1969 he was made Australia's first Knight of the Garter, a gift of the Queen, after he retired as Governor-General of Australia.

Casey's experience in intelligence began with his service in the Australian Army in the First World War. Thanks to the intervention of his father, who was well acquainted with Aust-ralian prime ministers and generals, he served in the comparative safety of the staffs of various military commanders.[6] He handled a large volume of military intelligence material in these positions. He witnessed the huge carnage induced by the incompetent generals under whom he served. While he seems to have accepted this military-mindedness at the time, it left him with the conviction that wars must not be left to generals alone but that other means such as intelligence-collecting and clandestine operations should be used to contain a foe.

Further experience was gained by Casey in the collection and application of intelligence as a result of his appointment between 1924 and 1939 as representative of the Australian Prime Minister, S.M. Bruce, in the British government. He acted as a type of post office, handling material sent by MI5 and the Special Branch of Scotland Yard to the CIS and the reverse flow of reports from Australia. These reports related to the movements of CPA members travelling to Berlin or Moscow via London or to Soviet activists travelling to Australia or parts of the Far East. Casey assessed each report to decide which intelligence organization should be the recipient.[7] During the Second World War, which brought a significant rise in importance of intelligence activities, Casey kept abreast of developments by being involved in several important areas of intelligence collection and usage. By 1940 he had accepted appointment to the US as Minister in the new Australian legation established in Washington. During his two-year appointment there, Casey worked closely with the British embassy in an attempt to persuade the US administration not only to join the Allies against Germany but also to demonstrate a firmer resolve against the imperialist expansion of Japan. The British, at Churchill's urging, appointed William Stephenson, 'the man called Intrepid', to be the Passport Control Officer in New York (he was later to be head of the British Security Co-ordination Office there) as a means of monitoring Germany's attempts to court US support and also as a means of countering the strong belief in the US administration that Britain would soon fall victim to a German invasion. These intelligence operations were relatively successful and confirmed for Casey who worked with some of Stephenson's staff, such as Alan Dudley, whose cover was in the British Library of Information in New York, the effectiveness of intelligence operations to counter the enemy and win allies.[8]

Casey also developed what were to be long-term contacts with US intelligence organizations including the Office of Strategic Services (OSS) under Bill Donovan and with whom Casey established a lifelong relationship. He visited the OSS offices in the Administrative Offices in E Street, Washington DC, and was enchanted to find when he returned in 1952 to discuss intelligence affairs with Donovan's successor, Walter Bedell Smith, in the succeeding organization, the CIA, that it maintained the same address.[9]

Casey's effective support for the British cause in the US, not to mention his now enlarged intelligence experiences, led to his being appointed by Churchill as Resident British Minister in Cairo in 1942 where he became even more deeply immersed in intelligence affairs. The British had two main aims after the North African war turned in the Allies' favour: to hold the Suez Canal and maintain access to the Arab-controlled oil resources. Casey, by covert and non-covert means, had to hold to these aims against a variety of forces marshalling in the Middle East for their own purposes, such as the Zionists, the Greek monarchists, the Lebanese, the Persians and, on some matters, the Americans. It was in this posting that Casey obtained his greatest insight into intelligence activities. Early in 1944 Casey became Governor of Bengal, again at Churchill's invitation, and in 1945 returned to Australia then governed by his political opponents, the ALP.[10]

Casey immediately got himself appointed as President of the Liberal Party so that he could bring together the two elements to have his party re-elected to power – money and supporters.[11] The Liberal Party won the general elections of 1949 and Casey accepted the portfolio of Minister of National Development, which, however remote from the management of intelligence affairs, did not prevent him from dabbling in such affairs, as we have seen with the appointment of Colonel Spry to head ASIO and, as we shall later see, in the placing of an agent in the CPA in order to feed official disinformation from his Department of National Development to that party's press.

It was not surprising that Casey and Spry worked closely together with Spry frequently visiting Casey's property or town residence and Casey visiting ASIO headquarters.[12] ASIO was under the ministry of the Attorney-General, with the right of direct access to the Prime Minister, and it was some indication of the status of Casey and his expertise in intelligence matters that he was able to bypass the Attorney-General and deal directly with his appointee – the Director-General.

By the time of Spry's appointment, ASIO's staff amounted to 141 people, and Spry added to this number, probably at Casey's instigation, by recruiting some university graduates. These included Michael Thwaites who had worked for the *Age* newspaper in Melbourne. He was an active supporter of another right-wing secretive group with whom Casey shared an affiliation, Moral Rearmament (MRA).[13] This body sought to oppose Communism by some form of Christian revival. Other recruits were Robert Swan, who had dabbled in poetry writing, and R. Campbell, son of Casey's friend H.A.M. Campbell, former editor of the *Age* newspaper. Spry also appointed people from military intelligence such as Max Phillips who had been his motor transport driver during the war. Casey visited ASIO's new headquarters in Melbourne in February 1952 to meet these and other staff as well as the MI5 liaison officer who knew Casey's former contacts at MI5, Peter Goodwyn and Guy Liddell.[14]

CASEY, ASIO AND ASIS

Casey also established Australia's external security force, the Australian Secret Intelligence Service (ASIS) and gave it firm direction after he became Minister for External Affairs in August 1951. It was established under the aegis of the British Secret Intelligence Service (SIS) also known as MI6. Between 1954 and 1957 ASIS had expanded to 60 staff and stations in Jakarta, Tokyo and Bangkok. It also maintained agents in the SIS stations at Singapore and Hong Kong.[15] Casey also selected the son of a friend to head ASIS, Alfred Deakin Brookes. Clandestine activities seemed to run in the Brookes family. His father was Herbert Brookes who with covert government support, attempted to establish a private right-wing army in 1918 and 1919 to counter the left-wing movements that had formed during and after the war.[16] Casey enlarged his earlier contacts with the OSS, by then the CIA, and found that the CIA was eager to help with the development of ASIS. On a visit to Washington in November 1952 Casey was told by its director, Walter Bedell Smith, and his deputy, Allen Dulles, that the CIA could train its officers and provide equipment. ASIS remained tied to the SIS and joined its covert radio network in 1953. A transmitter was established near Darwin in northern Australia to expand this ASIS/SIS radio net.

The CIA had established its own representation in Australia when Henry Balivet arrived in May 1953 to be replaced by Samuel Rowntree Sanders in May 1954. Sanders adopted the discreet cover of assistant naval attaché and assistant attaché for air in the US Consul's office in Melbourne. Casey continued to cultivate the CIA connection and on 11 September 1953 he visited its headquarters and discussed intelligence affairs with its new Director, Allen Dulles, his deputy, General Cabell, Frank Wisner, in charge of operations and Robert Amory, head of the intelligence section of the Joint Intelligence Bureau (JIB).[17]

By 1957 Brookes seems to have overstepped his authority and the government considered abolishing ASIS. Colonel Spry leapt to its defence arguing that its great value in watching Indonesian affairs could be lost. The CIA through its local agent, Lieutenant Colonel Collas G. Harris, urged its retention. SIS responded by sending its Vice-Chief, Sir James Easton, to Australia to lobby for its retention. ASIS was saved and Brookes was replaced by a new Director, Ralph Harry, a former diplomat.[18] In 1960 Casey resigned from politics for reasons that are still not apparent. Thereafter, ASIS had several ministers. The diminished Cold War and the departure of the generation nurtured on the evilness of the Bolshevik revolution such as Casey and Dulles meant that intelligence organizations like ASIS and ASIO had to begin searching for new roles for themselves. In 1975, under the Whitlam Labor government, both ASIO and ASIS received considerable shake-ups when their directors were removed for different reasons by Prime Minister Whitlam.[19]

ASIO AND THE SUPPRESSION OF THE CPA

Returning to the early 1950s, we can see that Spry, like his predecessor, Reed, perceived an opportunity for the expansion of ASIO under the proposals of Menzies to proscribe the CPA. The legislation proposed that a receiver be appointed to dispose of the Party's property, that fringe groups of the Party be dissolved and that people continuing to carry on the functions of the Party were to be jailed for five years. People declared to be 'Communist' under the Act were to be dismissed from their jobs in the public service and the defence forces or trade unions. People accused of being Communists could appeal to a court to have that declaration set aside. If they appeared in court and gave evidence it became the task of the government to prove that they were the persons named. If they did not appear in court the burden of proof fell upon the individuals to show that they were not the persons named. The role of ASIO would have been central to enforcing this unusual piece of legislation. It would be the task of ASIO to ensure that the CPA was suppressed and that the fringe groups were also dissolved. Those people bold enough to challenge through the court procedures the declaration that they were Communists, whether they appeared or not, would have directly involved ASIO because the evidence on which such declarations were made would come from its collection of dossiers. If the government opposed the appellant's claim it would be on the basis of ASIO's say-so, and it would again be on evidence produced by ASIO that the government's case would be sustained. ASIO agents would have had to appear in court and it is apparent now why Reed and later Spry were eager to have the CIS assume the responsibility for conducting the prosecution's case in order to conceal the identity of their ASIO agents. By this time ASIO had acquired all the records relating to CPA members from the CIS including what was then the latest haul of names obtained when the CIS conducted an extensive raid on CPA headquarters in Marx House, Sydney, in July 1949. By this time the Party membership stood at approximately 6,000 people.[20]

The importance of all this illiberal legislation was that it conditioned the Australian population to the belief that there existed an enemy within the gate; for ASIO it led to an increase in ASIO's staff numbers, particularly skilled people such as lawyers, and others who could handle all the administrative work that would accompany the implementation of this unusual banning measure. Had the Communist Party Dissolution Bill not been disallowed, ASIO staff numbers would have swollen considerably and made it more like the secret police force familiar in totalitarian countries. An analysis of the Ministerium für Staatssicherheit (MfS or Stasi), the former East German internal security service, has indicated that it was one of the

97

largest East German landowners with over 5,000 residences in East Berlin alone, one of the largest employers with 85,000 full-time and more than 109,000 unofficial employees, and one of the largest consumers of paper with 120,000 linear metres of files by the time its dissolution was undertaken in March 1990.[21]

The Communist Party Dissolution Act became law in October 1950 after passing through both Houses of the Australian Parliament. It would have been impossible for the Labor Party to have stopped this legislation in Parliament even though they had control of the Senate. The emotions of the electorate were thoroughly excited by Menzies and the media over not only the CPA at home but also the war against the Soviet-sponsored North Korea, in which Australian military forces were involved.

On the day immediately following the passing of the Act, the government discussed the appointment of a receiver to seize and commence selling all CPA property. ASIO was alerted and Menzies ordered the establishment of a secret organization under military command, identified by the code name 'Alien', which would rally mainly civilian forces to counter the effects of possible industrial actions and demonstrations in protest against the legislation. Spry had already anticipated the additional workload to be imposed on ASIO with the adoption of this legislation and wrote to the Attorney-General in October 1950 asking that the Prime Minister should enrol the support of the State Premiers to allow ASIO to call on their police forces for aid in 'searching covert places' seeking 'documents and other property belonging to the Party'. When the CPA was banned in 1940 they concealed their papers and printing presses and some members went underground in order to continue distributing Party propaganda and leaflets. Spry was aware that the CPA would conceal their operations more carefully the second time and that larger manpower resources would be required to uncover the covert activities. If doors were to be smashed down and printing presses seized it was better for the police to be seen doing it rather than ASIO agents.[22]

CPA rooms and offices were again raided and searched in Melbourne, Sydney, Hobart and Darwin on 23 October and large truckloads of paper and documents were again taken away. Nothing of value seemed to have been discovered indicating that the CPA might have already adopted the plan of going partly underground. In Western Australia ASIO officers tried to swell their small haul by taking possession of the CPA documents seized by the local police in May 1949 and still held by them.[23]

This hurried action to round up the Communists continued to gather pace until approximately 14 November 1950 at which date a challenge was initiated in the High Court of Australia against the Act being considered legal under the terms of the Australian constitution. This appeal was lodged by several industrial trade unions, for some of which Dr Evatt appeared as counsel, much to the ire of Menzies and the right wing of the Labor Party.

The court hearing dragged on into the following year and the judgment was not given until 9 March 1951. Meanwhile Colonel Spry, seeking to keep the anti-Communist mood alive and ASIO's index of names as full as possible, decided to publicize more widely the existence of ASIO and its capacity to flush out what it regarded as subversives. He intended to lower very slightly the screen of secrecy surrounding ASIO by allowing the telephone numbers for its branches to appear in the relevant telephone books, but not the addresses. He also proposed to follow the tactic of the Federal Bureau of Investigation (FBI) in the US which actually lodged advertisements in newspapers and broadcast on radio stations inviting the public to report the names of alleged subversives to their nearest FBI office. The advertisement was distributed, not surprisingly, given his penchant for self-publicity, under J. Edgar Hoover's name and signature. Spry sought the approval of Prime Minister Menzies to conduct similar self-promotional advertisements for himself and ASIO, but by that time the plan for banning the CPA had moved on to another stage.[24]

The decision of a majority of the High Court was that the Act was contrary to the Australian constitution. Menzies seemed eager to keep the anti-Communist issue alive and, because he lacked a majority in the Senate, took the politically prudent decision to exploit the continuing excitement and clamour over anti-Communism by obtaining a double dissolution and attempting to win large majorities in both houses. The elections of 28 April 1951 brought him success in this plan and he thereupon set about holding a referendum to alter the constitution to provide for the banning of the CPA. Menzies was an eminent constitutional lawyer and laid claim to being a liberal democrat and a man of tolerance and learning. He must have foreseen the serious constitutional problems that would emerge on the issue of civil liberties if the terms of the Dissolution Act had become entrenched in the Australian constitution. As one Australian jurist remarked, he was embarking on a proposal that was 'alien to our constitutional and legal traditions' and that it represented a negativism that clearly represented 'a vacuum in the philosophical underpinning of conservative politics in Australia which was to haunt those parties after they eventually lost government in 1972'. Such a judgement, while valid in itself, fails to understand how a government carrying its own convictions of the evils of Communism might not have been blinded to constitutional and human rights issues by the very brilliance and efficiency of its own counter-espionage organization.[25] ASIO was adding to its dossier collection of Communists every day. The accuracy of the reports might be questioned, but for a Prime Minister who had once before banned the CPA, these growing numbers of intelligence reports could not but have convinced him that the loss of civil liberties and the creation of constitutional problems in the future was a price worth paying for eliminating the demonstrable and documented evils of Communism once and for all from the Australian body politic.

ASIO EXPANDS

Between the election in April and the refendum to alter the constitution in September 1951, Spry continued to oversee the continuing expansion of ASIO. By this time ASIO had established within its head office four sections. These were to handle administration, technical work (such as operating electronic listening devices), records and police liaison work. Surveillance work was conducted by three branches at head office, the first being concerned with subversive organizations. Spry had also been attending a conference of British Commonwealth intelligence chiefs held in London. It was a precursor to the joint meetings of intelligence heads of Canada, New Zealand, Australia and Britain, to be known as CAZAB, and officially started in 1967. The intelligence officer who attended from New Zealand was impressed by the ASIO organization and at his request, placed via Spry, an outline of ASIO's structure and functions was sent by Menzies to Prime Minister Holland in New Zealand.[26]

ASIO acquired for itself another extension of its authority when, in conjunction with the Minister and the Department of Immigration, it arranged on 1 September 1950 to compel all those Australians wishing to visit Eastern Europe to obtain the permission of that Department and of ASIO to do so. ASIO immediately went into action against 29 Australian peace conference delegates, both Communist and others, who were already attending a peace conference in London which had been banned by the British government and which the organizers then transferred to Warsaw. This number included Jessie Street, an active feminist and peace-worker, Jim Healey, Secretary of the Waterside Workers' Federation, and John R. Hughes, Secretary of the NSW Clerks' Union. The Australian government learned of this switch on 13 November and warned the Australians that their passports would be cancelled if they went to Poland because they had not been endorsed under this new programme. The Australians thereupon left for Prague, presumably as a means of reaching Warsaw. The government asked the British authorities to seize and impound the Australians' passports if they returned to the UK and the Australian immigration officers were ordered to seize the passports when the delegates returned to Australia. ASIO's role thereafter was to interrogate Australians wishing to visit Eastern Europe about the reasons for their proposed journey and 'if no security risk was involved' the passport was issued. This arrangement was clearly a surveillance technique to watch and document more easily those Australians who were visiting Eastern Europe.[27]

ASIO also became the expert on compiling information for public distribution about the CPA. During the referendum campaign to ban the CPA, ASIO prepared a paper entitled 'Communism in Australia' for use by government speakers on 19 September 1951. The referendum was held on 22 September and it is not clear whether the paper's distribution to government speakers was late because of a delayed realization that the government's case might fail in the voting or because the ASIO officers had been tardy in preparing such material. Certainly Colonel Spry believed this document to be very worthwhile and suggested to Menzies that it should be distributed after the referendum as a White Paper.[28]

This new development whereby ASIO became a type of information distribution agency was, paradoxically, the result of ASIO's very effectiveness in curtailing the membership numbers and authority of the CPA. By this time CPA membership had dwindled to approximately 3,000 people representing many of the hard-core stayers. This decline of membership from the peak of approximately 20,000 in 1944 was of course not caused by ASIO's activities. It was brought about more by the Menzies government's withering attack supported by the public's knowledge that there was a type of secret police force silently and efficiently exposing the party's activities. Together these two factors led to diminishing membership numbers and collapsing support. With the prestige of the CPA permanently weakened by the thoroughness of this campaign, it became a matter of some irony that ASIO had to devote more resources to documenting and publicizing the activities of this remaining rump of the party in order to justify its continuing existence.

ASIO pushed its presence into the film-making media at this time. It learned that the government's Film Division of the Department of the Interior had been unwillingly prodded into making an anti-Communist propaganda film in the middle of 1952. Its minister, W.S. Kent Hughes, instructed that a film be made showing 'a scorching indictment of the menace of communism'. This was to be compiled mainly from clips of film supplied by 20th Century Fox Films, showing for instance weeping and bewildered French peasants unable to understand why France had been invaded by the Germans. The audience was expected to infer that the French Communist Party sapped the French will to resist. Spry sought to offer assistance to J.S. Allan, a director, in the section of the Film Division making this ten-minute film that bore the ominous title, *Menace*. ASIO's help was not required in the script-writing but it did manage to have itself invited into the studio premises where it began vetting the Film Division's staff, some of whom had objected to making such a propaganda film because it was outside the objectives of the film-making unit. Those staff who raised such arguments were investigated by ASIO agents and their names and details added to the Organization's growing data-base. Richard Casey was delighted that this piece of counter-propaganda had been made and after viewing it in a Melbourne cinema declared that it had been 'quite well done'.[29]

ASIO AND ITS QUARRIES

This brief review of ASIO's quarries examines both the old targets of ASIO, now familiar to readers, such as the left-wing trade unions, and the new targets that appeared following post-war changes in Australian society, such as universities, anti-war groups, cultural nationalists and immigrant groups. The individuals quickly reviewed here also reflect these categories of old and new targets. The common element in all these groups and individuals was that they were Communist or were perceived by ASIO as being sympathetic to Communism.

Of the many Australian trade unions that shed their Communist executive members as a result of the general anti-Communist hysteria, two industrial unions remained firmly attached to theirs. These were the Waterside Workers' Federation (WWF) and the Seamen's Union. James Healey was Federal Secretary of the WWF and as a CPA member had been a target of ASIO for decades. Healey had become an active leader in the World Federation of Trade Unions (WFTU), based in Paris and regarded as Communist-dominated. When the New Zealand waterside workers conducted a strike with WFTU backing, Healey supported the banning of all work on New Zealand ships in Australia and elsewhere. The government was galvanized into action. The army and navy were mobilized to work on the wharves and sail the ships. ASIO was also thrown into the fight. It helped compile material to aid the prosecutions under the Australian Crimes Act. It was also called upon to use its secraphone telephone network to help with naval intelligence liaison and keep track of union leaders believed to be masterminding the industrial stoppages. Healey was prosecuted and sentenced to six months' imprisonment in July 1951, but his appeal against being jailed was upheld.[30]

Ernest Thornton, General Secretary of the Federated Iron-workers' Union (FIU), was also a CPA member and active in the WFTU. The FIU had managed after a long struggle to unionize

Australia's sole steel-maker, Broken Hill Proprietary Ltd (BHP). This was of such a concern to ASIO, and no doubt the company, as to make the assistant director of ASIO's Sydney office report to Spry in October 1950 that 'the Union [FIU], with its General Secretary a figure in the world Communist organization, its National Council dominated by members of the ACP [CPA], and its close liaison with other communist dominated unions, is a perfect instrument for carrying out whatever policy the Kremlin has towards Australia's steel industry'.[31]

For this and other reasons ASIO established close links with the Special Branches of the State police forces, appointed their own Field Officers and hired informants in the unions, in order to monitor industrial actions and the elections of the union executives. In the more militant unions CPA members were kept under observation by ASIO. In union elections these CPA members were usually elected to the executive, but they did not advertise their CPA connections, much to ASIO's annoyance. ASIO officers also compiled information about the unsuccessful non-CPA candidates, apparently in an effort to identify men who could be put up against the Communists. The exercise seemed dispiriting. While their ALP and Catholic church adherences could not be questioned, the ASIO reports sadly identified them as suffering alcohol problems, indulging in financial mis-management or being plainly unpopular with their co-workers. Communists remained on most of the militant union executives; ASIO continued to watch them; and the unions continued to gain improved conditions for their members.[32] The intelligence authorities had always been suspicious of non-English speaking immigrants to Australia (see Chapter 1), but between 1945 and 1951 Australia absorbed 170,000 displaced persons from war-ravaged Europe. These were Yugoslavs, Ukrainians, Poles, Czechs, Russians and Baltic States' people who tended to estab-lish national clubs and cohere in the larger cities.

The Russian immigrants were mostly semi-skilled or unskilled, but ASIO kept track of them on the suspicion that they could be activated to serve some nefarious Moscow cause. ASIO agents visited them, inviting them to contact the Organization if approached by the Russian embassy. Those Russian immigrants who maintained contact with Soviet officials, such as Boris Petrov (no relation to the subsequent defector), were punished for maintaining these connections. He had been born of a Russian mother in Harbin, China, in 1923, and the family arrived in Australia in 1930. He applied for Australian nationality in 1950 but ASIO prevented this by claiming that he mixed with 'pro-Soviet elements' at the Russian Social Club and had been in close contact with Nosov, the TASS agent, that he and his mother 'entertained Soviets at their flat' and that the mother 'still held pro-Soviet leanings'. ASIO's word on questions of naturalization was usually final.[33]

The government and ASIO, like pre-war non-Labor governments and the CIS, feared that Communists from Europe would slip into Australia disguised as immigrants, and in October 1951 eight ASIO agents were attached to Australian embassies including Holland, Greece, Austria and Germany, disguised as migration officers, to vet intending migrants. Spry, in a deft but unchallenged manoeuvre, had their salaries and expenses met from Immigration Department funds.[34] In the early 1950s the British Crown colony of Cyprus experienced war between British forces and Cypriot nationalists, including the local Communist Party (AKEL), fighting for independent government. Some Cypriots sought to emigrate to Australia but ASIO, concerned that Communists might be concealed in those numbers, insisted that emigrants' names be checked with records held in Athens where Communists could be identified. Non-Cypriots were to be further checked by ASIO's Senior Service Officer in Europe because Greek Communists, who for some years after the Second World War challenged the government being imposed on Greece by the British and US governments, might attempt to enter Australia via Cyprus.[35] Nicholas Annousis, who had lived on the island of Leros in Greece, attempted to migrate to Australia but was stopped by the efficiency of ASIO's records which identified him as a Communist. His former teacher, Kyrikos Barris, then living in Australia, sponsored his application to enter Australia, resulting in Barris being summoned before the Royal Commission on Espionage. This Greek aspect of intelligence vetting shows how ASIO's operation was two-pronged: it caught both the Communists in Greece and their friends in Australia.[36]

Most of these immigrant nationalities established their own newspapers which reported sympathetically on their home governments even if they were then Communist. Some of the migrant groups, such as the Yugoslav Immigrant Association, had been pressing for socialist governments since before the war. This body attracted the post-war Yugoslav immigrants, much to ASIO's concern, and published two papers, *Napredak* and the *Macedonian Spark* which recognized the Tito Communist government in Belgrade.[37] The Polish Unity League and its paper, *Free Poland*, also supported the Communist government in Warsaw. ASIO viewed the League with great suspicion and established a large file on its leader, Mark Younger, who was active in establishing links with the new Warsaw government.[38]

When it came to taking action against leaders of Nazi collaboration forces who had managed to slip through the immigrant security screening net (with US, British and Vatican support), ASIO remained reluctant. Many of these quislings, working on behalf of the Nazis, had committed atrocities against their own people and their post-war governments sought their extradition from Australia to stand trial. The Menzies government chose to believe that these men were innocent and refused the extradition requests from Yugoslavia, Lithuania and the Soviet Union, despite protests from the ALP and Jewish anti-Fascist groups.[39] Most of ASIO's files have not been released on these embarrassing episodes, but what is known of events provides an apt lesson in how the uncritical and unthinking embrace of anti-Communism can lead an intelligence organization into the active support of the enemies of toleration.

The writers, artists and painters who promoted Australian nationalist concepts, those people who have since been identified as cultural nationalists, came under ASIO's surveillance because many were either associated with the CPA or were left-wing supporters. Their cultural interpretations clashed with the more conventional expressions of the established artists and their left-wing attitudes marked them as an identifiable group. ASIO had taken over the CIS dossiers on these artists who were in the CPA or the Fellowship of Australian Writers because the latter was regarded as a CPA front. The Australian Culture Defence Movement came under the surveillance of the Sydney ASIO office in September 1952 not so much because it sought to promote Australian films, writers and artists but because it was based in the rooms of Actors' Equity, a suspected group, and was supported by people already 'on file', such as the writers Alan

Marshall, Rex Ingamells, Gavin Casey and Leslie Rees. They were not CPA members but assisted in art functions of the CPA that were conducted to attract popular support.[40]

The exploits of ASIO in regard to the realist writer Judah Waten is a good example of how it tried to thwart leftist writers. Waten came to ASIO's attention as publicity manager of the Jewish Council to Combat Fascism and Anti-Semitism whose goal was to deport those Nazi fugitives who were infiltrated into Australia. ASIO was then markedly anti-Semitic partly reflecting the British campaign against Jewish terrorist fighters in Palestine. ASIO was watching Waten closely because of his Jewish connections and endorsed his file with the equivocal comment that he had been expelled from the CPA in 1945 but was 'still believed to be a communist'.[41] In January 1952 Waten was granted a Commonwealth Literary Fellowship and ASIO received a complaint from Geoffrey Fairbairn, later to be an academic historian at the Australian University. The Prime Minister's Department, which supervised the Fellowships, called upon Colonel Spry to provide a security check on Waten because anti-Communist members of the government were also displeased at his selection. ASIO's alarm bells began ringing in October 1953 when Colonel Spry noticed that an article by Waten had been published by the Immigration Department in its monthly bulletin, *The New Australian*, in August 1953. Spry wrote to the Department in sorrow and anger: 'I cannot feel it is in the best interests of migrants generally or for your Department for his writings to receive such favourable official publicity in such an official journal', and he offered to supply an ASIO agent to 'examine how this came about with a view to preventing any recurrence'. The implication was that covert CPA supporters located in the publishing wing of the Department might be supporting the likes of Waten.[42]

Another group to attract ASIO's surveillance was composed of those who could loosely be termed the intellectual left in Australia, located in the universities. Soon after its establishment, ASIO approached university staff known to be anti-Communist to have them report on fellow staff or students who could be judged to be security threats. By 1952 teaching staff in Melbourne and Sydney Universities had been classified according to their position on a left ideological spectrum. At the University of

Melbourne 63 academics were thus categorized, while at the University of Sydney 17 academics were identified for their closeness to the CPA or its fronts. Spry approached Prime Minister Menzies on 9 April 1952 seeking to place the Australian National University (ANU) under a special observation. Spry implied in his letter that he had received notice from MI5 that an Australian scientist, William Berry-Smith, who had been researching in nuclear physics at the University of Birmingham, was to take up a research position at the ANU and that 'in advice received from overseas' he was considered to be a possible security risk. Having inserted his foot in the university door by use of this implied MI5 contact, he sought Menzies' approval for ASIO to examine other lecturers at the ANU with the remark: 'I am sure that you will readily appreciate the inadvisability of employing, in any University, lecturers who are likely to infect students with subversive doctrines'. To this end he suggested that the ANU 'will submit to my Organisation [sic] for security checking the names of proposed appointees, at least for certain agreed departments of the University'. Menzies seemed to approve of the proposal and endorsed the letter with his own hand that 'I think Spry and Copeland [the Vice-Chancellor] should see me together'.[43]

Menzies appears to have supported this vetting procedure because by 1953 ASIO was examining the security backgrounds of research students offered scholarships at the ANU by distributing the names of these winners to its regional offices for local checking with the comment that 'In view of the present and future importance of the ANU, advice would be appreciated from the addressees as to whether any of the following applicants are adversely recorded in their respective States'.[44] In October 1953 Spry was sending to Menzies what he termed in his covering letter, 'brief background summaries' on particular staff and student members of the ANU.[45]

USES FOR ASIO DOSSIERS

What uses were the millions of ASIO dossiers put to? Some were used to check details when ASIO was vetting public servants or migrants seeking naturalization or for other purposes.

The remainder stood unused but ready to be produced at an appropriate time. The files on the left-wing political activists contained a wealth of detail collected from various intelligence sources in both Britain and Australia. Two examples of this thorough dossier compilation conclude this chapter. The files on the two men to be discussed here, David Morris and Bruce Yuill, illustrate how people first came under intelligence surveillance and also to what purpose the files were put.

The names of these two men were contained in the papers that Vladimir Petrov was alleged to have brought with him from the embassy on his defection. No explanation has been provided of why they appeared in such documents. The defection and its outcome for ASIO are analysed in the next three chapters. A discussion of the use of the dossiers of these two men will explore the assertion, made during the course of the subsequent Royal Commission, that their contents were used to fabricate parts of these Petrov papers. It was suggested during the Commission hearings that Soviet embassy staff, functioning as intelligence agents, could not have known of the detail to prepare the statements about these two men, or indeed about the other people mentioned in the papers. The dossiers could well have been the source.

David John Morris was described in the Petrov documents as university-educated and an expert on army tank design. It was one of the several vague and unspecific comments suggesting that a Russian-sponsored espionage operation existed in Australia. The Morris dossier stretched from 1926, when he was first watched because of his radicalism, until his death in 1968. Reports about him were collected from British intelligence sources, the Queensland police, military intelligence, the CIS and ASIO itself. His dossier was thick and very detailed. It contained a mine of information about a Communist Party activist. A dedicated ASIO agent could be forgiven for thinking that if Morris was not a Soviet espionage agent then he certainly should have been.

He was born in Brisbane in 1910 and studied science and engineering at the University of Queensland. He was active in student politics and joined the CPA in 1931. He travelled to Britain in 1936 to gain experience with engineering companies and became a member of the British Communist Party in Birmingham at Erdington. British intelligence agencies observed him and noted his failed attempt to obtain a visa to the Soviet

Union, information about which was retailed to Australia. He returned to Queensland in 1938 and joined the Grange branch of the CPA, a Brisbane suburb.

Following the declaration of war in 1939, he joined a group of engineers and other professionals who composed the Scientific Advisory Committee of Trades and Labor Council of Queensland to publish a booklet in 1940 explaining the method of constructing large and deep air raid shelters. They claimed, as did the CPA, that an attack on Australia by an imperialistic Japan was likely and such shelters should be constructed.[46] He joined the army as an engineering officer in the Ordnance Corps on 28 December 1941 and, because Australia was then seeking to manufacture tanks, he was sent to the Military College of Science in Britain in February 1949 to develop his skills in tank design and technology. He went on to further studies in the US at the Edgeworth Arsenal and the Aberdeen Proving Ground, returning to Australia in June 1945. He remained with the army for two years after the end of the war.

He did not conceal his CPA adherence while in the army and military intelligence, of which Spry was to become the Director, noted his postings from 1942 and informed his commanding officers accordingly. With the shift in the perception of the Soviet Union from being an ally to a potential enemy after the war, Morris came to be looked upon far less tolerantly. In 1946 he worked in the experimental and testing section of the army and after being promoted to Major he was sent to Britain again as technical officer with the Australian Army staff in London in August 1946. Then the axe fell. Colonel Spry now Director of Military Intelligence wrote to the Deputy Chief of the General Staff on 28 August 1946 outlining, with some exaggerations, Morris's involvement in the CPA both before and while in the army. Morris was quickly recalled from London four weeks after he had arrived and was effectively sidelined by being appointed to the reserve of officers in December 1946. The CIS in Brisbane placed his name on the 'Black List' and the Canberra CIS announced in August 1947 that he 'must be rigorously excluded' from missile experimental work. There was, of course, no likelihood of his being so appointed. On 2 July 1947 an anonymous letter signed *Pro Deo et Patria* was received by Colonel Spry on 2 July 1947 identifying Morris and his wife in detail and announcing that he must not be allowed to be sent to England for 'Atomic Research'. By then Morris had settled in Melbourne and worked for the State Electricity Commission. He salvaged something from his tank experimental work by writing a thesis on tank design for the University of Queensland, for which he was awarded a Master's degree in engineering. He found that he could obtain neither promotion in his work nor appointments outside and he resorted to chicken-farming with his wife for a living. He was also expelled from his returned servicemen's organization together with his wife, a former army nurse, for being in the CPA.[47]

By the time ASIO was expanding under Colonel Spry, Morris was in the unenviable position of having a large and up-to-date ASIO dossier compiled about him and was indirectly known to the Director-General himself. He was also identified as an expert on tank design who had appropriated army information for his study. It is not clear how ASIO thereafter blocked Morris's career as an engineer, but he found that numerous appointments offered to him were withdrawn a few days after he accepted. Thus disheartened, he left Australia with his wife and family to live in China and later the Soviet Union where he died of cancer in 1968.[48] With its operations based firmly on its dossier collection, ASIO had moved into that secretive activity of undermining those it believed, on the basis of its records and experiences of its officers, to be subversives. These were to be unchallengeable judgements covertly applied.

The second man in this study, Bruce Yuill, appeared only briefly in the Petrov papers. He was a clerk in the public service, but the Soviet staff were instructed to study him along with diplomatic staff. He was a trade union activist and opposed to the activities of the right-wing Industrial Groups who were attempting to dominate the Canberra labour movement. The Groupers, as they were known, falsely accused all of their leading opponents, including Yuill, of being covert CPA members. This, plus Yuill's public ridiculing of ASIO for its heavy-handed snooping on local public servants, seems to have led to ASIO's opening a dossier on him. If some of the Petrov papers were fabricated by ASIO agents it is possible that Yuill's name was casually included because he was under surveillance at that time.

Yuill was born in 1925 and graduated in economics from the University of Sydney in 1948. He worked for the Amalgamated Postal Workers' Union until 1950, then went to Canberra to work as a research officer in the Department of Immigration.

He had been an active member of the ALP in Sydney and took up similar interests in Canberra where he was elected President of the Canberra Trades and Labour Council (TLC) in 1952. Those trade unions opposing the Industrial Groups supported Yuill, which led to his being accused of being a Communist. Their attempts to defeat him in the presidential elections for the TLC in 1953 failed. Understandably there were links between the Groupers, principally based in the Catholic church and ASIO, because of their mutual interest in opposing all manifestations of Communism. Once opened, Yuill's ASIO dossier had reports filed in it of his attending at Canberra railway station to meet representatives of the Anti-Japanese Peace Treaty organization who were opposed to a hasty settlement with a former enemy and were attending meetings in Canberra to be addressed by Dr John Burton and Senator Morrow of the ALP.[49] What swelled his dossier out most of all, however, was a radio talk he gave during the weekly TLC radio programme in which he attacked the activities of ASIO in Canberra and its constant snooping on left-leaning public servants. It was well known in Canberra that ASIO officers noted the car registration numbers of people attending parties conducted by ALP activitists and diligently followed any member of the local CPA. This operation was particularly conspicuous at night because the ASIO vehicle had one constantly inoperable headlight. Canberra was then a small city of 30,000 people and it was known whose telephone was currently being tapped by ASIO because of the informal network of friendships in which telephone technicians who connected the tapping equipment mixed. ASIO was regarded in Canberra by the labour movement as somewhat menacing because of its secretive policing role. Yuill expressed these criticisms of this surveillance in a radio broadcast during a session devoted to labour movement activities. He concluded this general condemnation of ASIO with the remark: 'The Labour Government set this vicious organization up just before it went out of office. It can quickly disband it when it gets back.' ASIO quickly obtained a full transcript of the talk to add to his expanding dossier.[50]

In his role as President of the TLC little of Yuill's public life escaped ASIO's attention. Yuill was invited to a film-cocktail evening at the Soviet embassy on 22 May 1953. His attendance at the function would have been recorded by the ASIO agents observing those entering the embassy or noting their car registration plates. Yuill spoke briefly to a staff member, Karkovetz, who spoke poor English, and left the function soon afterwards. Yuill associated with the small but articulate group of ALP supporters in Canberra which included academics such as Manning Clark and C.P. Fitzgerald, diplomats such as Jim Hill, Ric Throssell and the former secretary of the External Affairs Department, Dr John Burton, all of which was noted by ASIO. But it was in 1953 when Yuill began sharing his flat with Fergan O'Sullivan that we can see that ASIO had accepted the Groupers' accusation that Yuill was a Communist. O'Sullivan, a journalist with the *Sydney Morning Herald*, became Dr Evatt's press secretary on 1 April 1953. Two years previously, O'Sullivan had prepared for the Sydney TASS representative, Pakhamov, a gossipy report on the various members of the Commonwealth parliamentary press gallery because Pakhamov wished to establish which of them would be more receptive to the publicity material he was to distribute. This account was later to become document 'H' in the Royal Commission on Espionage. ASIO had been monitoring Evatt and his staff and later in 1953 Colonel Spry advised Dr Evatt that O'Sullivan was sharing a flat with Yuill identified as 'either a Communist or an informant of the Communist Party'.[51] Dr Evatt instructed O'Sullivan to find other accommodation which he did. Yuill's involvement in trade union affairs ebbed thereafter and while he was on a short visit to Melbourne in September 1953, the Groupers mobilized sufficient numbers to have him expelled from the ALP. Yuill left Canberra in February 1954 to study for a doctorate in economics at the University of Glasgow. His short but active political life, fitted in between his work as a public servant, left a large collection of folios in his ASIO dossier. This provided the material for an ASIO investigation into him during the conduct of the Royal Commission on Espionage (RCE) in January 1955 after his name 'coincidentally' appeared in the papers allegedly produced by Petrov.

NOTES

1. See F.M. Cain, *The Origins of Political Surveillance in Australia* (Sydney, 1983), Ch. 5, for a study of the role of the Australian

police forces in this type of intelligence work before the Second World War.

2. *Nation Review*, 8 December 1976, p. 145. The author has no way of knowing whether these agents' 'names' are correct. They are taken from secondary sources such as this newspaper and could be incorrect and perhaps fabrications. The quoting of these 'names' here and elsewhere in the book cannot be taken as being an act of publishing ASIO officers' names.

3. Reed to Spicer 3 April 1950, CRS A1209, Item 72/10048.

4. F.M. Cain, 'Political Surveillance in Australia 1916–1983: Administrative Aspects' in J.J. Eddy and J.R. Nethercote (eds), *From Colony to Coloniser: Studies in Australian Administrative History* (Sydney 1987), p. 177.

5. Archives of Royal Military College, Duntroon, Canberra, Australia; Central Army Records, AA Victoria, B2458.

6. W.J. Hudson, *Casey* (Melbourne, 1986), Ch. 3.

7. Cain, *Origins*, pp. 241–2.

8. Casey Diaries, 30 Oct. 1953, National Library of Australia, MS6150.

9. Casey Diaries, 13 Nov. 1952.

10. Hudson, *Casey*, Ch. 7.

11. Casey Diaries, 1 Feb. 1952.

12. Casey Diaries, 18 Feb., 25 Aug. 1952, 3 June, 20 July 1953.

13. Casey Diaries, 29 Jan., 24 Sept., 10 Oct. 1952.

14. Casey Diaries, 1 Feb. 1952.

15. Hope Report on the Formation and Development of ASIS [hereafter the Hope Report], paragraphs 2–47.

16. Cain, *Origins*, pp. 169–72.

17. Casey Diaries, 16 Dec. 1953, 18 May 1954.

18. Hope Report, paragraphs 91–101.

19. Brian Toohey and William Pinwell, *Oyster: The Story of the Australian Secret Intelligence Agency* (Melbourne, 1989), pp. 172–9.

20. Frank Cain and Frank Farrell, 'Menzies' War on the Communist Party, 1949–1951' in Ann Curthoys and John Merritt, *Australia's First Cold War 1945–1953* (Sydney, 1984), p. 119.

21. *Intelligence Newsletter*, Paris, No. 142, 28 March 1990, pp. 5, 6, 7.

22. Cain, *Origins*, Ch. 7.

23. Menzies to Minister for Defence, 8 Nov. 1950, CRS 4816/1, Item 25/301/493.

24. Spry to Menzies, 14 Feb. 1951, CRS A 1209, Item 72/10048.

25. Mr Justice Michael Kirby, 'H.V. Evatt, the Anti-Communist Referendum and Liberty in Australia', Conference Paper given at Conference on the Life and Work of Dr H.V. Evatt, Bond University, 14–15 July 1990.
26. Spry to Menzies, 29 July 1951, CRS A 1201 Item 72/10048.
27. Report, 19 Dec. 1950, CRS A1209 Item 58/512.
28. Spry to Menzies, CRS A1209, Item 57/4416.
29. Allen to Spry, 4 June 1952; ASIO field officer's report n.d. CRS A6122/XR1, Item 158.
30. 'Influence of WFTU on Australian Trade Unions', report by ASIO, 1953, CRS A 6122/XR1, Item 347, Vol. 4.
31. Letter 'Re Broken Hill Proprietary Ltd – ACP Campaign – Use of Federated Ironworkers' Union', 30 Oct. 1953, CRS A6122, Item 322, Vol. 1.
32. See for example 'G.L. O'Brien, Waterside Workers Federation – a Report', 23 Nov. 1953, CRS A 6122/XR1, Item 340; Waterside Workers' Federation, Senior Field Officer's report, 3 March 1954, CRS A6122/XR1, Item 328.
33. 'Australian-Russian Society (NSW Section) report', 1 May 1950, CRS A6119/XR1, Item 66.
34. Spry to Hayes Dept. of Immigration, 7 April 1951, 7 Oct. 1951, CRS A6122/XR1, Item 163.
35. Spry to ASIO regional office, Melbourne, 3 Feb. 1953, A6122/XR1, Item 141.
36. Royal Commission on Espionage, transcript, Government Printer, Sydney, 1955, p. 1650.
37. Report 30 May 1950, CRS A6122/XR1, Item 172.
38. See all of file CRS A6119/28, Item 351.
39. Mark Aarons, *Sanctuary: Nazi Fugitives in Australia* (Melbourne, 1989), Ch. 6.
40. 'Australian Culture Defence Movement, Memorandum for Headquarters A.S.I.O. (2)', 8 Sept. 1952.
41. File Extract, Melbourne, 19 April 1950, CRS A6119/XR1 Item 101.
42. 'Minute, Judah Watan [*sic*]' ASIO Headquarters, Melbourne, 15 Jan. 1952, CRS A6119/XR1, Item 101; Brown, Prime Minister's Dept. to Spry 5 Feb. 1952, CRS A6119/XR1, Item 61.
43. Spry to Menzies, 9 April 1952, CRS A1209/23, Item 57/4264.
44. Memo for Regional Offices, 28 April 1953, CRS A6119/XR1, Item 271.
45. Spry to Menzies, 6 Oct. 1953, Item 278.

46. *Protect the People, Report on A.R.P. Presented to the Trades and Labor Council of Queensland by the Trade Union Scientific Advisory Council* (Brisbane, 1942).
47. File, David John Morris, CRS A6119/XR1, Item 61.
48. Bernice Morris, *Between the Lines* (Melbourne, 1988), Chs. 5, 6, 7.
49. File, Bruce Ford Yuill, A6283/XR1, Item 7.
50. 'Broadcast by Bruce Yuill', A4321/1, Item 53/71.
51. Evatt to Attorney-General, 2 March 1955, Evatt Papers, Flinders University.

6

ASIO and the Road to the Petrov Affair

Historians of the Petrov affair describe it as unexpectedly bursting like a bombshell on the political landscape of April 1954 just after Menzies had announced the holding of general elections in which the predictions were that the government might not be returned. The excitement of a revelation about Soviet spying helped to reverse this expectation and while the Menzies' government went on to enjoy another twelve years of office, the political fortunes of the ALP and its leader Dr Evatt suffered a severe reverse, leading to the wrecking of his political career and the splitting of the ALP that ensured its exclusion from office for the next 16 years. The release of Petrov Royal Commission papers and some ASIO documents by the Hawke ALP government in 1984 allows us to view the affair in a new light showing that it was not the spontaneous affair it was initially believed to be. The archival evidence is that ASIO was documenting the activities of Communists and radicals who were to be the future participants in the Royal Commission that was to be held into the 'unexpected' defection. The seeming coincidence of these people's names afterwards appearing in the documents that Petrov produced and of their being called before the Royal Commission on Espionage is analysed in this chapter, in which a study is made of how ASIO positioned itself on the road that led directly to the Petrov affair.

The first step taken by ASIO in this direction occurred when Ray Whitrod instructed Mercia Masson, one of his agents who had worked in wartime naval intelligence, to join and become friendly with members of Communist Party fringe groups in Sydney. She was then 'appointed' to a position in the Department

Rex Chiplin, a Communist journalist with that Party's paper, upon whom ASIO planted an agent with disinformation in order to link Chiplin to Petrov's alleged spy network. (*Age*, Melbourne)

Doctor by day and ASIO agent by night, Michael Bialoguski had so gained Petrov's confidence that ASIO had to increase payment to him to ensure Petrov's defection at the appropriate time. (*Age*, Melbourne)

of National Development in Melbourne on 4 January 1950 working under its director, Commander Robert Jackson, whom Casey knew from his days as Minister in Cairo and had borrowed from the British Treasury to fill the directorship of this Department. Casey probably appointed him as much for his intelligence background as his administrative experience, which was not very considerable. In this new and seemingly important position Masson was instructed to offer 'secret' reports to the Communist friends with whom she became acquainted in Melbourne. Jackson and Whitrod selected the documents she was to 'leak' to her Communist friends, particularly to Rex Chiplin, editor of the Party's Sydney newspaper, the *Tribune*. Certain words were altered before the document was handed over in order to prove that the arranged 'leak' was the real source. One document was a draft of a proposed treaty of friendship with the USA which Masson gave to Chiplin while both were visiting Canberra early in November 1951. As part of her 'official duties' she was permitted to fly frequently between various Australian cities. An article based on this 'document' was published by Chiplin in the *Tribune* on 14 November 1951 and it is of little surprise that there was no official reaction until 29 August 1952 when the *Tribune* office and Chiplin's house were raided to trace the 'leaked' document. As a means of maintaining the consistency of this intelligence double-game, A.A. Wilkes of the CIS was instructed to conduct an investigation into this matter. He presented an interim report on 17 October 1952 and a final report on 13 January 1953. No solution, of course, to the mystery 'leakage' was discovered.[1]

This covert ASIO operation was to have considerable ramifications. On 27 May 1952, W.C. Wentworth, who proudly wore the epithet 'anti-Communist crusader', asked a parliamentary question of R.G. Casey, by then Minister for External Affairs, about how Chiplin obtained the information. Casey implied that it could have been leaked by Dr John Burton who had been Secretary of the Department of External Affairs when Dr Evatt had been the minister. There was now great antipathy towards both Burton and Evatt in the new government and, accordingly, in the Department of External Affairs as well. He then made the significant announcement that there was a 'nest of traitors in our midst' but that this nest within the public service would be uncovered.[2] Casey's 'nest of traitors' speech has come to be regarded not only as an attack on Dr Evatt and Dr Burton, but also as an indication that ASIO had become confident that it could unravel the mystery that was assumed to surround 'the Case', and it might also have represented a point in time when ASIO believed that the possibility of Petrov's defection could become a reality.[3]

Another important outcome of ASIO's agent-planting operation was that in the documents brought from his embassy by Petrov, the code name 'Charlie' appeared which Petrov claimed specifically referred to Rex Chiplin. These references to him were innocuous, but Petrov added to them by claiming that he used Chiplin to obtain information clandestinely from the Department of External Affairs. Chiplin was called before the Royal Commission to answer Petrov's accusation and he not only denied this but also refused to reveal the source of the government documents, including the draft treaty of friendship with the US discussed in the *Tribune*. For some unexplained reason, ASIO then produced Mercia Masson for examination by the Royal Commission and although she agreed that she had passed some documents, she denied having given the treaty document. Chiplin now revealed that it was she who gave him the treaty document thereby demolishing Casey's claim about the existence of a 'nest of traitors' in the public service.[4] The 'traitors' were in fact a single ASIO agent. Clearly ASIO's left hand did not know what the right was doing. Both Masson and her evidence about handing over some documents were offered to demonstrate that Chiplin did have access to public servants, that he obtained secret information from them, and that his claim to not know officers in External Affairs from whom, by implication, he would have obtained documents like the draft treaty, was probably false. The ASIO officers managing the Organization's case at the Commission seemed to be unaware that Masson had been *instructed* to give Chiplin the draft treaty and that the vague accusation that it was an External Affairs officer who gave it to him, the allegation first raised by Casey in his parliamentary speech implicating Burton, was now seen as a fabrication. Masson produced her diary to demonstrate that she was not in Canberra early in November 1951 in an attempt to recover the situation, but circumstances of her close involvement in the leaking process tended to counter what appeared as a piece of *post facto* evidence to help her and ASIO wriggle out of the situation.[5]

A much more successful use of the double agent by ASIO (and one that did not rebound embarrassingly on it) was the employment of the Russian-speaking Pole, Dr Michael Bialoguski. He had worked as a part-time agent with the CIS to infiltrate Polish national groups in Sydney, and on the establishment of ASIO he was immediately given employment as a part-time agent to infiltrate the Russian Social Club which maintained permanent club rooms in Sydney, the Sydney peace groups, the Australian-Russia Society, the Polish Alliance and the Slavonic Congress. Bialoguski was born in Kiev in the Ukraine on 19 March 1917, but his parents (his father a veterinary surgeon and his mother a dentist) moved to Poland to live in Vilnius in 1920. After schooling there Bialoguski attended the medical school at University of Vilnius for five years. He married Irena Vandos about this time, but divorced her soon afterwards, on 17 February 1941. By then the Soviet Union had occupied Vilnius in the carve-up of Poland between Germany and the Soviet and Vilnius was then reincorporated back into Lithuania. Before the Germans marched in to occupy Lithuania, Bialoguski left, travelling through the Soviet Union to Vladivostock, then to Kobe, Japan, where he caught a boat to Sydney landing there in June 1941.[6] It is not clear how he was able to obtain all the transit documents to make this extensive journey. He enlisted in the Australian Army in March 1942, as a citizen of an Allied country, and was fortunate in being selected by the army to attend the Sydney University medical school in order to complete his medical degree. The medical faculty accepted his application in September 1942 granting him credit for three years of his studies, although it is not clear what documents were produced to prove his claim for advanced status, and he started at the university in 1943.[7] He married Patricia Ryan on 17 May 1943 and was discharged from the army on 23 November 1944. Thereafter he seemed to be supported by the Repatriation Department training scheme and his wife who kept a small shop. After repeating his third year of studies (he seemed to be working as an agent with CIS watching the Russian club by this time), he graduated in October 1947. With finance from the Ex-Servicemen's War Loan Department he purchased a share of a medical practice in the rural town of Thirroul, but soon returned to Sydney to practise. His application in August 1946 for naturalization as a British citizen of Australia was granted in October 1947. He sought Immigration Department assistance to bring to Australia his widowed mother and also his brother, Stefan, who had been with the Polish forces in Italy. Stefan arrived, but his mother died in 1949 before arrangements could be completed.[8]

While working as a medical practitioner during the day, Bialoguski maintained his surveillance for ASIO during the evenings on the target groups including the Polish nationalists who were supporting the new Communist government in Warsaw and, of course, the Russian club. Soviet embassy and TASS staff visited the club and Bialoguski became acquainted with them and other members posing as a friend of the Soviet Union and offering his medical practitioner skills. It was here that he met Vladimir Petrov in July 1951, and established a close association with him by encouraging and exploiting Petrov's tastes for drinking, carousing and the company of prostitutes.[9] In its counter-espionage role ASIO watched members of the Russian embassy and the TASS journalists in Sydney very closely in order to see what Australian citizens they associated with and who might be giving them information of a secret nature. This did not seem to be very rewarding because most Soviet embassy staff spoke little English and tended not to mix with any other people outside their embassy in Canberra. The gaining of an embassy official's confidence by one of its agents in the face of these restrictions was considered to be an important advance by ASIO in its attempt to spy on the Soviet mission.

Given that Petrov appeared to be a valuable catch, it was not surprising that ASIO officers kept a close watch on Bialoguski. They tapped his surgery telephone to record his conversations and early in 1952 they hired another Polish-speaking agent, George Marue, to establish an acquaintance with Bialoguski to obtain further information about him. Both Marue and his ASIO handler, Fred Ommundson, were told that Bialoguski was being watched because he was a possible Communist, and that his heavy spending on expensive night-life and gambling on horses might be financed by funds from the Soviet embassy. This wide surveillance on Bialoguski shows that even in his early relationship with Petrov the entrapment operation was being carefully planned and monitored by the senior officers of ASIO.[10]

With what seemed to be limitless resources, ASIO left no stone unturned in its endeavour to watch every move made by Soviet officials in Australia. The TASS journalists were employees of the Telegraph Agency of the Soviet Union (Telegraphnoe Agenstvo Sovietskago Soyuza) and were based in Sydney where cultural and commercial life could be better observed and reported to Soviet newspaper readers. The TASS office had been opened in Sydney by Vladimir Mikheyev on 1 September 1942, soon after the diplomatic relationships had been established between the two countries. From this Sydney base Mikheyev visited the US war zone in the South Pacific in September and October 1944. He was joined by the personable Fedor Nosov in August 1943 and Mikheyev returned to the USSR in January 1945. Ivan Pakhamov arrived in June 1950, followed by Victor Antonov in July 1952. This agency closed when the Soviet embassy staff departed in 1954. TASS journalists were usually well-trained in the language and culture of the country to which they were posted. They tended to mix as much as possible with the community in order to collect information. However, these were the very characteristics that ASIO viewed with great suspicion, believing that they were more likely to be collecting intelligence information from the Australians they met. ASIO's surveillance of these TASS journalists, beginning with Nosov, was accordingly an expensive and elaborate operation. A flat overlooking his apartment and office in King's Cross, Sydney, was occupied by two female ASIO agents, the pretence of their being innocuous residents being sustained by ASIO offices around Australia sending them letters or postcards so as to maintain the fiction for the benefit of postmen or people inspecting their letter box. This apartment, according to Alan Reid, a journalist with the Sydney *Sun*, was, to use Reid's expression, 'wired for sound'.[11] Nosov was also followed about Sydney by ASIO agents and his visits to trade union offices, particularly the Federated Ironworkers Union before the Communist members of its executive were deposed, was a source of concern for ASIO. The number plates of the cars parked near the union office on these occasions were noted and their owners identified through the motor registry department in order to contribute generously to ASIO surveillance files of people having contact with Soviet officials.[12]

THE PETROVS

The two Petrovs, Vladimir and Evdokia, arrived in Australia on 5 February 1951, and it is perhaps symptomatic of the uncertainty they were to create about who they were and what they actually did, both before and during their official stay in Australia, that the news of their arrival was marked by some confusion. In the initial newspaper report of his arrival, Petrov was described as a first secretary and his colleague Koukharenko as counsellor. The Soviet embassy was quick to point out to the External Affairs Department the incorrectness of this report, stating that Koukharenko was in fact a chauffeur and Petrov was not of diplomatic rank, but a type of office worker.[13] This description possibly better reflects his real status of cipher clerk in the Soviet embassy.

It is not just the misrepresentation of the Petrovs in newspapers that has made them so difficult to judge in the Australian historical context. The problem they pose for historians is of a larger dimension: it is one of historiography. It concerns the question of documentation about their lives and the events they claim to have been involved in. Such questions arise because the history of the Petrovs is mostly what they themselves have asserted it to be. The Soviet archives are closed and, therefore, the official careers of these two in both the Soviet Union and Australia cannot be corroborated in any way. Some ASIO sources have been released, but only after heavy weeding and self-censorship. Historians have no alternative source against which to verify the Petrovs' own account of themselves. This need not be so. Some aspects of Petrov's activities in Sydney during his frequent visits spent in the company of the part-time ASIO agent, Dr Bialoguski (214 of which were said by ASIO to have occurred), could be verified if ASIO was prepared to release the reports prepared by Bialoguski for his ASIO handler and by those other agents who monitored the activities of these two men. There is also evidence that ASIO tapped the Soviet embassy telephone, and it too could produce evidence to support Petrov's assertions about the spy ring he was conducting if it could be persuaded to release the transcripts.[14]

Bialoguski published his biography in 1955 in which he discussed his relationship with ASIO and the Petrovs. The alleged spy ring and Petrov's role in it were not mentioned.[15] The Petrovs published their joint biography in 1956, but it was ghost-written by Michael Thwaites, the ASIO agent who was involved in examining them after they defected, and it adds nothing to the other material about them,[16] that is, the reports about themselves which they gave to ASIO and the evidence they gave to the RCE. In the absence of any supporting material about themselves, historiographical questions concerning what the Petrovs have asserted about their activities in Australia must remain unanswered.

Petrov claimed that he was a Colonel and his wife a Captain in the Ministerstvo Vnutrennik Del (MVD), the Ministry of Internal Affairs. Later it became known as the Committee for State Security (KGB).[17] Both were supposedly sent to Australia to head a local spying team. Petrov claimed that this team had been led by senior embassy officials of at least first-secretary level since it was formed by Semen Makarov in 1943. On Petrov's account the network was handed to Valentin Sadovnikov, another first secretary, for the period 1949–51, and then it was handed to the TASS agent in Sydney, Ivan Pakhamov. The key to the KGB safe in the Canberra embassy was given by Sadovnikov, before he departed, to none other than Evdokia Petrov then a book-keeper and cipher clerk. Questions that might naturally be asked at this stage about how a Soviet journalist could run this spy network from a source 200 miles from its base, with no access to the KGB safe, remain unanswered. Petrov declared that he was soon promoted from cipher clerk to third secretary and took control of this network in February 1952, although Pakhamov did not return to Moscow until June 1952. The all-important key to the KGB safe was then presented to him by his wife.[18]

This account by Petrov indicates that if a spy-ring had existed it must have sunk to a lowly state to be placed in the hands of an officer only recently promoted from the level of a cipher clerk. Neither he nor his wife was trained in intelligence work or skilled in the English language.[19] They both understood English but so poorly that they were unable to give their evidence in English to the RCE. A skilled translator, Major Arthur Birse, had to be brought from Britain in order that they could give evidence in Russian.

Dr John Burton, in evidence given to the RCE, said that the two Petrovs obtained what intelligence knowledge they did claim to possess from their sighting during their ciphering duties of the cables to and from Moscow, including the KGB material. It is likely too that after his arrival in Australia and his involvement in such rewarding capitalist enterprises as being the middle-man in the sale of hard-to-procure Scotch whisky purchased on embassy imprest, Petrov decided that he would remain in Australia at the termination of his posting. Like another Soviet cipher clerk, Igor Gouzenko, who defected in Canada in 1945, he rightly believed that his reception by intelligence authorities and the granting of local citizenship would be more assured by presenting himself as an intelligence agent and delivering what could be regarded as intelligence documents to Australian officials.

Dr Burton, knowledgeable in the ways of diplomatic staffs, gave evidence that he saw Petrov as typical of disgruntled embassy staff members whose view of their own importance is not matched by their actual status in the system. 'Every foreign and cipher service has its Petrovs,' reported Dr Burton:

men who reach middle age, who have not been promoted to carry out responsible duties, who have some knowledge of secret matters which some of their seniors do not possess because of documents and messages they handle, who have become disgruntled believing that they should be given greater responsibilities and who stop at nothing in their attempt to compensate and build up their prestige. Several examples could be given in our own Administration.[20]

There are some perhaps minor aspects of Petrov's life in Australia that can be corroborated by alternative sources. Among the most interesting of these was his involvement in what was termed black-marketing of duty-free Scotch whisky, then a scarce commodity, obtained from the importers Crawford and Company in Sydney in the name of the Soviet embassy at wholesale prices. News of this leaked out during the RCE, no doubt from disgruntled retailers who had lost their business to the enterprising Dr Bialoguski and Petrov. At first the government refused to hold an investigation into the allegation, but after constant pressure from the Commonwealth MP, Eddie Ward, the Customs Department had an officer conduct an investigation. This disclosed that while 64 gallons of whisky were cleared free of duty to the Soviet embassy for the six months ending March 1953, for the six months ending March 1954 (on the eve of Petrov's defection) more than ten times as many (650) gallons were cleared from bond.

Ward said that he had been informed that Petrov had bought the whisky for $2 per bottle and sold it to hotels and restaurants for $4.70. Petrov and Bialoguski told the Customs investigator that the embassy would have purchased all this whisky because it 'gave considerable quantities of liquor as presents to individuals, to peace conventions and the like'. At this time the Soviet embassy was seventh largest in Australia with seven diplomatic staff – well behind France with 16 and Holland with 14. The importing company delivered the whisky to Dr Bialoguski's residence. The reason for this, the doctor explained to the investigator, was that it could be held there until a driver from the embassy could bring a car from Canberra to collect it. This, said the doctor, overcame the language problem that an embassy driver might face in negotiating the collection from the

The 'spy-master' Petrov (left) with the ASIO agent, G.R. Richards, who helped arrange his defection. It is possible that Petrov could have been 'planted' on ASIO as a defector by the MVD. (*Age*, Melbourne)

wholesalers. When questioned before the RCE on these events, Petrov denied any knowledge of them.[21] It would have been unlikely that the ASIO in tailing Petrov and Dr Bialoguski or in tapping their telephones – particularly so close to Petrov's defection – would have been unaware of these dubious commercial transactions and may have discussed the ramifications with the two men.[22] Such enterprises would not have been related to Petrov's spy-ring activities, but if ASIO was prepared to release documents reporting on its monitoring of these events, it may help to give more of a commercial or economic explanation of why Petrov defected when he did.

Other small aspects of Petrov's public life can be verified from ASIO's records, but it is possible that their analysis may provide more questions than answers about whether he was a spy leader. He seemed to enjoy the privilege of frequent travel during his three-year posting in Canberra. ASIO seemed to maintain surveillance officers at the main airports, or it may have been that they had agents in the ticket-selling departments of the airlines, because they seemed to keep close watch on Petrov's arrivals and departures at the Canberra and Sydney airports.[23] He seemed to be followed in Sydney, and the few reports available on this surveillance process indicates that he escorted the Soviet diplomatic couriers and could have been responsible for their travel arrangements within Australia. It was this apparent freedom of movement and frequent travel that seemed to convince ASIO, and perhaps Petrov himself, that he was the leader of a spy-ring.[24] One element to explain his frequent travelling could be his involvement in promoting the activities of the Soviet Cultural Office (VOKS) and assisting Russians who wished to return to the Soviet Union. Reports were collected by ASIO from people who followed up invitations from him to call on the embassy for books, music or ballet scores, and possibly six or so accepted his offer. His apparent independence was also marked by the fact that he and his wife lived in a house, albeit a very simple one provided by the local Housing Commission, whereas most staff lived in the embassy grounds. He also had the use of an embassy Skoda motor car, although how much it was for his personal use is not clear.

In his account to ASIO, the Skoda car assumed some intelligence importance. Petrov told ASIO that Pakhamov had been

The wreck of the Skoda car from which Petrov claimed to have walked away unharmed. ASIO accepted that his 'ownership' of this car demonstrated his senior KGB status. (ASIO photograph)

authorized to purchase it from TASS funds, but Petrov said the money had come from KGB funds. The new TASS representative, Victor Antanov, was too frightened to drive it in the busy Sydney traffic, and Petrov claimed at first that he had purchased it from Pakhamov, but later that he had decided to move it to Canberra and register it as the embassy car. It was given the diplomatic vehicle registration DC290. Petrov told ASIO that the ambassador, Lifanov, guessed that Pakhamov was a KGB agent because Petrov purchased his car. This appears to be a *non sequitur*, but Petrov managed to get away with the making of illogical statements to ASIO. Perhaps both parties were seeking to demonstrate his status in the KGB to their mutual satisfactions. He told ASIO that he did not discuss this matter with the ambassador and that he was questioned by both the embassy staff and others about how he managed to purchase Pakhamov's car. After he had crashed the Skoda car on his way to Cooma, the embassy reported the accident to both the External Affairs Department and the Canberra police, claiming that it was their embassy car. The affair of the car and its ownership seemed to have been part of that false scent that Petrov and ASIO have laid across the trail of historians seeking to establish the truth of the Petrov affair. Because ASIO agents followed Petrov's comings and goings, it is highly likely that its records of these events would help cast light on these questions. Discussion about purchasing and use of the car also appeared in the Moscow letters, although these do not help clarify the matter.

The crashing of the car also raises questions about Petrov's veracity. He claimed that he was driving it to Cooma to meet Madame Ollier, of the French embassy, on a secret assignation when he was hit at 6 a.m. by a motor truck travelling in the opposite direction. His car appeared to be rolled over and wrecked, after which it caught alight and was destroyed (see photograph on p. 129). A remarkable feature of this accident is that there was no sign of the truck with which he collided and which would have been damaged by the force of the impact. To add to the mystery, Petrov escaped unharmed; he was given a lift to Cooma by a passing motorist and returned to Canberra by train that evening. Remarkably, he retained the train ticket and brought it with him when he defected. ASIO maintained its watch on him and noted him travelling to Sydney on 29 December and returning the next day. The impression remains that the meeting with Madame Ollier, which she claims was purely a social one, had to be marked as noticeably as possible. The destruction of a car by fire, it could be said, was probably going too far in making the point.[25]

PETROV AS A SPY-MASTER

It is difficult to accept Petrov's assertion that he was a spy-master. Not only did he lack training in an intelligence school but also he had a fatal attraction for alcohol. Dr Bialoguski reported on his heavy drinking during his frequent visits to Sydney in his book. Bialoguski's wife, Pat, reported on how her husband complained that the constant drinking with Petrov was making him ill, although this could have been a situation where one was leading the other on. Joan Ferguson of the Australia–Soviet Friendship Society in Sydney noted the same drunken behaviour when she met Petrov in Sydney and also sometimes in Melbourne as he performed his duties associated with cultural activities. She only refrained from reporting his poor behaviour to the embassy because she understood that he was to return to Moscow in July 1953. He stayed on in Australia, where his drunkenness and inefficiency in conducting his duties continued to such an extent that she reported him to the ambassador Lifanov and also to Antonov, the TASS representative, for transmission to the next ambassador, Generalov.[26] Pakhamov, from whom Petrov took over the spy-ring, was quite aware of Petrov's deficiencies, and on his return to Moscow in 1952 began action to have him recalled. He told a journalist, Rupert Lockwood, in 1956 that he had 'knocked on every door' pleading 'recall Petrov before it is too late'. His pleas seemed to fall on deaf ears.[27] Such events indicate that the Soviet intelligence organization suffered from the laxity and inefficiencies that marked – and still do – much of Soviet governmental organization. Alternatively it indicates that Petrov was planted in Australia with a view to his 'defecting' and that his provocative behaviour had to be tolerated in order to maintain the implementation of this programme.

Petrov achieved no intelligence gains during his office in Australia. Robert Manne, in his thorough analysis of the RCE

131

hearings, the few ASIO documents then released, and his discussions with Colonel Spry, suggests that Petrov did not tell all when he was debriefed by ASIO. Manne suggests that this applied specifically to Petrov's relationship to the CPA official, H.B. Chandler, about which he may have concealed facts. Given ASIO's monitoring of Petrov and his movements – not to mention the telephone tapping – it is unlikely that ASIO was ignorant of the details of any of Petrov's contacts. Robert Manne's argument that Petrov concealed some of his spy management operations could be quickly answered if ASIO could be persuaded to release its records on the Chandler incident.[28]

PETROV AS A 'PLANTED' DEFECTOR

It is difficult when analysing Petrov's behaviour to avoid the conviction that he was a Soviet official seeking an invitation to defect. While all other Soviet officials in Canberra kept to themselves, Petrov mixed widely in his travels about Canberra and Sydney. He formed a close friendship with Dr Bialoguski, a Russian-speaking Polish emigrant, by no means a typical Australian citizen and about whom any Soviet diplomatic official would naturally be suspicious. Because Soviet officials have been the object of great attraction to Western intelligence agencies, they have behaved in most instances with considerable caution and circumspection. Where they have been intelligence officers as well, they have been even more watchful – particularly those who sought to defect. Petrov, however, behaved in a manner noticeably contrary to this. He drank heavily in public, lived in Dr Bialoguski's apartment when visiting Sydney, caroused, engaged the services of King's Cross prostitutes and indulged in sly grog-selling. His behaviour guaranteed the attention of ASIO, who were in any case watching him from his arrival in 1951, but more importantly, guaranteed the attention of the embassy in Canberra. Not only was the embassy chauffeur witness to some of his exploits, but the diplomatic circuit in Australia, as in any country, has its discreet but effective bush telegraph system.

It is noteworthy, however, that the embassy showed little interest in Petrov's antics. Other embassy officers, who misbehaved far less publicly than Petrov, were declared to be in disgrace and quickly bundled aboard the next aircraft leaving for Moscow. This did not happen to Petrov, and his behaviour continued to become more outrageous. Instead of Petrov being sent home in 1953 at the end of his normal posting, the term was actually extended into 1954. He explained away this extension of his stay to his Australian intelligence contact by saying that he had to undergo medical treatment in Canberra for an eye complaint.[29] This total lack of acknowledgement of Petrov and his exploits by the Soviet officials, and also the extension of his appointment tends to confirm the argument that he was being 'planted' on ASIO as a defector. This is further strengthened by the report of the TASS agent, Pakhamov, that he could obtain no response to his pleas in Moscow to have Petrov recalled immediately.

Did ASIO suspect that Petrov was a 'fool spy', the term used to describe a false defector in those years? The answer is not clear although ASIO officers may have suspected this as they watched his behaviour become steadily more outrageous. What convinced them to reverse this apparent policy of not inviting Petrov to defect earlier was probably the belief by 1954 that he might be able to help them solve the riddle of the Case. This related to the episode of an alleged leak from the Department of External Affairs to the Soviet Union, which will be analysed later in this chapter.

False defectors have presented troubles of some magnitude to Western intelligence agencies. The most famous of these has been Anatoli Golitsyn who, unlike Petrov who allowed himself to be courted for some time, walked into the CIA office in Helsinki in December 1961 and offered to defect. Once accepted by the CIA, he then claimed that all previous Soviet defectors (Petrov was not mentioned) were 'planted' on the West by Soviet intelligence. These included Michael Goleniewski, Oleg Penkovsky, Yuri Nosenko and two Soviet intelligence officers working under cover in the United Nations in New York who were given the code names Bourbon and Scotch.

Some CIA officers were sceptical of Golitsyn's claims, but James Angleton, the chief of the CIA's counter-intelligence, was firmly convinced by him that all Soviet defectors and double agents had been 'planted' by the KGB and that all Western intelligence agencies had thereby been penetrated by Soviet intelligence. Angleton started a witch hunt within the CIA such that several sections of it were paralysed into inaction. The outcome was that Angleton himself was dismissed along with most of his counter-intelligence staff.[30]

British intelligence became concerned at the turn of events. The exposures that the 'defectors' had made to their US handlers all concerned leaks from British defence establishments of US secrets by Soviet-paid spies. The British saw these events as an apparent Soviet tactic to further damage US–British intelligence co-operation. The suspicions that motivated Angleton inspired MI5 officers like Peter Wright to look more closely at its senior officers including Sir Roger Hollis, the founder of ASIO and by then Director-General of MI5. The corrosive effects of internal suspicion built on the memory of the Cambridge moles continued to affect British intelligence circles for many years afterwards.[31]

Where Petrov fits into this schema is difficult to see at this stage. It could be that Australia – an English-speaking country where ASIO had been recently established and had proven to be free of any double agents that haunted the other English-speaking intelligence bodies – was selected as a test case by the KGB to launch a false defector. The fact that Petrov behaved in such a bizarre fashion before being invited to defect was possibly due more to the KGB not knowing how to instruct a false defector in that unusual role. Australia and ASIO could have been the test-bed for the KGB learning how to 'plant' their defectors. The Petrov case may have demonstrated to them the amount of 'secret material' the agents had to bring with them to 'prove' their bona fides, the amount of reward received and what lifestyle they and perhaps their wives could expect to be established in after the defections.

ASIO, PETROV AND THE CASE

Reference has been made in Chapters 2 and 4 about how the Case and its precursor, the Venona decrypts, led to the establishment of ASIO.[32] The Venona decrypts have come to assume an important role in the history of Western intelligence organizations although firm details sufficient to lift them out of the region of speculation are not available to historians. They have come to form part of the mythology of Western intelligence because they

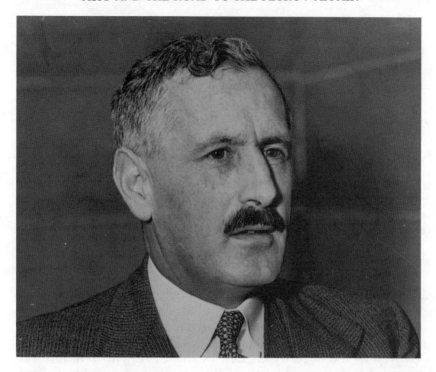

The Australian diplomat, George Legge, who befriended Petrov in Canberra and accompanied him on fishing trips, all observed by ASIO. Colonel Spry informed Prime Minister Menzies on 3 August 1953 about this liaison, reporting that signs of a spying operation were indicated. Menzies was to claim that he first heard of Petrov on 10 February 1954. Legge was dismissed from his Department because, it has been suggested, Petrov might have revealed his double-agent role to Legge. (*Canberra Times*)

are seen not only to represent the victory of Western brain-power and technology over the cleverness of Soviet espionage but also because they allegedly led to the exposure of moles and spies in Britain and the US who had long been concealed. Decrypts of Soviet radio traffic allegedly transmitted between Canberra and Moscow and collected at the Darwin intercept station through the agency of MI5 and discussed by Sillitoe and Hollis with Prime Minister Chifley in 1948, provide the foundations for the Case in Australia, however insubstantial that may appear to be from an historiographical point of view. The allegations and inferences that lay behind the Venona story seemed to have become a continuing riddle for ASIO and Colonel Spry as well as Richard Casey and his successor as Foreign Affairs Minister, Paul Hasluck.

In July 1953 Spry reported to Prime Minister Menzies on the latest developments of the Case. This was that Petrov, identified as third secretary of the embassy, had been observed to have been cultivating the company of an External Affairs diplomatic officer, George Legge, on fishing trips and that Legge was to be prosecuted for drunken driving after visiting Petrov's house.[33] Legge had a cousin, John, who was a physiologist at the University of Melbourne. He had led research in wartime poison gas experiments and because he was active in the CPA he was subject to close ASIO investigation.[34] George Legge, after this traffic offence prosecution, was transferred out of External Affairs to an appointment in Melbourne.[35] It has subsequently been suggested that George Legge had to be separated from Petrov in order that ASIO's delicate defection operation would not become known to Legge and others.[36] Spry also reported to Menzies that H.B. Chandler's house had been raided by ASIO on 17 July 1953 and there was evidence that he had replaced W.S. Clayton as the Security Officer for the CPA. This position was responsible for guarding the CPA secrets and possibly liaising with the KGB agent at the Soviet embassy. The Case was then at the forefront of the government's and ASIO's attention. Prime Minister Menzies appeared to be closely following the affair and although he may not have been aware that Petrov was soon to defect, he could have been aware that Petrov was an information collection agent for the Soviet embassy.

ASIO at this time was not fully aware of what comprised the Case, although its officers were probably familiar with one element of the matter. This related to the apparent disclosure to the Soviet Union of a British discussion paper from its Post-Hostilities Planning Group in approximately 1945 or 1946 and discussed above. The disclosure was reportedly made in Australia, although the related events, as shown below, are so vague that even this detail cannot be proved. The other aspect of the Case that seemed to be unknown to ASIO, related to Dr Burton's policy of releasing selected information to officials at the Soviet embassy. Jim Hill, a diplomatic officer, was involved in this closer official relationship with the Soviet Union instituted by Dr Burton. Dr Burton was seeking to help the Soviet Union appreciate the direction of Western diplomatic intentions as a means of overcoming their reserve and suspicion of the West.[37]

Unaware of Burton's and Hill's diplomatic endeavours, ASIO believed that the Petrov Case concerned only the vague information provided by Sillitoe and Hollis about possible leaks from the Department of External Affairs. Accordingly it focused its attention on three External Affairs diplomats, Jim Hill, Ric Throssell and Ian Milner. These had worked in the Post-Hostilities division of the Department and with the exception of Milner had either been in the CPA or had family relations in that party. Dr Burton, whom ASIO watched closely, had also been a member of that division.[38] These officers, however, had been mostly appointed by Paul Hasluck who by this time had become a senior member in the Liberal Party government.

ASIO's suspicion seems to have fallen mostly on Ian Milner mainly because he was then living in Communist-governed Czechoslovakia. He was born in New Zealand in 1911 and had studied at Oxford University in 1937 after graduating from his New Zealand university. After studying at American universities he visited China in 1937 on his way back to New Zealand. He was appointed a Lecturer in the Department of Politics in the University of Melbourne in 1940 and also became involved in the Civil Liberties Movement. He spoke at several meetings of the Australian–Soviet Friendship League, where in May 1943 he called for Australians to join in a militia force to fend off a threatened Japanese invasion. In November 1944 he was granted leave from the university to accept an appointment at the External Affairs Department in order to obtain public service experience in matters dealing with foreign affairs. He joined the Post-Hostilities Planning Division and his name thereby became linked with Hill, Throssell and Burton, all later subjects of ASIO surveillance.

As the External Affairs representative on the Defence Department's Post-Hostilities Planning Committee, Milner was given copies of papers sent by the British government to the Australian Defence Department. One paper dealt with the Security in the Western Mediterranean. In 1948 it was discovered – although details of the event could not clearly be established – that information on this topic had fallen into official Soviet hands.

Ian Milner, a former Australian Foreign Affairs officer whom ASIO was eager to cast as a Soviet spy. Petrov's semi-fictional evidence helped sustain the ASIO fabrication before the Royal Commission on Espionage. (University of Melbourne Archives)

Sir Percy Sillitoe visited Australia to discuss the matter with Prime Minister Chifley and although an inquiry was conducted, no explanation for the leak from Australia could be discovered. The Defence Department accounted for all copies it had received from Britain – not that the subject matter was very revealing or important – and it firmly claimed that none of its officers could have divulged the information. Some suspicion fell on the External Affairs Department because a certain rivalry existed between the two departments. By this stage Milner had resigned from the Department to take up a position early in 1947 with the United Nations in New York. With his copy of the paper having been returned to the Department of Defence and knowing that he had been a loyal officer, the inquiry also cleared him of being involved in any leak. Chifley reported to Prime Minister Attlee on the matter commenting that Sillitoe's report was so vague as to indicate that Australia may not have been the source of the leak.[39]

Suspicion of Milner seemed to linger, particularly in the Defence Department. He was friendly with members of the CPA and although there were allegations that he was a member of the

CPA, there is no conclusive evidence that he was a member. When he returned with his wife to Australia on leave from the UN in September 1949 the newly established ASIO closely monitored his movements in Sydney, Canberra, Melbourne and Adelaide. ASIO even noted that he visited Arthur Tange, later a secretary of the Department of External Affairs, although the ASIO agent added the rider that 'This, of course, may be an entirely innocent contact as they were both together at Rhodes Island'.[40] Brigadier F.O. Chilton, who was in charge of the Defence Department during Sir Frederick Shedden's visit overseas, obtained information about Milner's visit and wrote to Mr Justice Reed of ASIO remarking that 'I have no doubt Hollis passed on to you some important information about this man'.[41] But Reed had received information from other sources and this accounts for ASIO mounting the large watching operation. It appears that when Milner had studied at Oxford he came under the notice of MI5 and this interest in him may have been passed to the FBI while he worked with the UN. It was probably from such sources as these that Chilton and Reed obtained their information.

Milner, therefore, was in the unfortunate position of being recorded both in international intelligence files and in similar Australian files, including those of Military Intelligence which reported on the talks he gave during the war on arming for home defence.[42] He had also fallen foul of the intellectual right in Melbourne. Miss Leeper and Professor Bland, both of the University of Melbourne, complained of his appointment to the External Affairs Department basing their objections on the interpretation he had adopted in articles he had published in the *Australian Quarterly*.[43] In January 1947 he left the Department to work for the United Nations carrying with him the recommendation of Paul Hasluck, then acting as the Australian representative at the UN. Milner served as Senior Political Adviser on the UN Palestine Conciliation Commission and in 1948 as Deputy Principal Secretary of the United Nations Temporary Commission on Korea. By September 1949 he was Senior Political Officer with the UN Secretariat and resided at Long Island, New York. When his wife became ill in 1950 he obtained six months' leave from the UN for her rheumatism to be treated at spas in Prague, where he obtained a temporary teaching appointment in the Department of English at the Charles University. With his wife requiring permanent treatment in Prague, he resigned from the UN in October 1951 to become a full-time staff member at the Charles University.[44] He remained in Prague after retiring from the University and together with his second wife published English translations of Czechoslovakian poetry. He returned to New Zealand to give lectures during his university appointment and occasionally visited his brother who lives in Britain.[45] He died in June 1991 in Prague.

ASIO knew little of Milner's later career and remained fixated on the rumour emanating from the Defence Department that it might have been Milner who leaked the Post-Hostilities document to the Soviet Union. ASIO, through the Solicitor-General, K.H. Bailey, contacted Arthur Tange, then on the Australian Delegation to the UN in Paris, to verify that Milner had indeed resigned from the UN to work in Prague. Clearly ASIO's interest in him never dimmed.

It is very likely that had Milner remained in the service of the UN and not gone to live and work in Czechoslovakia, his name would not have been so closely involved in ASIO's attempt to solve the Case through the Petrov affair. In the planning of his defection, ASIO specifically requested Petrov to bring information with him about leaks in government departments. He was offered a reward of $10,000 with an additional $10,000 (totalling $122,000 in present-day terms) if the information proved to be revealing about spy networks in Australia.[46] In these circumstances it was not surprising that Petrov remembered receiving a cable from Moscow in October 1953 enquiring about none other than Ian Milner. Petrov, *mirabile dictu*, was also able to provide Milner's code-name, Bur. It was significant that he was not asked by ASIO to explain how he knew the code-name if he had received only one cable from Moscow mentioning Ian Milner. The cable was never produced by Petrov; we are dependent entirely on his oral report of it. And this, because of his poor English expression and his difficulty of recall, was a garbled affair. 'We got a cable from Moscow about his [Milner's] situation', Petrov reported to Richards in the early days of his debriefing in the ASIO safe house, 'how they appreciated that he was absent from External Affairs, and he has parents in New Zealand. His father is a church minister. They live in New

Zealand, and from Moscow they asked me how is his situation in External Affairs in Australia, and if it is possible for him to go to New Zealand and stay and live with his parents'.[47]

The only meaningful interpretation that can be extracted from this confused account is that Moscow or Milner were aware that his spying career had been revealed and he was trying to find out if it was safe to return to live in New Zealand without risking arrest or trial for spying. The truth of the matter, however, was that Milner had no wish to return to New Zealand at that time. He was about to be permanently appointed at the Charles University and was awaiting a 'foreigners' clearance from the Czech Ministry of the Interior. The episode seemed to be constructed in order to involve Milner's name in the subsequent inquiry. Petrov then claimed that he made elaborate plans to discover through contacts his spy network had with the External Affairs Department (in the person of Rex Chiplin), Milner's standing with that Department.

In January 1954, well after, even on the ASIO account of events, Petrov had made arrangements to defect, he claimed that he met Chiplin by appointment to obtain an answer for Moscow and a week later received Chiplin's report that Milner had been in the Department, but nothing else. Chiplin, however, gave evidence to the RCE that he met Petrov by chance on a Sydney tram in January 1954, went for a drink with him and was asked about a Yan Milner, of whom he knew nothing. He met Petrov a week later in the same area of Sydney for a further drink and discussion, but at no time conducted enquiries about Milner.[48] This course of events shows an elaborate structuring of arrangements and timings on the eve of Petrov's defection to ensure the involvement of Milner's name, and thereby the Case, in the Petrov affair.

This awkward means of involving Milner's name in the ASIO attempt to tie up loose ends of the Case through the Petrov inquiry may, in retrospect, appear to be a very amateurish approach to achieve that end. It did, however, in being based on the principle of vague coincidence match the tactics of 'verballing' and the extraction of police confessions that were used widely in police forces in those years. It was that type of environment where Richards, Redford and others, who were involved in the Petrov case, learned their intelligence skills. Why did Petrov agree to mouthing this exaggerated story? It may have been the inducement of earning the other $10,000 on offer or it may have been to earn his acceptance as a defector. If he were a 'planted' defector, he may have decided that it was a prudent action to take as a means of disguising his false status.

The keenness ASIO displayed to have Milner's name involved in these events and the lengths to which it was prepared to go in that direction must have been obvious to all involved in the affair. This possibly accounts for Mrs Petrov in her safe-house debriefing adding another dimension to the Milner episode. She enlarged on her husband's story by declaring that the same and solitary Moscow cable indicated that Milner had supplied secret information to Walter Clayton. Clayton was regarded by ASIO as the CPA official who delivered spying material to the Soviet embassy. She added that 'something had happened to Milner when employed by the Department of External Affairs'.[49] This story was closer to what ASIO was looking for as a means of totally implicating Milner in the allegations of spying. Curiously, however, Petrov rejected his wife's elaboration, saying it was 'both inaccurate and dangerous'.[50] Petrov may have challenged his wife's account because the offer of the additional $10,000 had now faded. If he were a 'planted' defector he might have rejected this additional material because while implicating Milner more deeply in the spying allegations, he could perceive that it added factual material to his vague cable-story which would release only more wild hares that he would have to invent stories to account for.

The RCE began examining the Milner story in February 1955 and ASIO had to resolve the differing accounts of the two Petrovs before then. In November 1954 ASIO confronted them both in the safe house with the contradicting stories and Mrs Petrov backed away from her account, saying that she had confused Milner with Ric Throssell.[51]

Unfortunately for Milner, he was unable to keep up with all the hearings of the RCE. He could have been called before the RCE because his address in Prague was known to the British embassy there. ASIO officers travelled to Glasgow to interview and collect evidence from Bruce Yuill, and while there may have been delays in obtaining visas to enter Czechoslovakia, it is possible that Milner would have been able to meet them outside that country and even to have come to Australia to give evidence to the RCE on his own behalf. He did submit an 11-page statement to the Prime Minister early in 1956 asking that it be incorporated in the official record of the RCE. It was decided that it was too late to do this and nothing came of his statement.

The RCE did not examine the Case in itself, but it did agree that Milner's handling of documents while working in the Department 'gave rise to grave suspicion as to the use he made of them'. It was a vague piece of legalese that said and meant very little. The Commissioners accepted Petrov's garbled account of the alleged Milner cable from Moscow saying that it showed Moscow's fear 'that the Australian government might have knowledge of something to his [Milner's] detriment'. Although Mrs Petrov had withdrawn her allegation that Milner had been accused in the Moscow cable of passing departmental information to the Soviet embassy, the Commissioners decided to accept her account of it declaring that along with other anti-Milner evidence 'there was a probablility of correctness of Mrs Petrov's recollection'. It was a clear example of how the three legal experts happily accepted what ASIO thought was too unbelievable even by its own uncritical standards. These three top legal practitioners justified this contradiction between the two Petrovs over the Milner spying allegation with the astounding throwaway line 'That he did so is supported by other material which we have seen'.[52] Milner in his absence was 'tried' and found guilty. The Case was concluded to ASIO's satisfaction and Milner has gone down in Australian intelligence history if not as a Soviet spy, then certainly as a guilty man who 'defected' to the East to avoid discovery.[53]

Colonel Spry was determined to remain convinced of Milner's guilt. In what could be a totally predictable response to Milner's lengthy statement, he commented to the Solicitor-General, K.H. Bailey, on the document 'that it does not accord with the situation as I understand it'.[54] On 18 May he wrote to Prime Minister Menzies further attacking Milner's statement with the remark: 'It is my belief that the preparation of this statement and his submissions are part of a pre-conceived plan in which others could be concerned. I think Milner has been assisted in its composition.' Somehow he believed that it was wrong for the beleaguered Milner to seek assistance to reply to allegations against him made by a bevy of lawyers and intelligence agents. Spry seemed to perceive Milner as a rallying-point for those who played a central role in the RCE in challenging many of the assumptions put to it by ASIO. Spry informed Menzies that Edward Hill, who had represented many witnesses at the RCE, Rex Chiplin and none other than Dr Evatt were, to his knowledge, intending to travel to Czechosloavkia. He added darkly: 'I feel that this visit could also be connected with the activities of Milner, if not the primary reason.'[55]

It was perhaps understandable that ASIO did not wish to see Milner fade from the Australian intelligence landscape. The lengthy and expensive Royal Commission produced no positive results. No spies or other persons could be recommended for prosecution and with the legal cloud left hanging over Milner, questionable as that may have been, it was necessary to maintain the fiction that Milner was the real spy behind the Case. His behaviour matched the spy novels of that era. He was the Australian spy who 'went into the cold'. This wider and deeper examination of Milner's career and an analysis of how his name became involved in the events surrounding the Petrov affair, may help to dispel that piece of fiction from Australian intelligence history.

NOTES

1. Royal Commission on Espionage, hereafter RCE, Proceedings, Vol. 6, pp. 2744–51; Wilkes Report in CRS A6291, Item 401; ASIO's summary for counsel to examine Chiplin in RCE, A6283/XR1, Item 45; 'Report of Lost Papers Dept. National Development', 13 July 1955, A6213/1, item RCE/N/I.
2. CPD, 27 May 1952, pp. 808, 871–2.
3. Nicholas Whitlam and John Stubbs, *Nest of Traitors, the Petrov Affair* (Brisbane, 1974), pp. 48–9.
4. RCE, Proceedings. Vol. 9, pp. 2677, 2684–6.
5. RCE, Proceedings. Vol. 9, p. 2714.
6. 'I Got Petrov', *Sun*, Sydney, 10 June 1955.
7. 'Dr Bialoguski by His Wife', *Argus*, Melbourne, 2 June 1955.
8. CRS A1533/XR1, Item 1955/2375.
9. CRS A6213/1, Item RCE H/4.
10. Manuscript by Marue in Evatt Papers, Flinders University.

11. 'Personnel and Structure of Soviet Intelligence Services in Australia 1943–1954', CRS A6201/1, Item 92; Sydney *Sun*, 24 Nov. 1953.
12. CRS A6122/XR1, Item 322, Vol. 1.
13. *Daily Mirror*, Sydney, 5 Feb. 1951; Report from Legal and Consular Section to Secretary, External Affairs Department, 6 Feb. 1951, A1838 T14, Item 1300/1/3/2 Pt 1.
14. ASIO report from Senior Section Officer, B2, 27 August 1954, A6119/XR1, Item 1.
15. *The Petrov Story* (Melbourne, 1955; reissued 1990).
16. *Empire of Fear* (London, 1956). Of the 27 chapters 19 are about their lives before arriving in Australia.
17. Soviet intelligence has undergone general reorganizations and name changes. The recent title KGB will be used hereafter for this organization to avoid confusion.
18. 'Personnel and Structure of Soviet Intelligence Service In Australia 1943–54'. Report prepared by ASIO for RCE, 21 July 1954, CRS A6201, Item 92.
19. ASIO report, n.d., circa late 1955, A6122/XR1, Item 64.
20. 'Submission by Dr J.W. Burton to the Royal Commission on Espionage'; A6213, Item RCE/1/9.
21. RCE official transcripts, pp. 1796–7, 18 Jan. 1955.
22. Ward Papers, NLA, Ms 2396/7/1765/ -1838; Questions in Parliament, A6213/1, Item RCE/G/7.
23. See 'A.C.T. Summary of Surveillance on V.M. Petrov' for a sample of observation maintained on Petrov. A6283/XR1, Item 3.
24. See ASIO report 'Defection of Vladimir Mikhailovic Petrov' for how ASIO convinced itself on these points that he was a spy. A6283/XR1, Item 15.
25. Interview with Mme Ollier, Paris, 27 Aug. 1990, ASIO report on accident by Senior Officer B2, 5 Jan. 1954, A6283/XR1, Item 81.
26. RCE official transcripts, pp. 2257–8, 15 Feb. 1955.
27. Rupert Lockwood, 'Vladimir Petrov: a Decoy for the MI5 Moles', *Bulletin*, 2 Oct. 1984.
28. Robert Manne, *The Petrov Affair: Politics and Espionage* (Sydney, 1987), pp. 198–201.
29. ASIO Report on Defection of the Petrovs, A6283/XR1, Item 15.
30. See Tom Mangold, *Cold Warrior: James Jesus Angleton, the CIA's Master Spy Hunter* (New York, 1991), *passim*.
31. Nigel West *A Matter of Trust, MI5 1945–72* (London, 1982), Ch. 7; Christopher Andrew and Oleg Gordievsky, *KGB, the Inside Story*

of its Foreign Operations from Lenin to Gorbachev (New York, 1990), p. 446.

32. See Ch. 2, pp. 24–37 and Ch. 4, pp. 82–6.
33. Spry to Menzies, 31 July and 9 Sept. 1953, A6119/XR1, Item 91.
34. See ASIO file, John Williamson Legge, A6119/XR1, Item 78.
35. See ASIO file, George Williamson Legge, A6119/XR1, Item 19.
36. 'Non-Spy Comes in from the Cold', *Bulletin*, Sydney, 22 May 1990.
37. Evidence given in camera to RCE by Dr John Burton, 2 Nov. 1954, CRS A6213, Item Z/9.
38. See ASIO file Dr John Wear Burton, A6119/XR1, Item 128.
39. Shedden to Burton, 7 April 1948, A 669/1 Item A33/1.
40. Report to Director, Sydney, 22 Sept. 1949, A6119/XR1, Item 53.
41. Chilton to Reed, 10 Nov. 1949, A6119/XR1, Item 17.
42. Extract from Military Intelligence file 2/7, 1942 in CRS A6119/XR1, Item 17.
43. ASIO report on Milner n.d., circa 1952, CRS A6213, Item H9.
44. Personal statement by Ian Frank George Milner, March 1956, CRS M1505, Item Box 65.
45. Interview with Professor Ian Milner, Prague, 14 Sept. 1988.
46. Richards to Spry, 22 March 1954, CRS A6283 Item 94.
47. Interview with Petrov at Safe House starting Tuesday 6 April 1954, CRS A6119/XR1, Item 18.
48. RCE transcript, pp. 2235, 2392, 2398, 2397.
49. Information from Mr and Mrs Petrov, CRS A6119/XR1, Item 18.
50. ASIO Report 23 Nov. 1954, CRS A6119/XR1, Item 18.
51. Report by Agent E.O. Redford, CRS A6119/XR1, Item 18.
52. *Report of the RCE*, NSW Government Printer (Sydney, 1955), p. 146.
53. See, for example, Richard Hall, *Rhodes Scholar Spy* (Sydney, 1991).
54. Spry to Bailey, 21 May 1956, CRS M1505, Item Box 65.
55. Spry to Menzies, 18 May 1956, CRS M1505, Item Box 65; see letter by Milner to Dr Evatt, 29 May 1956, from Prague rebutting the charges made against him, Evatt Papers, Flinders University.

7

ASIO and the Petrov Defection

It is difficult to estimate with the unavailabilty of most of ASIO's records relating to this topic, when it was that ASIO formed the conclusion that Petrov was either seeking to defect or could be the recipient of an invitation to defect. From the material available it does appear, however, that both parties, Petrov and ASIO, kept signalling to each other that an offer and an acceptance were a real possibility. The unmentioned question in these unspoken negotiations was one of what goods were to be exchanged for what reward. At the centre of these negotiations stood the self-seeking Dr Bialoguski calculating what benefit he might be able to collect from either side. The manner in which this highly intelligent freelance agent was able to get himself employed by ASIO to watch closely and report on Petrov has been analysed in the previous chapter. What is of interest at this point is when the good doctor also came to the conclusion that Petrov was seeking, or offering, a defection package and how he manoeuvred to ensure that he got something out of the arrangement. The outcome was a compromise – ASIO got their defector; Petrov got his cash reward and Australian citizenship; Dr Bialoguski got his financial reward and every assistance from ASIO to publish the book of his experiences. The judges and lawyers involved in the RCE, as well as Colonel Spry, gained knighthoods from Prime Minister Menzies for their endeavours. It would have been an equally fitting tribute for Dr Bialoguski to have been similarly honoured for his political services to the Menzies government in playing such a central role in ensuring that Petrov and his documents were delivered safely into ASIO's hands.

PETROV AS A DEFECTION TARGET

It is not clear at what point in time ASIO decided to make Petrov a target for defection. Dr Bialoguski seems to have established himself in Petrov's confidence as early as July 1951 by which stage he was chauffeuring Petrov and Pakhamov, the Sydney TASS agent, between the Russian Club and their Sydney hotel.[1] It was probably towards the end of 1951 that ASIO decided that Petrov was a defection target because that was the time when ASIO allocated a more senior and skilled agent to collect Bialoguski's reports about his contacts and observations of Petrov. This closer attention ASIO paid to Petrov was reflected in the increased number of occasions on which Dr Bialoguski met with Petrov. He met Petrov 19 times in 1951 and 64 times in 1952 – an average of more than once a week.[2] The question of having Petrov defect seems to have been a topic of discussion in ASIO circles by early in 1952. Among the ASIO files on this topic is a hand-written memorandum, which marks it as being unusual because all ASIO documents were typewritten. It is unsigned and addressed to D/B2 (Director, Counter-Intelligence) with the date 14 January 1952 and raised the following question: 'In view of Petrov's apparent discomfort and other *vague* [underlined] reports that he is drinking hard and has been ill, could he be considered as a Cabin candidate?' A diagonal line was drawn across it with 'no' written at the foot. A stronger piece of evidence is found in a report of 15 April 1952 from the Regional Director of ASIO in the Canberra region with the following comment: 'It has been suggested that Petrov might become a suitable candidate for a planned defection but so far there is insufficient evidence to implement such a plan'.[3] Although hesitant, these comments indicate that many ASIO officers recognized Petrov's signals that he was willing to defect.

Further evidence that the Petrov defection had become a likely possibility can be gained from such simple details as the movements of Colonel Spry and his deputy, Michael Thwaites. It was in January 1952 that Colonel Spry took Michael Thwaites, his chief counter-espionage agent, whose section had then assumed responsibility for monitoring Petrov's movements, to meet the political supremo of Australian intelligence, R.G. Casey, at his country estate.[4] With little intelligence information committed to paper, it was appropriate that Casey should be given only verbal reports by Thwaites. Thwaites himself has reported that he was introduced to the Petrov affair earlier, on 4 September 1951, in fact.[5]

It is known that Spry was looking for clues to solve the riddle of the Case and the planning for Petrov's defection gave his efforts new impetus. Cecil Sharpley, a defector from the CPA who was the main witness for the Lowe Royal Commission into the Party in the State of Victoria, was about to migrate back to Britain in January 1952. Spry gave instructions that he was to be questioned immediately about people outside Victoria who Sharpley considered might be involved in spying for the Soviet Union. Sharpley provided the names of people who, by an amazing coincidence, were to appear in the papers Petrov brought from the embassy when he defected in April 1954. Sharpley's list included such people as Jim Hill, Ric Throssell, Walter Clayton and Frances Garrett, formerly Bernie and formerly Gluck. She was described by Sharpley as 'Typist in Federal minister's office, suspected communist sympathizer'. Sharpley added orally to his list by remarking that Ian Milner was an 'undercover Party member' and that 'Dr Burton was sympathetic'.[6] Both men were to become a focus of interest for ASIO and the RCE.

The evidence of an important intelligence coup in the offing can be gleaned from other related sources in Canberra at that time such as the discussion by Cabinet on 9 September 1952 of subversion in the public service.[7] Casey himself had already documented his conviction about Communism in terms that were to be repeated in the RCE and which he committed to his diary in these alarmist phrases: 'spying – breaches of security – interference with loyalty – disruption generally – inciting unrest – theft of documents – malicious perversion of truth etc'.[8] The conviction of Casey about Soviet spying in Australia was further confirmed for him in September 1952 after a discussion in Melbourne with the visiting Professor Clyde Kluckholm, Director of Russian Research at Harvard University. He told Casey that 'there is a spy ring in Australia and in practically every country of the world; they [the Russians] are working actively and on a long view'.[9]

DEFECTION TACTICS

The leasing by Dr Bialoguski early in 1953 of an expensive flat in Sydney where Petrov was able to stay with him more easily on his trips to Sydney could have been the point at which negotiations began between Petrov and ASIO over his possible defection. These new domestic arrangements led to the curious conduct of an artificial game of intelligence-collecting. Petrov would travel to Sydney with the names of CPA contacts or other people who were associated with the left wing of Australian politics. While the diplomat slept, Dr Bialoguski would empty Petrov's wallet and pockets, inspect his diary and copy down any names he discovered. On his next visit Petrov would arrive with another collection of names in his pockets and the ASIO part-time agent would repeat the transcription operation in the middle of the night. Dr Bialoguski's report on these events carries the implication of serious ethical breach on his part. He reported: 'At 12.30 p.m. we went for a walk along Victoria Street, then at Petrov's request I gave him a prescription for indigestion powder in which I incorporated a sleeping drug'.[10] Dr Bialoguski's self-revealing comment could have been made to give the pocket-picking report some verisimilitude. Given the quantities of alcohol Petrov was reported to have consumed and the numbers of prostitutes he kept hiring, a sleeping draught would have seemed totally unnecessary to ensure his undisturbed sleep while his pockets were allegedly picked. It was by this means that the name of Madame Ollier, second secretary of the French embassy, was brought before the Royal Commission. ASIO, of course, already knew her because she had always been friendly to the staff of the Soviet embassy and would have been kept under surveillance by ASIO when watching the Russians. Other names consisted of people known to ASIO and who were subsequently brought before the Royal Commission. These names appeared in corrupted form such as Fergus for Fergan O'Sullivan and A.A. Fridenburg for Friedenbergs.

This apparent game of rehearsed intelligence revelations was also marked by a falling out between Dr Bialoguski and ASIO. ASIO's freelance agent was concerned, probably justifiably, that he might be thrust aside by ASIO just when his years of patient cultivation of Petrov might culminate in some rewarding intelligence coup. The pocket-searching charade was clearly a signal by Petrov that he was in possession of intelligence information about the CPA and other left-wing activists in Australia. While it must have then been apparent that Petrov was interested in defecting, there was also a general agreement among the parties that Dr Bialoguski should remain the central negotiator for that event.

Dr Bialoguski quickly seized the initiative if only as a means of demonstrating his primacy in the affair. First he demanded a higher remuneration from ASIO. When this was not forthcoming, he approached the US consul's office in Sydney and the CIS to invite them to share in the Petrov revelations. His old friend in the CIS, Bill Barnwell, told him the CIS was not interested but the US consul, Harry Mullin, who was more aware of the significance of the event, reported the matter to ASIO. The reactions within ASIO to these entrepreneurial activities of Dr Bialoguski have not been divulged. The event did not go unnoticed in US intelligence circles because it was at this time, May 1953, that the CIA established a representation in Melbourne in the person of Henry Balivet. It is apparent that the US consul, if not trained in intelligence work, was sensitive to an intelligence issue when he saw one. Dr Bialoguski claims that he resigned from ASIO at this time, but the Organization was unwilling to lose its freelance agent who maintained such a valuable contact with a possible Soviet spy-master and the resignation seemed to lapse in the face of an increase in his weekly remuneration.[11]

The pace of events in this affair had begun to increase towards the middle of 1953. Petrov announced that he was to make a short visit to Moscow and return to Australia in July. It is not clear why the Soviet government would have required a comparatively junior employee to have incurred the costs of making such a hurried trip to Moscow. The journey was postponed because Petrov complained of eye trouble, which was diagnosed as retina apathy, and Dr Bialoguski referred him to Dr Beckett, an eye specialist with whom he shared rooms. After treatment in the Canberra hospital by Dr Lodge, Petrov announced that the trip had been cancelled altogether. Dr Bialoguski has suggested that Petrov was shamming the eye complaint. 'He acted as a much sicker person than he was in fact,' he reported to ASIO.[12] If

Petrov were a false defector this is highly likely. The trip to Moscow may also have been fictitious and planned with a view to prompting an offer to Petrov from ASIO. The likely possibility of Petrov not returning to Australia could have been the means of inducing ASIO to respond more quickly with a defection invitation.

Whatever was the scheming at Petrov's end of events, ASIO was by then beginning to compile evidence which was later to be placed before the RCE. Information about people who had been mentioned by Cecil Sharpley, and referred to above, had been analysed. The ministerial typist, Frances Garrett (her maiden name, Bernie, was always used), was interviewed in June 1953 by G.R. Richards himself, then Regional Director of New South Wales.[13] She revealed that she had been a typist in Dr Evatt's office between 1944 and 1946 where she attended to the unimportant office matters. She was then a member of the CPA and recalled someone suggesting that she deliver documents she saw in that office to Walter Clayton at the Party's headquarters in Sydney. She had done this six times, but confessed that the documents she selected were of no importance.[14] ASIO believed Clayton to be the leader of the local Communist spy ring and that he carried information collected by that ring, to the Soviet embassy for transmission to the KGB. ASIO has never revealed why or how it made this judgement of Clayton. Garrett's evidence was seen by ASIO as reinforcing their suspicions of Clayton and the anticipated defection of Petrov would have been a means of confirming those suspicions.

Another of Clayton's alleged spying exploits was uncovered by ASIO in March and June 1953 when it interviewed June Barnett who was a diplomatic officer in the External Affairs Department. She confessed to ASIO that she had been a member of the CPA during the war while she was in the Australian Air Force, but then left the Party. After the war she joined the Department and in 1950, during her diplomatic training in Canberra, she became acquainted with a fellow officer, George Legge, through whom she met Fred Rose and his wife who were associated with the Canberra CPA. While visiting Rose's house, she was introduced to a person resembling Clayton – she was not certain it was him – who asked for information about her Department. She refused to tell him anything and never saw him or the Roses again.[15] Barnett's evidence added to the expanding dossier ASIO was compiling on this Clayton-led spy ring.

The snippets of information obtained from Petrov's pockets, his closely observed telephone calls and visits to the Australian cities plus his entertainment of George Legge, the left-leaning diplomat in the External Affairs Department, did not in themselves bring ASIO any closer to identifying the people or the means by which it believed information passed from the CPA to the KGB. The Clayton connection did not seem to be leading to a definite source. ASIO also seemed to be looking at a wider canvas. It was seeking to solve the mystery of the Case and also to make an exposé akin to the Gouzenko case in Canada in which connections between the Soviet embassy in Ottawa and several trade unionists, members of Parliament and the outlawed Communist Party were identified. These led to important prosecutions and jailing by the security branch of the Royal Canadian Mounted Police. As ASIO searched more diligently for the connecting links to the KGB it began to focus more on Herbert Chandler. He was a senior CPA figure who was deeply involved in the CPA's publishing and administrative domains.[16] Petrov was identified as having clandestine contact with him from which even Dr Bialoguski was excluded. This was an event worth remarking upon because Petrov seemed to take his medical companion wherever he went in Sydney. The opportunity to make a raid on Chandler's house and seize any papers which might reveal this assumed CPA–KGB connection occurred on 17 July 1953 following the publication in the *Communist Review* of an article criticizing the British monarchy. This publication was considered to be seditious and raids were conducted on the homes of Chandler, Rex Chiplin (the recipient of ASIO disinformation via Mercia Masson discussed in the previous chapter), the CPA press, its book shop and offices. Among the papers seized from Chandler's wardrobe in his bedroom was a bundle of papers which contained a list of car registration numbers including ones used by ASIO.[17] At the RCE, Chandler denied having seen the list before and other than showing that the CPA might have been spying on ASIO it threw no light on the assumed CPA–KGB link.[18]

THE MARGINALIZATION OF DR BIALOGUSKI

The problem of how to marginalize Dr Bialoguski from the impending affairs remained for ASIO. A solution was found by Michael Thwaites of counter-intelligence who suggested introducing a second person to negotiate with Petrov for his defection. This was to be Dr Beckett, the eye specialist, who readily agreed to sound out Petrov about defecting when he was checking his eyesight on 23 July 1953. Dr Bialoguski was kept in the dark about this development and was justly annoyed when he learned of ASIO's new tactic. The offended doctor obtained his revenge by taking leave without pay from ASIO on 26 August 1953. ASIO responded by simply asking him to keep it informed of any information he found. Further irritated by this off-hand treatment, he drove to Canberra on 3 September 1953 to obtain an interview with Prime Minister Menzies to complain about his treatment and poor pay. He put his complaints in writing and gave the letter to Geoffrey Yend, Menzies' private secretary.[19] Yend fobbed off the incensed doctor, although Bialoguski claims that he was under the impression that Menzies was made aware of the episode.

This question of whether Menzies knew of Petrov's proposed defection before he was officially told of it on 10 February 1954, when Spry visited him in his Canberra office, has become an important point in Australian history. Critics of Menzies suggest that he knew well before 10 February of the defection and planned his May election around the proposed defection. Others argue that Menzies knew nothing of the affair although, as has been mentioned, Spry wrote to him on 9 September 1953 to report that Petrov of the Soviet embassy was closely fraternizing with government officials and an External Affairs Department diplomat.[20] Whether Menzies knew of Dr Bialoguski's visit in September or read his letter remains an open question. The reaction of Colonel Spry to the visit was swift and certain. On 22 September 1953 he ordered that 'all use of Dr Bialoguski as a source of information is to cease forthwith'.[21] Such a command may have been appropriate in a miltary situation but was totally unsuitable in the uncertain world of counter-espionage. Even the Colonel's choice of words was inapplicable. Bialoguski was far more than a 'source of information'. He was the doctor who was about to deliver, not a newborn baby, but a Soviet spy-master bearing diaries, documents and information into ASIO's hands. It was at this stage that ASIO temporarily lost control of events. It was ironic that it was not ASIO that marginalized Dr Bialoguski, it was Bialoguski who, having control of Petrov, marginalized ASIO. Whatever was done by ASIO to insert Beckett between Petrov and Bialoguski, Petrov remained firmly attached to his doctor friend. Petrov, the object of this tension, continued on his travels about Australia. He escorted his ambassador, Nikolai Generalov, and his wife on one trip to Sydney and travelled to Brisbane with Janis Plaitkais, the embassy attaché, on another trip.

In an attempt to avenge his dismissal by ASIO and as a means of earning some money, Dr Bialoguski approached the *Sydney Morning Herald* about 20 October 1953, offering to write articles about Communist front-organizations in New South Wales. He would have enjoyed the knowledge that this would have exposed both his cover as communist sympathizer and his ASIO connections.[22] He also mentioned Petrov's name to the newspaper but claimed that he did not intend to use it in his articles.[23] ASIO, with its network of unofficial journalistic agents, would have learned quickly of Bialoguski's proposed exposé and moved to stop its publication. Frustrated by ASIO again out-manoeuvring him, Bialoguski made his last throw. It was a tactic that left ASIO with no alternative than to put him back on its payroll. On the afternoon of 23 November, the doctor told ASIO that both Petrovs wished to defect because Mrs Petrov had been dismissed as embassy book-keeper and that unless ASIO put 'him back on his former work' he would take both Petrovs to the newspapers to reveal all.[24]

This event threw ASIO's top management into turmoil. Telephone conversations were hastily arranged on the secraphone between Colonel Spry and Michael Thwaites in Melbourne and Max Phillips, the Regional Director in Canberra, and Richards in Sydney. An ASIO memorandum which may have been prepared for these discussions put ASIO's two options in the matter as follows:

> Courses open are:
> (a) Not deal with BIALOGUSKI, which means if defection eventuates he will take PETROV and wife to Press.
> (b) Deal with BIALOGUSKI.[25]

With the astute doctor holding all the cards it was not surprising that ASIO adopted the latter course.

What was most surprising in this plan of action prepared by ASIO was the instruction given to Phillips that he advise the External Affairs Department of a possible defection in the immediate future. It is difficult to believe that the Prime Minister was kept in the dark on this particular event especially after Spry had notified him on 9 September 1953 about Petrov mixing with public servants and an External Affairs Department diplomat.[26] If Spry had warned Menzies in September because he had suspected a Soviet spy scandal erupting, the question arises of why he would not have advised his Prime Minister on the eve of a defection which would have had ramifications much more far-reaching. Either he knew that Bialoguski was bluffing and that a defection was not to occur, so that he need not inform the Prime Minister, or else he had decided to keep the Prime Minister ignorant of events and warn him an hour or so before the defection. The question also arises of how Spry expected that the External Affairs Department would keep the secret of the possible defection to itself. The Secretary of the Department in the face of such an important impending event would be duty-bound to warn his minister, R.G. Casey, of this possibility and Casey would accordingly be obliged to warn Prime Minister Menzies.

Another indication that Colonel Spry must have advised Menzies of impending events can be seen in a memorandum headed 'Points to be put to BIALOGUSKI' and labelled 'Top Secret' which seems to have been prepared at this time. This document described the role of the government in the affair as follows: 'the Government would not consider granting PETROV and wife political asylum if they are not under the protection of this Department.' Another clause declared: 'If these people wish to defect we are prepared to accept the responsibility of their protection until such time as the Government has made a decision with regard to them.'[27] While it would be considered not unusual for a departmental head like Colonel Spry to make a commitment in a formal sense on behalf of his employer, the government of Australia, it would be unlikely that he would do this on such an occasion as the proposed defection of a Soviet embassy official without at the same time advising his overseeing department and its head, the Secretary of the Attorney-General's Department. The Secretary would advise the Attorney-General who again would be obliged to advise the Prime Minister of an incident likely to have international ramifications.

The immediate result was that the troublesome doctor was restored to the ASIO payroll on 23 November. He was remunerated for the period during which he had been sacked and his pay was increased thereafter.[28] A strategy plan for dealing with the doctor was formulated at an ASIO meeting in Sydney attended by Spry. Richards was given instructions to brief Bialoguski over the three days, 27–30 November 1953.[29] It is significant that Petrov visited Sydney over these same three days and that he stayed at the doctor's flat.[30] It is not impossible that he was made aware of the events by Dr Bialoguski at that time. The contents of this briefing have not been released by ASIO, but it appears that Dr Bialoguski's relationships with ASIO were put on a more professional basis. The loss of his professional time, the use of his motor car and the loss of his private time were to be recognized by ASIO. There was also a hint in the re-engagement arrangements that he was to be recompensed for the loss of income through not having his newspaper articles published.

These new relationships had an immediate effect. Petrov had decided to travel to Melbourne on 1 December and suggested to the doctor that they travel together in the doctor's car, a distance of more than 500 miles. ASIO happily agreed to this expenditure. In the event Petrov flew to Melbourne, but he was watched more closely than ever before by local ASIO agents. It was reported that he was frequently drunk and in his desire for female company he abandoned discretion to the extent of accosting women in Melbourne's streets.[31]

DEFECTION DEFERRED

While Petrov appeared to continue to conduct himself in the style to which he had become accustomed, the question remains of what happened to the plan for himself and Evdokia to defect.

Was it a figment of Dr Bialoguski's imagination and put to ASIO as a means of being re-employed as an agent? Did Petrov feel sorry for his doctor friend being sacked (Bialoguski claimed that he had never revealed his intelligence agent role to Petrov) and allowed the proposal of a defection to be put to ASIO as a means of having his friend re-engaged? Until ASIO files on this matter are released, any answer to these questions must remain speculative. Petrov remained a trusted employee of the embassy flying to Sydney on 12 December 1953 to attend a reception given by the Czechoslovakian consul, Kafka, and again on 23 December to attend the departure of Soviet couriers. Despite being replaced as embassy book-keeper, his wife travelled to Sydney on 6 March 1954 with the wife of A.G. Vislykh, the first secretary to the embassy, to attend a function arranged by the International Women's Day Committee. Even after Petrov defected, his wife was reported to have maintained her contact with KGB business. She was responsible for handing over the KGB documents (or what was left of them) to Kavalenok and for discussing the people named in the documents.[32]

The course of these events suggested no possible defection of Petrov on the grounds of being insulted and offended by the embassy senior officers, as Petrov himself has suggested. The passage of these events also fails to explain why Colonel Spry ordered the renting of a house, named 'Operation Cabin 11', to be established in Sydney on 8 December 1953 at the time Petrov was in Melbourne where, among other activities, he was accosting Melbourne ladies. It may have represented a second attempt by Petrov to defect but again ASIO has not released the documents to explain the background to these events. Richards reported that he had rented the house for one month 'on the same basis as in a previous occasion' indicating that this safe house operation had been staged before.[33]

It is evident that ASIO had come to some agreement with Petrov, and perhaps his medical friend, about defecting. While ASIO has released some of the documents dealing with what could be called the third round of defection planning, the first round, starting with Dr Bialoguski's telephone call to ASIO, has had few documents released on it. Even less has been released on the second attempt, beyond the discussion of Cabin 11. The importance of these earlier negotiations on the course of the succeeding events would have been crucial. The agreement between ASIO and Petrov probably contained two important elements – an undertaking for his safety and protection from Soviet retribution and a guarantee of a cash reward and continuing financial security. This latter point seems to have been settled in the three-day briefing session in November when Petrov was in Sydney, because the brief account of it mentions that Petrov 'was interested in farming'.[34] What Petrov offered ASIO, other than his defection, is not clear. However, as revealed in the third-round discussions, particularly with Richards, information on the Case was of primary importance to ASIO. Petrov would have confessed that he knew nothing on that matter, but he possibly offered the contents of his diary giving details of people he had dealt with. He could have supplemented this source with a list of names of CPA members and others associated with the Soviet embassy or the Russian Club in Sydney with whom he had no direct dealings.

DEFECTION RESUMED

The direct outcome of these negotiations was that during his visit to Sydney on Saturday 12 December 1953 to attend the Czechoslovakian reception, he went with Dr Bialoguski to inspect a chicken farm that ASIO seemed to be prepared to purchase for him for $7,600 ($50,000 in present-day values) and give to him as a gift.[35] Petrov liked the farm and seemed to accept the proposition and returned with his doctor friend on 9 January 1954 to pay a $100 deposit given to Dr Bialoguski by ASIO.[36] On this trip he nominated 5 April 1954 as the date for his defection because he was then due to return to Moscow on completion of his posting. The defection actually occurred two days earlier on 3 April. This coincided with the arrival of his replacement, Eugenii Kavalenok, and adds to the evidence suggesting that he was a false defector and that it suited his masters to have his successor arrive before he left the Soviet service. Meanwhile Petrov continued his frequent travelling to Melbourne and Sydney and Dr Beckett, who Bialoguski had previously believed was being hired by ASIO to displace him, became further involved in the defection programme.

What planning arrangements had been made between Petrov and ASIO at this time has not been revealed, but exactly one month after Petrov fixed his defection date, Colonel Spry travelled to Canberra on 9 February to reveal the defection arrangements to the Prime Minister, his other ministers and the heads of the associated departments the next day. It was during these interviews that the mention of holding a Royal Commission was first made. Both the Solicitor-General, Kenneth Bailey, and Prime Minister Menzies mentioned conducting a Royal Commission and the one in Canada dealing with the Gouzenko Case was referred to. This development seems to confirm the point that ASIO had already reached some form of agreement with Petrov about what he would produce and what reward he would be given. If ASIO had not struck such an agreement and if it was the case that they knew no more about him than what they had learned from their surveillance operations over the previous years, such as whom he had spoken to, whom he had slept with and where he had travelled, then it could not have been anticipated that at that early stage a Royal Commission would be necessary. The contents of the papers he was expected to bring with him were supposedly not known and could not at that stage be a reason for planning to hold a Royal Commission.

In the case of Gouzenko in Canada, his papers were read and analysed, those named were arrested and jailed and then a Royal Commission was held. The fact that Prime Minister Menzies agreed to hold a Royal Commission into Petrov's information nearly eight weeks before he was to defect implies that it was already known what names and what events were to appear in the papers he was expected to bring with him. There seemed to be no expectation that Petrov would simply leave his embassy to seek political asylum in a democratic and free Australia empty-handed. There was clearly an expectation that he could produce information casting serious reflections on a number of important and unimportant Australians that would have to be investigated.[37] Such developments could account for ASIO's investigation of Frances Garrett and June Barnett, and the raids on the CPA premises and its officials' homes in July 1953.

The events relating to what could be identified as Petrov's third defection attempt are described in documents readily made available by ASIO. This action is in stark contrast to the withholding of the documents relating to his other two defection attempts. Drs Beckett and Bialoguski and Petrov met for dinner where the Soviet diplomat was sounded out about his remaining in Australia. G.R. Richards, the Regional Director in Sydney, was ceremoniously introduced to him in Bialoguski's flat on 27 February 1954. He met Petrov thereafter twelve times, almost half in Sydney and half in Canberra, and each meeting was recorded on a portable wire recorder, sometimes with Petrov's knowledge and other times apparently not. These recordings and some typed manuscripts have been released by ASIO, but they contain little detail other than the statement by Richards that ASIO was seeking material on the Case and Petrov would be paid $10,000 ($61,000) if he produced useful information in this regard and double that if it was very revealing about the Soviet spy-ring in Australia.

One meeting, among this otherwise unrevealing collection of meetings, was that of Friday 26 March, at 7.00 p.m. On that date Petrov met Richards in his ASIO car parked behind the Kingston Hotel which was directly opposite the Soviet embassy and little more than a stone's throw away. Richards suggested driving away to conduct their conversation as they had done in the past, but Petrov said they could conduct their conversation parked there. In meeting Richards so close to his embassy, given also that it would be in autumn twilight, Petrov showed that if he was a KGB spy-master on the verge of defecting he was either very bold or very stupid. If he was a 'planted' defector he and his managers were, at the least, displaying a considerable degree of over-confidence and they ran the serious risk of arousing Richards' suspicion.[38]

PLANNING PETROV'S DEFECTION

ASIO's plans for Petrov's third defection attempt went ahead. Three safe houses were hired, two in Sydney and one in Melbourne. Staffing for the first safe house was to consist of four interrogators, four typists, a technical officer (presumably to attend to the wire recorder and other equipment), four guards, two Russian interpreters and an unspecified number of officers to analyse the material. The operation this time was identified as 'Cabin 12'.[39]

The most important and most expensive part of the defection, the exchange of Petrov's papers for ASIO cash, throws more light on the question of the extent to which the defection was planned and arranged. It appears that while Petrov was unable to provide any documents about the Case he promised to bring other documents pointing to espionage activities involving Australians. ASIO records so far released do not indicate whether he produced such documents for ASIO's inspection late in 1953 or early in 1954 when ASIO negotiations seem to have been conducted with him. ASIO, however, agreed on a sum of $10,000 as payment for such papers and this must have been arrived at after making an inspection of what Petrov was offering. It is noteworthy that the offer of $20,000 for more revealing material was never pressed very far.

That ASIO may have had some knowledge of the papers' contents and their value is indicated by the fact that it was officially admitted by ASIO that these documents were not actually inspected until Friday, 2 April, one day before Petrov defected. ASIO's records indicate that Colonel Spry was handed them by Petrov at 8 p.m. that night as an indication of Petrov's good intentions, that he quickly inspected them (more than half were in Russian which he could not read) and returned them to Petrov.[40] The handover of the papers for cash was not to occur until Petrov had officially defected and had arrived in the safe house. The money was handed to Petrov, it was then put in a safe and the key given to Petrov. If the explanation is accepted that ASIO was ignorant of the contents of the papers for which it had already offered Petrov $10,000 and that they were not inspected until Spry quickly perused them one day before Petrov defected, it means that ASIO was embarking on a considerable gamble of paying a large cash sum for unseen goods. Some justification can be offered for what appeared an irresponsible ASIO action. It could be argued that ASIO knew that it would be holding Petrov and that if his unseen and unread documents were found to contain no intelligence of any substance, ASIO could make him give evidence about the alleged espionage events which could fill out the case ASIO knew it would have to put before the proposed Royal Commission.

The ASIO plans for Petrov provided for him to defect in either Canberra or Sydney. If it occurred in Canberra, he was to be transported to Sydney at night in a three-car convoy, each one fitted with special lights to assist identification in the traffic. Petrov, however, flew to Sydney on 2 April to bid farewell to Soviet officials, and to receive his successor. He carried with him his very valuable collection of papers and showed them to Colonel Spry that evening in an ASIO flat, and then slept that night in Dr Bialoguski's apartment. The artful doctor does not appear to have arisen in the middle of the night to inspect his guest's collection of papers on this occasion.[41] Completing his official duties the next day, Petrov then drove with Richards to the safe house, handed over the all important papers and began to dictate to the ASIO Russian interpreter, W. Marshall, an account of his spy-master's role in Australia and his career in the KGB.

He also wrote a letter in Russian to the wife of the first secretary, A.G. Vislykh, returning his unspent travel money and declaring that he was committing suicide. He repeated the point which he had made to Dr Bialoguski and Richards that he was defecting because of the abuse he and his wife received from their senior embassy colleagues. Petrov claimed that he had been driven to suicide because he had been branded as an 'enemy of the Soviet people' by Kovaliev, Party Secretary, Commercial Attaché and reputedly a member of Petrov's KGB team, as well as the ambassador, Generalov, together with his predecessor, Lifanov.[42] He wrote that he and his wife had become bundles of nerves, that the attacks were a disgrace, they were against regulations and his nerves could not hold any longer.[43] This letter may have been written for two reasons – the first being to sustain the verisimilitude that he was defecting because of the clash with embassy officialdom by his wife and himself. The second reason, based on the assumption that he was a false defector, could have been that he wished to send a message, concealed in the wording of the suicide letter, that he was well and the defection plan had succeeded.

ASIO AND THE POLITICS OF DEFECTION

With Petrov surrendering himself and his papers into ASIO's hands, ASIO initiated a train of events it had already planned.

Prime Minister Menzies was officially shown the papers by Spry the next day, 4 April, but they seemed to contain few surprises for him.[44] The decision to hold a Royal Commission was confirmed at that time not only with the intention of obtaining the maximum publicity for the defection but also as a means of publicly compelling those people who had been watched by ASIO, plus others mentioned in Petrov's papers, to explain their connections with the alleged CPA–KGB spy-ring. The evidence of these people was to be acquired compulsorily by amending the Royal Commission Act in order to compel the attendance of those people at the RCE. Nine days later, the Prime Minister announced Petrov's defection and the evidence pointing to a Soviet espionage and subversion operation in Australia. Capitalizing on this revelation, the Prime Minister announced on the following day, 14 April, that a general election would be held on 29 May and then immediately prorogued Parliament.

Because of its failed economic policy, the electoral fortunes of the government had declined significantly in the previous years. Whereas it had been unlikely that the government would have been returned some months previously, the visit of the British monarch to Australia followed by this revelation of a Soviet spying operation, confirming all that Menzies had preached for years about the continued threat that Communism and the USSR posed for Australia, seemed to assure the return of the Menzies government.

The Labor Party leader, Dr Evatt, instinctively believing that events had artificially been manipulated to achieve these electoral ends, telephoned Colonel Spry to seek details of the defection. Spry informed him that he 'was not empowered to do this' and referred him to Menzies.[45] Even given that there was suspicion of Dr Evatt in US, British and Australian intelligence circles, it was a highly inappropriate response for Spry to have given an alternative Australian Prime Minister. Evatt refused thereafter to have any communication with Spry and the foundation was partially laid for the development of a deep animosity and suspicion by the Australian Labor movement towards ASIO.

The general elections produced a swing of votes to the Labor Party but insufficient to win government. How much the revelations of the Petrov affair swung voters back to the Menzies government is hard to say, but it must have been an important element in persuading the electorate to stick with the devil they knew. The role of ASIO, however much it might wish to deny it, was fundamental. Without ASIO the defection would not have occurred. The outcome was largely due to ASIO's patience in constantly watching Petrov, adapting itself to Dr Bialoguski's mental moods, but most of all to its investing $10,000 in inducing Petrov to defect complete with his documents.

The historian to write most recently on the Petrov affair argues that the defection was linked to the election date only by coincidence. Robert Manne argues that it was as late as 7 December 1953 that Petrov set his defection date as approximately 3 April 1954.[46] That was close to the date on which he expected to return to Moscow on completion of his posting. ASIO material thus far released does not indicate that the two Petrovs were to return to Moscow at that time. Whereas ASIO agents monitored his aircraft bookings in July 1953 when he announced that he would be making a short trip to Moscow, similar observations of his movements for April 1954 do not seem to be available.[47] The Petrovs would have had to dispose of possessions acquired in Canberra before departure, including their Alsatian dog Jack. They would have had to give and attend farewell parties and even obtain British visas to transit through Singapore. No indication of this activity being put in train is apparent in the ASIO documents at present available. The defection date, therefore, may not have been fixed close to what seems like an indefinite departure date. It is not known when Prime Minister Menzies selected 29 May to be the election day. Nor is it known whether he settled on that date early in December when he might have first learned of Petrov's proposed defection date that was to occur eight weeks before the election. Settlement of the question about the linkage between the defection and election dates will have to await the release of more ASIO documents.

Petrov's defection was not to be the end of this pre-election drama because on 19 April Evdokia also sought political asylum in the most dramatic of circumstances. She was to return to Moscow with the escort of two Soviet diplomatic couriers. A large crowd seems to have been assembled at the Sydney airport to prevent her departure. This incident appeared to have had some sort of official approval and there is confusion over whether the State

165

police were informed that their services would not be required. The result was that there were few policemen present to control the crowd. The throng of people got out of hand and airport workers had to man firehoses in order to protect the aircraft from damage.[48] In the event the plane did leave with her on board. After discussing the defection with government officials at the Darwin airport and speaking to Petrov by telephone, she decided to accept political asylum and soon joined Petrov at ASIO's Sydney safe house. She too provided an account of her intelligence work for the KGB although, except for confirming that harassment by the embassy staff provided an excuse for Petrov to defect, she never assumed the importance in the Royal Commission inquiry that her husband achieved.[49]

NOTES

1. Bialoguski, Michael. 9 July 1951, A6119/XR1, Item 1.
2. ASIO Report, 27 August 1954, A6119/XR1, Item 1.
3. Petrov, Vladimir Mikhailovich – Pt 1, A6119/XR1, Item 7 (emphasis in original).
4. Casey Diaries, NLA, M56150, 25 Jan. 1952.
5. Michael Thwaites, *Truth Will Out. ASIO and the Petrovs* (Sydney, 1989), p. 77.
6. Report for B1, 31 Jan. 1952, A6119/XR1, Item 187.
7. Casey Diaries, 9 Sept. 1952.
8. Casey Diaries, 25 Aug. 1952.
9. Casey Diaries, 10 Sept. 1952.
10. Report by Dr Bialoguski 22 Aug. 1953, Petrov, Vladimir Mikhailovich, Part 3, A6119/XR1, Item 9.
11. ASIO Report, 3 Nov. 1954, A6119/XR1, Item 1.
12. Report by Dr Bialoguski, 3 June 1953, A6119/XR1, Item 9.
13. RCE, official transcripts of proceedings, p. 1328.
14. Report by ASIO of interview with Frances Garrett (Bernie) 10 June 1953, A6283/XR1, Item 18.
15. Miss June Barnett, interview, 13 March 1953, A6119/XR1, Item 19.
16. For Chandler's comprehensive ASIO dossier see Herbert Bovyll Chandler, A6119/XR1, Item 76.
17. Report of Raid by L.E. Watson, 17 July 1953, A6201/1, Item 311;

Report of Raids and Sedition Charges, 17 July 1953 and 1 August 1953, A6122/16, Item 1004.

18. RCE official transcript of proceedings, p. 2839.
19. ASIO Report, 3 Nov. 1954, A6119/XR1, Item 1.
20. Spry to Prime Minister, 9 Sept. 1953, A6119/XR1, Item 19.
21. ASIO Report, 3 Nov. 1954, A6119/XR1, Item 1.
22. RCE, official transcript of proceedings, p. 998.
23. Ibid.
24. Operation Cabin 12, A6122/XR1, Item 18.
25. Ibid.
26. Spry to Menzies, 9 Sept. 1953, A6119/XR1, Item 19.
27. Memorandum, Mr and Mrs V.M. Petrov, in Operation Cabin 12, A6122/XR1, Item 18.
28. ASIO Report, on Bialoguski, Michael, A 6119/XR1, Item 1.
29. Re Petrov-Diary 30/11/53, in Operation Cabin 12, A6122/XR1, Item 18.
30. Report on Petrov, 27/11/1953 and 29/11/1953, A6119/XR1, Item 10.
31. Observation on Petrov, A6119/XR1, Item 10.
32. See, for example, Report of the Royal Commission on Espionage, p. 260.
33. Richards to Headquarters ASIO, 8 Dec. 1953, A6122/XR1, Item 18.
34. Re Petrov-Diary, 30/11/53, in Operation Cabin 12, A6122/XR1, Item 18.
35. Bialoguski, *Petrov Story*, pp. 161–2.
36. RCE, official transcript of proceedings, pp. 795–6.
37. Memorandum For File, Operation Cabin 12, A6122/XR1, Item 18.
38. Report of meeting 26/3/54 in Transcript of Minifon Recordings, A6119/XR1, Item 9.
39. Safe House Report in Operation Cabin 12, A6122/XR1, Item 18.
40. ASIO Report in RCS Cabin 12 Folder A, A6283/XR1, Item 70, f.24.
41. Ibid.
42. MGB/MVD Network in Australia, chart 'E', a6201/1, Item 92.
43. Translation of Letter, A6283/XR1, Item 3, ff.13,14.
44. CPD, 13 April 1954, pp. 325–6.
45. Report of Colonel Spry, A6213, Item 97.

46. Robert Manne, *The Petrov Affair: Politics and Espionage* (Sydney, 1987), pp. 94–102.
47. Petrov, Vladimir Mikhailovich Part 3, A6119/XR1, Item 9, f.56, f.58.
48. For Mrs Petrov's defection, see Evatt Papers, Flinders University.
49. Soviet Embassy Canberra, Director-General's Letter to PM re Petrova, A6122/XR1, Item 8.

8

ASIO and the Royal Commission on Espionage

The Royal Commission on Espionage (RCE) was the culmination of a long ASIO operation. It stretched from early 1951 when Petrov arrived, to April 1954 when he defected. The second stage ran from May 1954 when the RCE began until March 1955 when it concluded its hearings. These two contiguous episodes absorbed a large proportion of ASIO manpower over those four and a half years and when comparing the benefits obtained with the cost involved it was very doubtful if the operation was worthwhile. However, on the basis of the increased stature and importance bestowed on ASIO and the stimulus it provided for the government's anti-Communist crusade, the episode was of inestimable benefit. This chapter explores some aspects of ASIO's operations in relation to the RCE to provide some insight into the Petrov affair which still attracts the attention of political and intelligence historians in Australia.

The Royal Commission started immediately on Petrov's defection, thereby demonstrating the government's resolve to expose any spying scandal. The opportunity to win back the swinging voter, however, was not to be discounted in the government's calculations in this regard. These hearings paused between 19 May and 11 June 1954 which allowed ASIO to expand on the documentation which it had collected. Richards was promoted to be in charge of the ASIO case, although Colonel Spry also attended most session hearings. Richards was made Director-General (Operations) and also Controller of ASIO's Royal Commission Unit. W.R. Blackett was appointed as Deputy Controller and a large number of ASIO agents were appointed as Case Officers. Their task was to compile comprehensive briefs on the many people summoned to appear before the Commission. The sources for this information were the dossiers that ASIO had been compiling over the previous years, supplemented by information provided by the ASIO Interviewing Officers who travelled about Australia interrogating those mentioned in Petrov's documents. Other information came from statements made by Petrov himself in the safe house and translated there.[1] The Case Officers liaised with the legal counsel putting the case for the government to the commissioners. To the spectator it appeared that ASIO and not the commissioners was conducting the inquiry. These Case Officers frequently had whispered conversations with the counsel at the bar table in order to prompt questions to be put to the witnesses. This performance further demonstrated how central ASIO was to the Royal Commission. ASIO also held the two prime witnesses incommunicado in its safe houses, and it held all relevant documents and dossiers and directed what evidence was to be conducted in camera. Just as there could have been little chance of a Petrov defection without an ASIO, so could there have been no Royal Commission without ASIO. Bereft of ASIO, the Commission would have been unable to collect the huge body of information to assist the commissioners in their almost year-long inquiry. No other organization in Australia could match the detail in the dossiers of ASIO. However, the Royal Commission did have powers that even ASIO lacked. It could compel witnesses to appear and to give truthful evidence. This was information that ASIO on its own could never have obtained, particularly when such witnesses were hostile towards ASIO. The combined powers of ASIO and the RCE meant that no shred of evidence they wished to pursue could escape the attention of the commissioners and their counsel.

The other important ASIO role in the conduct of the Royal Commission was its management of the safe houses for the Petrovs. This was a doubly important operation. It allowed the ASIO officers to continue to collect information from the Petrovs while they relaxed in an informal domestic environment. More importantly, it prevented the Petrovs from divulging information to others which could be used to counter the evidence that ASIO produced to the commission. The staff in the houses consisted of four male agents, one woman agent and a non-ASIO agent

Major Birse, the Russian translator lent by the British government to assist the Petrovs in their debriefing by ASIO and the Royal Commission on Espionage. (*Age*, Melbourne)

Allan Dalziel, Dr Evatt's Private Secretary. ASIO maintained close surveillance on him, but nothing compromising could be established. (*Age*, Melbourne)

cook. One male was responsible for the house maintenance, lawn-mowing and shopping, two were dedicated to guarding duties day and night, and one to escorting Mrs Petrov together with the female agent, as they toured local shopping centres and attended picture theatres. Petrov entertained himself by fishing and shooting in company with his guards. All five agents were expected to collect statements from the Petrovs as the occasion arose.[2]

Male agents who carried out household chores objected strongly to the ridicule of the Petrovs who were accustomed to the Russian lifestyle where only women performed domestic work. The agents also disliked the Petrovs' Alsatian dog, which they described as 'a stubborn, ferocious animal', and expressed amazement that Petrov took the animal to bed with him. In the Melbourne safe house, the dog menaced the children living nearby and attacked and tore the clothes of another neighbour. The ASIO agents managed to divert a complaint being made to the local police by the offended neighbour. One Sydney safe house was located in a small urban settlement where the local butcher, who took a great interest in his customers, guessed that the ASIO agent doing the shopping was an ex-policeman and assumed that he was guarding the Petrovs. After returning from a stay in the Melbourne safe house, another safe house was selected in Sydney in an endeavour to avoid the percipience of the local butcher.[3]

The main purpose in isolating the Petrovs with their ASIO guards was to encourage them to divulge information. Petrov, aware of the adage that knowledge is power, offered his information sparingly. This greatly annoyed the ASIO agents who described him as a:

> lazy worker who preferred to give a statement of fact with little detail . . . The view was held that he purposely withheld information which was of vital security value. He objected to questioning, and made the task as difficult as possible . . . As a consequence, the extraction of information resolved into a tactical battle. On one occasion he refused to eat or associate with ASIO officers, refused point-blank to answer any further questions, and threatened to refuse to attend court.[4]

The ASIO agents confronted his stubbornness with a mixture of moral persuasion and mild threat by telling him that 'he could not take everything from a country without giving something in return, and in his case he was expected to assist with intelligence information for the freedom he had accepted.'[5] Another tactic employed was to pamper him, but his response was to demand more. Another was to emphasize his importance to the inquiry but this merely boosted his ego and produced no additional information. A further tactic was to use the tried and tested police technique of a tough police interrogator followed by a kindly interrogator. The ASIO agents would play such roles, timed so that Richards would arrive at the safe house soon afterwards to assume the position of middle man to extract information from a confused Petrov. The ASIO agents had to perform these antics because in the forefront of their minds was the fact, as the ASIO report put it, that 'He had the tactical advantage – the Commission could not function without him, and ASIO could have been discredited.'[6]

This reluctance by Petrov to divulge information to ASIO (he also refused to work with representatives of foreign intelligence services until compelled to do so) lends credence to the two assumptions already made about Petrov. If he were a genuine defector, but was little more than a cipher clerk who had been recently and temporarily promoted to a third secretary's position, his apparent reluctance to provide information could have been accounted for simply by his lack of knowledge about espionage or any other topic. He was neither 'lazy' nor incapable of adding details to the basic 'facts' he provided. The unfortunate man had very little information about Australian events to divulge in the first place. If he were a 'planted' defector his tactic of providing information reluctantly and sparingly would have been eminently practical. He would avoid exposing his false position by giving information that might subsequently prove to be incorrect.

Towards the conclusion of the RCE the number of agents was reduced to three, two males and a female. This reduction occurred because the cook, while retaining her culinary occupation, added to it by becoming a female escort and companion to Mrs Petrov. By similar multiskilling, Michael Thwaites, formerly the Director of Counter Espionage at ASIO's headquarters in Melbourne, became the full-time ghost-writer of the Petrovs' biography *Empire of Fear* published in 1956. He took up permanent residence in the Sydney safe house to work with the Petrovs where he was reported as being 'of great assistance in the guard and escort aspect, further in keeping the Petrovs occupied and also in maintaining the good relationship between the Petrovs and members of ASIO'.[7]

THE PETROV PAPERS

The papers which Petrov brought with him from his KGB safe consisted of four categories. The first, later to be identified as document J, became the point of lengthy legal debate in the RCE which led to Dr Evatt being barred by the Commissioners from further hearings. Rupert Lockwood was accused of having written it but he denied this. He had prepared reports for Antonov on Australian political and economic life amounting to nearly 165 pages and document J of 37 pages seemed to have been compiled from those, but not by him, he said. They discussed such topics as the activities of and inroads made by US and British capital on the political and economic life in Australia. Document J became a very controversial document. It discussed the allegation that business leaders and right-wing activists in Australia had been collaborating with the Japanese military and intelligence agents before the Pacific war, with a view to acting as quislings should Japan invade Australia. It listed as the sources for information three members of Dr Evatt's staff, Allan Dalziel, his private secretary, Albert Grundeman, his assistant private secretary, and Fergan O'Sullivan, his press secretary.[8]

The second document, later to be known as document H, was prepared by the same Fergan O'Sullivan at the request of the TASS agent, Pakhamov, to provide him with the backgrounds of the journalists in the parliamentary press gallery to whom he intended to send publicity material about the Soviet Union. O'Sullivan prepared this document of three pages when working for the *Sydney Morning Herald*, but when Petrov gave it to ASIO he had been working since April 1953 as Dr Evatt's press secretary. Dr Evatt immediately dismissed him, but the names of his three staff members being implicated, however indirectly, was seen to reflect badly on him. This also explains why he leapt to their defence to protect his own reputation as much as theirs.[9]

THE MOSCOW LETTERS

The Moscow letters formed the largest collection of material produced by Petrov. Unlike the two previous documents prepared by Australians, these letters and document G, to be discussed later, were written in Russian and consequently carried much more weight as genuine intelligence documents. This was unfortunate because it led to their contents and alleged origins remaining almost unchallenged in the RCE. The commissioners, lawyers and successive historians have uncritically accepted the Moscow letters as being genuine KGB documents. Few questions have been raised suggesting that they may be local fabrications at best, or the work of petty-minded Russian bureaucrats lacking intelligence skills at worst. They could have been a combination of both.[10] The Moscow letters were alleged to have arrived in Australia in six batches on dates between January and November 1952 and totalled 71 individual letters. Each letter averaged five to seven short paragraphs, although some were longer. They were reputedly written by two KGB officers using the code names Pavlov and Vadim who Petrov claimed were Colonel Raina and one Gosky. Petrov claimed that the letters were to be destroyed early in 1954 but he kept them instead and had Mrs Petrov sign a false declaration of destruction for despatch to Moscow.

The letters covered roughly 93 topics. Of these 63 related to individuals, sometimes more than once, and the remaining 30 were what could lightly be called intelligence instructions to Petrov. There were repetitions among the 63 names and also names of people unlikely to meet with a KGB agent, such as Prime Minister Menzies, his deputy Arthur Fadden or the Leader of the Opposition, Dr Evatt. There were also the names of 16 journalists who appeared in Fergan O'Sullivan's list which proved either that document H had arrived in Moscow or that some of the Moscow letters could have been prepared in Australia. Excluding the repetitions and the type of names mentioned above, there were 39 names which fell into the five broad categories of public servants, businessmen trading with Communist countries, Russian immigrants, CPA members and others. It is worth observing that the name of Dr Bialoguski did not appear. Being a close ally, Petrov claimed that he reported on him to Moscow and it is curious that Petrov was not instructed to use his medical friend to collect information as he was directed to do with other Australians less close to him.

Those public servants whose names appeared were mainly low level officers in the External Affairs Department. One was H.S. North who had served in the war in naval ciphers. He was later employed as a Cipher Clerk in the Australian embassy in Moscow and married his wife there in the Moscow Catholic church. His inclusion possibly helped to promote the notion that the KGB was interested in obtaining entry to the Australian diplomatic code. F.J. McLean, a press officer with the Department of External Affairs and known to be close to Dr Evatt, was mentioned as a source for Petrov to obtain information on such a topic as Australia's voting intentions in the UN General Assembly. In the letter of 25 November 1952, the name of Bruce Yuill appeared. The means by which this public servant and trade union activist had come to the attention of ASIO for, among other things, his strong criticism of ASIO in a Canberra radio broadcast has already been discussed in Chapter 5. The appearance of his name in the Moscow letters was accompanied by the instruction that a study should be started on him with no reason given. However vague or imprecise was the context in which his name was given, it was sufficient to ensure that Yuill's life and background was publicly and thoroughly analysed by the RCE.[11]

The Russian immigrants and the Russian businessmen mentioned in the Moscow letters were also known to ASIO. Their immigration and naturalization dossiers were all acquired when it took over most of the records for the CIS. Again, however, there is no explanation why their names appeared other than that they were of Russian origin or traded with Communist countries. One, Solomon Kosky (codenamed Priyatel) was probably included because he was a furrier in Melbourne, whose customers, as ASIO would have known, included the Russian women attached to the Soviet embassy. Mrs Petrov had considered purchasing a mink coat from him for $5,400.[12] Kosky purchased his stock at the Leningrad fur sales and engaged in the trade to sell wool to the Soviet Union worth $120,000 ($722,000 in 1990s values) for which he was paid two per cent commission.

In spite of Kosky being a wealthy merchant, ASIO maintained a large dossier on him because of his connections with the Soviet embassy trade officials, and his past support for both the Australia-Soviet House in Melbourne and the war-time activity to send Australian sheepskins to aid the Soviet people. The writers of the Moscow letters mentioned him twice in letters six months apart. This time-gap may explain why they confused the role they wanted him to play. In the first letter of 2 January 1952, he is recorded with the comment 'Kosky is our agent'. In the second letter of 6 June 1952, the earlier remark was disregarded and our wealthy furrier was then to be studied by Petrov with a view to 'establishing an agent relationship with him'.[13]

Similar circumstances prevailed with another expatriate Russian businessman, Arkadie Wassilieff, who conducted a prosperous business manufacturing bearings in Melbourne. He had been born in Russia and arrived in Australia in 1911. ASIO observed his friendliness towards Soviet embassy trade officials, as well as Petrov, when they had visited Melbourne. He asked these trade officials to send samples of his hard-wearing bearing shells to the Soviet for use in aircraft engines with a view to obtaining sales there. As with Kosky, the Moscow letter-writers seemed not so much interested in providing tasks for this immigrant engineer to perform as in ensuring that his name appeared in the Moscow letters and that he would be hauled before a subsequent inquiry, if only to provide some insight into how the Soviet embassy trade officials functioned.[14]

Given that ASIO strongly suspected a CPA–KGB connection, it is worthy of comment that the names of CPA members did not predominate in the Moscow letters. Six letters mentioned them although Rex Chiplin's name (code name Charlie) occurred in three of them. These emphasized his supposed role as a spy who clandestinely collected for Petrov information from the Department of External Affairs. Albert Keesing's name appeared (although he had no code name) because he was manager of the CPA paper, *Tribune*. He often met with Kovaliev, the commercial attaché at the embassy, to discuss, among other things, the importing of literature from the Soviet Union. It was this type of meeting that would have been closely monitored by ASIO.[15]

In the category of other groups can be included Dr Max Stephens, born in Poland. He had completed two medical degrees, one in Paris and one in Sydney, and he maintained a popular medical practice in a Sydney suburb. He was discussed in two Moscow letters and was recommended to Petrov to be cultivated with a view to having his house used as a secret meeting place.[16] Presumably the spies could exchange their material in his busy waiting room. Dr Stephens had mixed in Polish circles in Sydney in which Mark Younger, the supporter of the new Warsaw Communist government, was involved. He also met Dr Bialoguski in these circles with whom he had a serious conflict. Dr Stephens treated Pakhamov's wife for an illness over three visits to his surgery which would have been closely observed by ASIO. It was probably the dislike of Dr Bialoguski for Dr Stephens that led to his name appearing in the Moscow letters. Some evidence pointing to this possibility can be seen in a letter sent by Dr Stephens' counsel, B. Conway, to Dr Evatt on 5 August 1955. Conway reported that Dr Bialoguski had been criticized by Dr Stephens particularly after Dr Bialoguski had made unsought advances to Dr Stephens' married sister. Conway implied to Dr Evatt that Dr Bialoguski had obtained some revenge by having

Dr Stephens brought before the RCE which, of course, could only have occurred if his name appeared in the Moscow letters.[17] Given that the world of intelligence, like life, is often larger than fiction, the comments of Dr Stephens and his counsel could well have been true.

More substance to the claim that some of the Moscow letters could have been prepared in Australia from ASIO records was argued by Norman Russell and Neville Isaksen when they were summoned before the RCE to account for their names appearing in the Moscow letters. Both men had visited Moscow as members of a trade union delegation and the letter described some of their activities there. Information about Russell was very detailed:

> Norman Herbert Russell was born in 1922 in Sydney; he is non-Party, of middle school education – he completed an accounting course. At the present time he works as a clerk in the Sydney port. He is a member of the clerks' trade union. He is financially secure, lives in his own house and has his own motor car.[18]

The letter was sent to warn Petrov that Russell's behaviour in Moscow could indicate that he might be working for British intelligence and that Petrov should avoid him. The counsel for these two men, B.R. Miles and Clive Evatt QC, argued that such detailed information about Russell could not have been collected by the KGB in the short time he was in Moscow. Russell gave evidence that while he was overseas his bank had informed his wife that intelligence officers had visited to check on his financial position and what property he owned. He also gave evidence that his telephone was being tapped. Isaksen gave evidence that his papers and diaries had been seized by Customs officers on disembarking and returned some weeks later.[19] Their joint case was that through the information obtained from the bank, the seized diaries and reports from the British embassy in Moscow which they had both visited, the Moscow letter could have been manufactured in Sydney. The commissioners were unwilling to accept this proposal. But all indications pointed to the letter being prepared in order to embarrass the executive of the Federated Clerks Union, which then contained some CPA members. Sending its members on a heavily subsidized trip to

Victor Antonov, the bashful non-English-speaking TASS correspondent in Sydney. Petrov, the former cipher clerk, was supposed to train this unpromising candidate to be a local KGB agent. (*Canberra Times*)

the Communist heartland, however innocuous the trip may have been, could be portrayed in those Cold War years as touching on the subversive. Petrov stuck to his claim that the letter was an important warning from KGB headquarters to avoid these two lowly paid waterfront workers. He confessed that he had taken no action to familiarize himself with what they looked like. He also confessed it to be unlikely that these humble toilers would be invited to attend any Soviet embassy receptions.[20] Petrov maintained to the end the genuine nature of the documents despite the absurd position this placed him in.

INTELLIGENCE INSTRUCTIONS

Thirty of the letters, representing nearly one-third of those received, contained intelligence directions ranging from the trivial to the absurd. Ten of these contained instructions to recruit embassy officers, including his wife; four related to that all-important Skoda motor car previously mentioned; and 16 were directions on intelligence tasks to be pursued. The contents of the ten letters giving recruitment instructions show how they must be judged as either fabrications or the work of incompetent intelligence managers. Petrov who was untrained in intelligence work and had a low level of general education and spoke little English, was instructed, for example, to train Antonov, the TASS agent in Sydney, and Kislitsyn, the second secretary, both of whom spoke less English than Petrov. The conduct of intelligence activity, other than making clippings from the local press, which is not intelligence work in any case, would have been beyond their capacities. Indeed Mrs Petrov described Kislitsyn as being 'completely dumb, and that he was afraid of talking to anyone'.[21] It is difficult to resist the suggestion that these letters were prepared to sustain the image of there being a Soviet spy network operating in Australia and that Petrov was a more important intelligence agent than he actually was. Dr Evatt argued before the RCE that the letters could have been produced by people with access to a Russian typewriter and photographic processes.[22]

The sixteen operational instruction letters covered a wide range of intelligence work from compiling information about the External Affairs Department to infiltrating Australia's non-existent spy network. The information sought on the Department of External Affairs ranged from the innocent, such as its addresses and which trade unions its employees joined, to the serious such as how the Department's highly important documents were guarded.

It was the instruction to establish an 'illegal apparatus' that held the attention of the Royal Commissioners, particularly W.F. Owen and Roslyn Philp. This lengthy letter of 6 June 1952 was headed 'Plan of Work' and contained 21 paragraphs. To the Commissioners who were convinced that the Moscow letters were genuine intelligence instructions and that Petrov was a genuine KGB agent, this long letter seemed to confirm all of their ideas about the dangers of the KGB in Australia. To those of a more sceptical frame of mind the letter was further evidence that a person totally unskilled in intelligence operations wrote it or that it was composed to create a false picture of the strength of local Soviet intelligence.

Petrov was instructed that in view of the international situation and the necessity to reorganize all intelligence work, the 'timely collection of data concerning the situation should be put in hand'. He was to recruit 'lawyers of your acquaintance, members of the Australian-Russia Society, etc, without disclosing our intentions to them'. How the bumbling Petrov was to instruct such people in this 'timely collection of data' was not revealed. He was also given the absurd instruction to discover how Australian spies in the Soviet Union transmitted information back to Australia. This was followed by the more outlandish instruction to place trusted agents in the spy force operating within the USSR and its allies so that they could expose those who were genuine agents. After completing that simple task he was to train agents (apparently his legal friends again) 'for work in extraordinary circumstances' but he was not to let them think of 'these preparations as a sign of inevitable war in the near future', which was exactly what they would think. The Royal Commissioners did. He was reminded that he was not to recruit people 'whose progressive activity is known to counter-intelligence' (hence the lawyers, no doubt), but to concentrate on 'persons engaged on secret work of the government' (thereby excluding the lawyers). The letter continued in the same vein, making it quite impossible to take the contents and their instructions seriously.[23]

DOCUMENT G

What made the Moscow letters so difficult to accept as intelligence documents was that they proposed impossible tasks and made improbable demands. Even if Petrov had spoken good English and been trained in intelligence work or had the urbanity to mix in all circles he could never have implemented them. In addition, these letters were verbose, frequently punctuated with hortative and propagandist phrases and they showed no awareness of the political and social structures in Australia. Their importance for ASIO and the RCE was that the names of people, often together with their code names, were scattered as important clues through their pages.

Document G, on the other hand, written in Russian and containing a list of 63 names, appeared more like an intelligence document. It became very suspect, however, because of the contradiction over its origins. It was supposed to have been compiled by Sadovnikov, the KGB agent between June 1949 and April 1951, and copied by Petrov. It was said to have lain in the KGB safe in a sealed envelope marked 'N' for *navodki* meaning 'inquiries'. When the origins of the envelope were first raised at the RCE in October 1954, Mrs Petrov said she took the contents from Sadovnikov early in 1951 and placed them in the KGB safe.[24] In February 1955 she said that she had not seen the contents of this envelope but then quickly changed her evidence saying she saw them early in 1951 for a few moments before they were resealed. In that quick reading she said she saw that they were the names of agents 'put on ice' or ones being studied or no longer studied. But then she converted the single envelope into two. One, the original from which Petrov withdrew some papers before defecting but left in the safe, and the second which Petrov presented to Colonel Spry.[25] In sharp contrast, Petrov, in June 1955, said that there was a single envelope containing Sadovnikov's lists of names. He had not examined this envelope in the three years before defecting. It had lain in the safe unopened since Sadovnikov's departure in April 1951.[26] But on the eve of his departure he claimed that he had removed some of these lists and copied others in longhand. Given these contradictory explanations it is not certain what part these lists played in the alleged KGB spy ring.[27]

Like the Moscow letters, it could be argued, document G consisted of the names of people familiar to ASIO and about whom it could discover more by having them brought before the RCE for questioning. The 63 names included those people discussed in previous chapters such as Frances Garrett, née Bernie, who was alleged to have taken papers from Dr Evatt to give to the CPA. June Barnett, the diplomat who had been in the CPA during the war, appeared under the vague description of the girl who had completed training in the Department of External Affairs. David Morris, the suspect army tank expert, was mentioned and the External Affairs Department officers who were suspected of being involved in the Case, Jim Hill, Ric Throssell and Dr John Burton were listed by their code names. Clues to identify them were, not surprisingly, included so that 'Tourist' could be identified as Hill, 'Ferro' as Throssell and 'B' as Dr Burton. Ian Milner had been previously identified by Petrov. Madame Ollier, second secretary at the French embassy, appeared only as her code name 'Olga'. Jack Legge, the wartime gas expert and academic, was described as having a relation working in External Affairs. This relation was George Legge, who took Petrov fishing and who was hastily transferred out of the Department when this became known. George's name also appeared on this list.

Other names appeared who were not summoned before the RCE such as Arthur Calwell, Deputy Leader of the Opposition,

Sir William McKell, former Governor General, and Allen Fraser. The common link for these men was their parliamentary background in the Labor Party. Their inclusion gave verisimilitude to the lists not simply being the means of hailing ASIO suspects before the RCE. Don Woods was a name not seen before. The correct name was Woodward and he was described as the 'Secretary to the adviser of Doctor E. on atomic energy'. Suspicion about Dr Evatt was thereby again emphasized, especially when it was discovered by RCE questioning that Woodward had been a member of the British Communist Party, a fact probably passed to ASIO by MI5.

The question of atomic energy became a focus for the RCE because the British authorities had begun testing their nuclear weapons in Australia in great secrecy. John Kaiser, a scientist with the Council for Scientific and Industrial Research (CSIR) who had been dismissed from that body for demonstrating outside Australia House in London in 1949 against the previous Labor government's industrial policy, also appeared in document G described as 'a physicist working in atomic energy'.[28] This statement was quite incorrect even in June 1949 when Sadovnikov became the KGB chief and allegedly began preparing this document. The raising of the spectre of atomic spies in Australia provided a vague link to the more important defection of another Soviet cipher clerk, Igor Gouzenko, in Canada in 1945 which led to the exposure in 1946 of Dr Alan Nunn May, the British nuclear bomb scientist. The spectre also linked the Petrov affair to the exposure of Dr Klaus Fuchs, another atomic physicist, in February 1950, as a result of the Venona decrypts which also had an alleged connection to the Petrov affair.

MADAME OLLIER, 'THE FRENCH SPY'

The allegations of Soviet spying against the French embassy in Canberra and Petrov's attempts to subvert its second secretary, Madame Ollier, who was also in charge of its diplomatic cipher, was the factor that gave the largest international publicity to the Petrov affair. Madame Ollier's name appeared in several documents, and the Petrovs gave evidence about her in a closed session of the RCE indicating that the Russians believed that she might help them to collect intelligence information.[29] Unfortunately for Madame Ollier, she knew nothing of these allegations made against her. R.G. Casey reported these accounts to her ambassador, Louis Roché, who bundled her off to Noumea to be held in detention. Roché already held an antipathy towards Madame Ollier and probably seized the opportunity to be rid of her. She was later sent under arrest to Paris to be tried on the basis of the Petrov allegations and although she was acquitted, her subsequent career in the French foreign service suffered.[30]

It was Madame Ollier's knowledge of Russian culture and her inability to identify with the Russophobia then so prevalent in Australia that brought her to the attention of ASIO soon after she arrived in the Canberra embassy as a widow with two teenage sons. Her other interests such as motoring, horse-riding (she obtained her own horse soon after arriving) and rifle-shooting also made her prominent in Canberra. In addition, she entertained other ambassadorial staff in her home, including Soviet diplomats.[31] Her ability to be at ease with the Russians and other nationals arose from her cosmopolitan family background. Her father, Dr Pietri, a nose and throat specialist in Bordeaux, had worked in a Russian military hospital in Kiev during the First World War helping to reconstruct the damaged faces of Russian soldiers. Her mother learnt Russian in order to work with him, but the Russians would not let her travel to Kiev. He returned to France in 1918.

She knew the Petrovs socially and met Petrov occasionally while shopping at a delicatessen owned by a Greek in nearby Queanbeyan to which she often drove in the evenings to purchase continental-style food. She noted that towards the end of 1953 Petrov appeared to be very depressed about his future and worried about who would care for his Alsatian dog, Jack. Following a discussion at a diplomatic function on 23 December 1953, she agreed to meet him along with the dog at Cooma, a nearby country town, on 24 December because they would each be driving through that town on their way to their respective Christmas holidays.[32] Petrov's car was destroyed on that trip, but he and Jack were given a lift to Cooma where they met briefly.

Madame Ollier's name appeared in no fewer than four of the Moscow letters. In them, Petrov was given a series of outlandish instructions which would have been totally impractical to implement. For example, he was directed to obtain details of the secret French diplomatic cipher from Madame Ollier at clandestine meetings, to bribe her or compromise her with the gift of a wristlet watch to be purchased from KGB funds and to obtain details of Australian arms shipments to the French Army fighting Vietnamese nationalist forces.[33] Such instructions were clearly in the realm of the absurd. The most junior official in intelligence or diplomatic activities knows that information on diplomatic ciphers is never openly divulged by senior officials, particularly if the request for it is accompanied by a clumsy attempt at compromise. The shipment of the arms was a public issue because the waterside workers were objecting to the loading of them. The unrealistic nature of these Ollier Moscow letters tends to add further weight to the argument that they were fabricated with the intention of publicly exposing the names of people who were observed to have some connection, however indirect, with Soviet officials or the CPA.

The Ollier affair soon became an important sub-plot of the Petrov affair. This arose because of the interchange of information between ASIO and French intelligence authorities. Following Madame Ollier's despatch to Noumea, ASIO presented a copy of the transcript of evidence given by the Petrovs at the RCE on 20 July 1954 to Colonel Ramier of French intelligence who then travelled to Noumea to interrogate Madame Ollier.[34] He then sent a copy of this interrogation to ASIO on the understanding that it would not be divulged in the RCE hearings although the commissioners were given copies.[35] They would have been less than human if they remained uninfluenced by this secret French intelligence information. By 24 August 1954 when Dr Evatt was making successful gains in the RCE and was about to have Richards and Dr Bialoguski put into the witness box (Bialoguski's role in the affair was not then publicly known), the government was considering releasing the in camera evidence against Ollier. It did so on 4 September 1954 in an effort to demonstrate the international nature of the Petrovs' spying endeavours. The government's action and the nature of the evidence were condemned by Dr Evatt.[36] He said that it was a pathetic attempt by the government to brand Madame Ollier as a spy on the statements 'of two paid informers' (the Petrovs).

The commissioners were stung by this rebuke and barred him from further hearings of the RCE on 7 September 1954.[37]

The charge of 'violating state security' against Madame Ollier was dropped on 27 July 1955, soon after her interrogation in Paris, and she then stood trial for 'not revealing a violation of the external security of the state'. The main evidence against her seems to have been that given by the Petrovs to the RCE, but it failed to impress the military tribunal and she was acquitted on 20 October 1955.[38] Meanwhile, the government was eager to have Colonel Ramier's interrogation report released because it compromised Madame Ollier and bolstered the accusations of the Petrovs. The French government regarded the report as simply an account of a discussion having no legal status and it refused the Australian government's request. News of the acquittal coincided with the parliamentary debate accompanying the release of the RCE report. Dr Evatt was able to take advantage of the news to demonstrate his earlier assessment that Madame Ollier had been framed. Prime Minister Menzies had the Australian embassy procure a copy of the Ollier trial transcript hoping to obtain some morsel to sustain its case against Dr Evatt's claim. The Australian ambassador sent a brief account of the trial because no transcript was available, but it provided no ammunition for Prime Minister Menzies to use against Dr Evatt in the parliamentary debate on 25 October 1955.[39]

ASIO AND THE CONCLUSION OF THE PETROV AFFAIR

Two important intelligence developments marked the conclusion of the Petrov affair. The first was the introduction to the RCE by ASIO of the evidence by the Petrovs that they had been involved in a KGB operation to deliver a parcel containing $25,000 in US currency of $5 and $25 bank notes to Lance Sharkey, general secretary of the CPA. This represented $100,000 in current Australian values. Mrs Petrov first mentioned this to ASIO on 10 June 1954 in the safe house, but ASIO officers did nothing to investigate the matter immediately such as making inquiries at the banks in Sydney to discover who had been changing US currency into Australian money or investigating the state of the CPA bank accounts. Indeed it was not until 24 August 1954 that a statement was taken from Petrov of that very important event. He was then uncertain of the dates of the arrival of the parcel from Moscow or of when he took it to Sydney to give it to the TASS agent, Antonov, who was to deliver it to Sharkey.[40] By 10 December 1954, Petrov had prepared with the assistance of ASIO another report containing greater precision of dates and details. By this stage the ASIO officers had become aware that the $25 denomination did not exist in US currency, and in Petrov's second statement the bank notes appeared as $5 and $10 denominations. More significantly, he fixed the date on which Antonov delivered the parcel to Sharkey at exactly 8 p.m. on Friday, 16 October 1953. While not witnessing the handover, he claimed to have collected the receipt, given by Sharkey for the money to Nosov, the next day, 17 October, and despatched it to Moscow.[41]

The RCE seemed to be as lethargic as ASIO in following up this important revelation and did not call evidence on it until 8 February 1955. The hearing took a strange turn on 10 February 1955 when Sharkey gave evidence that he had been attending a meeting of the Central Committee of the CPA at 8 p.m. on 16 October and could not have been in the suburban house, as Petrov's ASIO report had it, to accept the parcel of money.[42] ASIO evidence indicated that Sharkey had been under surveillance by ASIO agents at that meeting. This contradiction of Petrov's evidence pointed to ASIO not keeping proper account of the evidence Petrov was supposed to present to the RCE. George Richards shouldered some of the blame for this débâcle by telling the RCE that he knew of the conflict of evidence. But then he shifted the blame to Victor Windeyer, counsel assisting the commission, by saying that he believed that he had written to Windeyer reporting that ASIO knew Sharkey was at the CPA meeting on 16 October.[43] The implication was that ASIO by itself had not bungled the evidence Petrov was to give and that Windeyer was also responsible for allowing Petrov to fix the wrong date. The Royal Commissioners were not concerned at the lateness or contradiction in this apparently important revelation. They blandly accepted that the money had been received in Australia and given to Sharkey 'at some date in or about October 1953'.[44] They showed no interest in how such a large amount of US currency could have been converted into Australian money nor in how it was disbursed. Understandably the account of the Petrovs, with all its flaws, was too good a witness of a KGB/CPA link to be questioned let alone rejected by these judicial experts.

The second important intelligence occurrence was the despatch of a letter from Dr Evatt on 10 February 1955 to V.M. Molotov, Foreign Minister of the Soviet Union, explaining the background to the Petrov affair. He pointed out that Petrov had been under the supervision of ASIO for two years via Dr Bialoguski and that few of the Petrov documents appeared to be genuine. He asked Molotov to intervene to establish with the Soviet authorities whether these documents were fabrications.[45] Dr Evatt was a friend of Molotov, having met and debated with him on numerous occasions at the UN and elsewhere. The answer was predictable. Any government in similar circumstances would have branded stolen intelligence documents as fabrications. Molotov himself did not reply to Dr Evatt and the letter sent on 9 April 1955 came from an unknown official, L. Ilyichev, who signed himself Chief of the Press Department of the Soviet Foreign Ministry.[46]

The legal mind of Dr Evatt seized on this letter as supporting evidence for his strengthening conviction that the Petrov affair was an ASIO/government fabrication. He briefly quoted from it in the parliamentary debate that started with the tabling of the report on 19 October 1955. It was greeted with jeers from the government benches. His lengthy and detailed attack on the RCE and the Petrov affair was totally sustained by the evidence he produced, but his mention of the letter only detracted from the overall effect.

With the conclusion of the RCE, ASIO began looking to the future for the Petrovs. They were taken to Adelaide and Brisbane to see if they would like to live in either city. The preparation of their biography was under way with the ghost-writer, Michael Thwaites. Dr Bialoguski was quicker off the mark getting his book launched by the middle of 1955. He too received the support of ASIO officers who furnished him with daily copies of the transcripts of the RCE and read drafts of his chapters. He was also assisted in writing his book, titled *The Petrov Story*, by Eric McLoughlin, a journalist with the *Sydney Morning Herald*. The Petrovs resented some of Dr Bialoguski's disclosures about them in his book and wanted Thwaites to answer them. To boost sales of their book, the Petrovs also sought to delay the public release of the RCE report until the middle of September when their book was to be issued.[47] As it happened the report was issued on 14 September 1955.

Colonel Spry was obviously pleased with the RCE report because it strongly praised his organization. It represented the successful conclusion to four years of active ASIO operations and, claimed Spry, it established the reputation of ASIO in the eyes of other intelligence bodies. He claimed, with perhaps more than a tinge of exaggeration, since he produced no supporting evidence, that 'the Petrovs had identified some 500 Intelligence Officers. This information is invaluable to the Free Democracies'.[48] The Colonel ordered 40 copies of the report of the RCE to be sent to Britain via MI5 and 100 copies to the CIA. Another 60 were to be distributed within ASIO.[49]

Spry's rejoicing over the successful conclusion to the RCE was short-lived because the political divisiveness that was apparent from the very beginning of the Petrov affair became more pronounced with its ending. Dr Burton attacked the report of the RCE, calling on his knowledge as former Secretary of the External Affairs Department and claimed in the following terms that it contained nothing new:

> I wish the Commission had more thoroughly examined the background in which Petrov and his documents appeared. For example, the Crown Law Authorities, Security and the Prime Minister knew that the substance of what was produced in the Petrov document was already known to Security years previously. They knew that investigations had then been made and all necessary action had been taken. Petrov and his documents gave an excuse to re-hash and to add to, in a way valuable from a political point of view, material already on the files of security. I know they knew this because I had this knowledge as Secretary of External Affairs and was aware that this knowledge was shared by them at the time.[50]

Colonel Spry could not reply publicly to Dr Burton's reproach, but that it rankled with him was clear from a secret and personal letter he wrote to a British intelligence colleague remarking:

Our old friend Burton is endeavouring to be thoroughly mischievous and distortful (if there is no such word there should be!!). In all I shall be glad when the Parliamentary debate, which begins tomorrow, ends.[51]

The debate that Colonel Spry hoped would finally settle the Petrov affair had the opposite effect by renewing with fresh vigour the attacks on the government and ASIO for fabricating much of the Petrov affair. In launching this debate on 19 October 1955 in Parliament, Dr Evatt examined in fine detail all the issues he had spoken on before such as the conflicting evidence, the lies and contradictions, the motives of ASIO, the complicity of the Petrovs, the unjudicial behaviour of the commissioners, the secret role of Dr Bialoguski and the official exaggeration of the importance of the Petrovs.[52] ASIO tape recorded his speech and prepared a rebuttal on many of the points for Colonel Spry to pass to Prime Minister Menzies.[53] Wisely, however, Menzies did not use this prompt-material. Unlike Dr Evatt who possessed a detailed and extensive knowledge of the tangled affair, Menzies had left the matter entirely in the hands of ASIO. He could not be expected to absorb the vast amount of detail to answer Dr Evatt. It is possible that by revealing more information Menzies could have aided rather than undermined Dr Evatt's attack. The Prime Minister, therefore, replied only in generalities.[54]

The development of events by this stage raised the dilemma that has come to face many intelligence organizations in countries functioning under liberal democratic governments. The dilemma arises through the realization that intelligence organizations are as much involved in national politics as they are in government administrative matters. During the Cold War years in Australia ASIO and the non-Labor governing coalition under R.G. Menzies shared a harmony of interests. Their mutual foes were the CPA and the Soviet Union in all their manifestations. Just as the British Conservative Party was once regarded as the Church of England at prayer so was ASIO regarded as the unofficial wing of the Australian Liberal Party and the Country Party – that is, the governing coalition. The Petrov affair was exploited to the full by R.G. Menzies in winning two general elections (1954 and 1955), and because ASIO was central to the affair it was popularly regarded as a political agency of the government.

The political division in Australia caused by the Petrov affair demonstrated to Colonel Spry the extent to which ASIO had become politicized. Although the RCE had then progressed no more than half-way, the Colonel knew that if an Evatt ALP government was elected ASIO would be dismantled or drastically overhauled. ASIO was still functioning under the 1949 government charter with modifications made by Menzies. The anxieties of Spry about his own future and that of ASIO were to be allayed by Prime Minister Menzies accepting the Colonel's offer on 15 October 1954 to draft legislation to establish ASIO as a permanent government department. The course of that and other legislation to preserve and strengthen ASIO is discussed in the final chapter of this book.

AFTERMATH OF THE PETROV AFFAIR

As with the outcome of all important national events there were winners and losers to be identified in the aftermath of the Petrov affair. Colonel Spry and his ASIO staff clearly benefited. Their jobs were made secure and the right to a retirement pension guaranteed. The Australian woolgrowers were losers. During the period the Soviet embassy remained closed, sales of Australian wool to the Soviet Union declined from $52 million in the year before the affair to an average of $124,000 over the following five years.

The lives of those individuals caught up in the affair suffered. Ric Throssell's career in the External Affairs Department ceased to prosper, although he was totally cleared by the RCE; George Legge and Jim Hill were virtually forced out of the public service and the CPA members such as Rupert Lockwood and his family recovered only slowly from the harassment and personal abuse they suffered as a result of their names being involved.

The Petrovs had a 'D notice' placed on them by Colonel Spry. This was an agreement by the public media not to discuss their whereabouts. They settled in the Melbourne suburb of East Bentleigh under the names Sven and Maria Allyson. He worked as a storeman with a photographic company and she as a typist-clerk with an agricultural machinery company. He spent the last 17 years of his life in a nursing home suffering

191

from senile dementia and died there aged 84 on 14 June 1991.[55] Their adjustment to Australian life was not easy. Despite all of ASIO's help their book did not sell well and Petrov lapsed into alcoholism. He was attacked while trying to break into a house in Surfer's Paradise in Queensland in November 1956 and he was taken in his trouserless condition to the local police station and charged under the name he gave, John Olsen, with drunkenness.[56]

Dr Bialoguski faced financial and emotional problems after the inquiry. Sales of his book and its serialization in the Australian and the US press earned him $18,000, almost twice the amount ASIO paid Petrov, which says something about the earning capacity of the writer versus the defector. The book was reportedly translated into Arabic by US intelligence for distribution in Egypt.[57] The doctor's financial affairs did not prosper in spite of this and in 1957 his failure to make alimony payments to his second wife landed him in jail for a very brief spell.[58] He had difficulty resuming his medical practice in Sydney and after marrying his third wife in January 1957 departed for Britain where he established a medical practice near Epsom.[59] He returned to Australia in 1961 to pursue a libel suit against his second wife and the newspaper publishers which had printed in 1955 her account of their marriage and of the Petrov affair. He took particular offence at her published comment that he had grown a beard to look more serious (and about which he had become very vain) and that he had used perfume. 'In an Australian community what more could you say to ridicule a man?' he asked of the court when seeking damages.[60] He died in Epsom in 1984.

It is still difficult, even at this distance in time, to give a final judgement on the Petrov affair as a counter-espionage operation. The main players, including George Richards, are dead and Colonel Spry lives in secluded retirement in Melbourne, refusing attempts to interview him by quoting the secrecy provisions binding him. He did provide interviews to Robert Manne to assist in writing his valuable book, *The Petrov Affair*. The most recent judgement about the importance of the affair remains the statement of Colonel Spry, made in 1955 and referred to earlier. This was that the information provided by the Petrovs about the '500 Soviet Intelligence Officers' was the affair's lasting legacy.[61]

Neither at that time nor since has Colonel Spry substantiated such a statement with any details.

Linked to this assertion is the claim that the Petrovs provided valuable information about Soviet spying in Sweden where they worked before coming to Australia. The Australian government asked the British government in 1955, when the Petrovs' book was published, to establish the Swedish government's response to the revelations of the Petrovs about their spying experiences in Sweden. The reply was that the Petrovs had added nothing to what the Swedish authorities already knew. 'Nothing revealed by Petrov suggests any need to strengthen Swedish legislation' was the final judgement.[62] When the new Swedish ambassador to Australia, J. Martin Kastengren, arrived, he too was pumped for information. He told a representative of External Affairs that in comparing the spying operations that his government had to counter with the affair in Australia 'the whole thing seemed very slight and rather ridiculous'. He went on to remark that 'Petrov, of course, was a liar in any case and might have made much of it up'.[63] The Swedes in their long experience as neighbours possibly know the Russians better than any other nation. It could be that from this point of view Ambassador Kastengren's statement stands as the best informed judgement about the Petrov affair.

NOTES

1. Report, Senior Field Officer, South Australia, A6199/XR1, Item 96, f. 22.
2. Report, Senior Field Officer, South Australia, A6199/XR1, Item 96, f. 76.
3. Report, Field Officer, B2, A6199/XR1, Item 96, f. 69.
4. Report, Senior Field Officer, South Australia A 6199/XR1, Item 96, ff. 74,75.
5. Report, Senior Field Officer, South Australia, A6199/XR1, Item 96, f. 71.
6. Report, Senior Field Officer, South Australia, A 6199/XR1, Item 96, f. 75.
7. Report of Leo Carter, 13 March 1955, A6283/XR1, Item 72, f. 411.
8. See A6202, Exhibits letter series, 1954; Exhibit 'J'.

9. See A6202, Exhibit letter series, 1954; Exhibit 'H'.
10. See A6201, Item 51.
11. See Letters D16, D17, D18 for North, F8, B10, B11, B12 for McLean and F5 for Yuill, A6201, Item 51.
12. RCE official transcript of proceedings, p. 358. Kosky had some heated correspondence with the embassy ladies because he refused to take back fur collars sold 18 months previously.
13. Letters A9, B4, D11, A6201, Item 51.
14. Letter F9, A6201, Item 51.
15. See letters E6, E9, F7 for Chiplin and A9 for Keesing, A6201, Item 51.
16. Letter A18 and A20, A6201, Item 51.
17. Conway to Dr Evatt, 5 Aug. 1955, Evatt Papers, Flinders University.
18. Letters B14 and B15, A6201, Item 51.
19. RCE official transcripts, pp. 1788–90.
20. RCE official transcripts, p. 1792.
21. RCE official transcript of proceedings, p. 710.
22. RCE official transcript of proceedings, p. 2008, para 301.
23. Letters D7, D8, D9, D10, A 2601, Item 51.
24. RCE official transcript of proceedings, p. 1299, paras 284–93.
25. RCE official transcript of proceedings p. 1735, paras 173–5, p. 2006, para 246, p. 2005 paras 177–88.
26. RCE official transcript of proceedings, p. 1566, para. 55.
27. RCE official transcript of proceedings, p. 1752, paras 136–8.
28. Letter G5, A6201, Item 51.
29. See A6213, Item Z/46 for those in camera transcripts.
30. See Mme Ollier's account of events in Kylie Tennant, *Famous Australians, Evatt Politics and Justice* (Sydney, 1981), Appendix C.
31. Ollier File, A6213, Item G2.
32. Author's interview with Mme Ollier in her apartment in Paris 27 Aug. 1990.
33. Letters B6, D12, E7, E8, A6201, Item 51.
34. Tennant, *Evatt*.
35. Cablegram Australian embassy, Paris, to Canberra 15 June 1955, A6213, Item RCE/H/13. Colonel Ramier's report being given to the commissioners in Colonel Spry's report to R.G. Menzies, 21 Oct. 1955, A6213, Item, RCE/G/7.
36. Top Secret cable Department External Affairs to Australian embassy, Paris, 23 Aug. 1954. A6213, Item RCE/H/13.

37. Draft of Dr Evatt, pp. 15, 16 in Evatt papers, Flinders University.
38. Tennant, *Evatt.*
39. Cable Australian embassy, Paris, to Tange 22 Oct. 1955, A6213, Item RCE/H/13.
40. Statement by V. Petrov, witnessed by Leo Carter, 24 Aug. 1954, A6283/XR1, Item 143 Vol. 1.
41. Statement by V.M. Petrov Re Lance Sharkey, A6283/XR1, Item 146.
42. RCE official transcript of proceedings, p. 2173, para 647.
43. RCE official transcript of proceedings, p. 2321, paras 8–36.
44. Report of Royal Commission on Espionage, op. cit., p. 110, para 363.
45. Dr Evatt to V.M. Molotov, 10 Feb. 1955, Evatt papers, Flinders University.
46. Ilyichev to Dr Evatt, 9 April 1955, Evatt papers, Flinders University.
47. Whiting and Byrne, Solicitors to Solicitor-General, 18 July 1953, A6127, Item 72.
48. Report by C.C.F. Spry n.d. A6213, Item RCE U/7. In another letter to the Prime Minister Colonel Spry said, 'I am afraid it is not possible to make a statistical survey of identification of Soviet operatives made by the Petrovs.' Letter 26 Aug. 1955, A6123, Item RCE/G/7, folio 50.
49. Director-General of Security to Secretary, Prime Minister's Department, 6 Sept. 1955, A6213, Item RCE U/7.
50. Petrov Inquiry – Statement by Dr Burton, 15 Sept. 1955, A45954/17 Item [3].
51. Letter from C.C.F. Spry, 19 Sept. 1955, A6122/XR1, Item 407.
52. CPD, 19 Oct. 1955, pp. 1694–718.
53. Spry to Secretary Prime Minister's Department, 21 Oct. 1955, including 'Notes on Dr Evatt's Speech', A6213, Item RCE/G/7.
54. CPD, 25 October 1955, pp. 1858–75.
55. *Age*, 17 June 1991.
56. Report 27 July 1957 in Correspondence Misc. Re John Olsen (Vladimer [*sic*] Petrov) Evatt Papers, Flinders University.
57. Report from Australian ambassador Cairo to Department of External Affairs, Canberra, A1836 Item 6a/1/3/7.
58. *Daily Telegraph* (Sydney) 9 April 1957.
59. Ibid. 25 May 1957.
60. Ibid. 18 April 1961.
61. Statement by C.C.F. Spry, n.d. A6213, Item RCE U/7, folio 257.

THE AUSTRALIAN SECURITY INTELLIGENCE ORGANIZATION

62. Letter J.D. Fraser, British High Commissioner's Office to A.T. Griffith, Prime Minister's Department, 13 Oct. 1955, A6213/1, Item RCE/K/8.
63. Report by F.H. Stuart of conversation with H.E. Mr J. Martin Kastengren, Minister of Sweden, 25 Nov. 1954, A6283, Item 11.

9

ASIO in the 1960s and 1970s

The closure of the Soviet embassy from May 1954 until early in 1959 was a mixed blessing for ASIO. On the one hand the monitoring of the Soviet officials ceased, thereby promising unemployment for ASIO agents. But on the other hand ASIO was able to expand its activities elsewhere, thus ensuring continuing employment for its workers. This included the vetting of military trainees then being commissioned as army officers to handle the ever-increasing numbers conscripted under the compulsory military training programme. This scheme marked Australia's domestic response to the burgeoning Cold War. Colonel Spry had already decided that vetting procedures for military personnel should concentrate on the four following categories: persons having access to top secret information, persons employed on intelligence duties, cipher staff and persons employed on educational duties.[1]

Soviet officialdom had contemplated selling the contents of their embassy, and questions were raised in Canberra whether the English-style typewriter, allegedly used to type document J, would appear. But that plan was reversed and an Italian caretaker was placed in the building and Soviet affairs were looked after by the Swedish ambassador. ASIO remained concerned, however, that Soviet propaganda material was being sent to Australia from the Soviet embassy in New Zealand.[2]

In 1959, when it appeared that the embassy would be reopened, Colonel Spry visited MI5 in London to obtain bugging equipment for installation in the embassy. The technical expert in MI5, then Peter Wright, recommended a device he had developed identified as 'Satyr'. Wright advised installing it in the woodwork surrounding a window. This was carried out secretly by one of Wright's assistants flown specially to Australia. Wright had advised not activating the device for twelve months to avoid detection by early anti-bugging sweeps made by Soviet technicians. ASIO found that the equipment worked satisfactorily in that it transmitted every footstep in the office and every rustle of paper, yet it transmitted not one spoken word. Either the Soviet technicians had identified the bug and staff were warned not to converse near it, or information of its installation had been leaked from ASIO to the Soviet officials.[3]

ASIO's questionable bugging skills had been sought earlier by the External Affairs Department late in 1955 when it began discussing the ramifications of re-establishing relationships with the USSR. Colonel Spry recommended that a one metre-deep trench be dug around the outer walls of the embassy proposed for Moscow (Indonesia had taken over the former embassy) in order to destroy wires that could connect microphones hidden in the embassy to an outside listening station. He also recommended that an ASIO agent be included in Australian embassy staff. The Department prudently thanked the Colonel, suggesting that the trench-digging would be impracticable and that the ASIO agent would be quickly identified by the Russians. Undeterred by this, Colonel Spry went on to suggest that travel restrictions be imposed on all Soviet embassy staff in Australia including the TASS agents, and that the Soviet government be compelled to provide full details of their staff members. 'We could then', he claimed, 'check with our voluminous Soviet Intelligence identifications, plus reference to our friends overseas.'[4]

THE SKRIPOV AFFAIR

The Skripov affair of 1963 was for ASIO, in marked contrast to the Petrov affair, a public relations and intelligence success. Briefly, it was the entrapment of the Soviet diplomat and KGB official, Ivan Fedorovich Skripov, by a female ASIO agent, which led to the demand by the Australian government for his immediate recall. News of the affair was released on 3 February 1963 by the Minister for External Affairs, Sir Garfield Barwick, who had succeeded, after a short time, R.G. Casey as minister.

Sir Garfield, however, was a leading barrister rather than an intelligence expert. The announcement was accompanied by the release of nine pages of foolscap describing events, together with 30 photographs, taken by clandestine ASIO photographers, of the two agents meeting. Others were of the spying equipment he gave to her. The account of the affair was therefore entirely reliant on the descriptions and photographs provided by ASIO. As with much of the Petrov affair, information on these events has been tightly regulated by ASIO, and a proper analysis of the Skripov affair must await ASIO's release of the appropriate documents.[5]

Skripov, as first secretary, was in the diplomatic advance guard which assisted in the reopening of the Soviet embassy in 1959. He spoke excellent English and mixed in many circles in Australia. He addressed Rotary clubs and other public functions and sought Russian exchanges with Australian sporting, cultural, scientific, journalistic and trade union delegations. The woman ASIO agent made contact with Skripov in 1960. There are two conflicting accounts of her background: one was that she was thirtyish, a brunette and a linguist lent to ASIO by MI6 (Colonel Spry has since denied she was MI6); the other was that she was a woman immigrant who ASIO hoped would lead them to Soviet contacts in Australia.[6] He was reported as having given her various tasks to perform such as collecting material from secret drop-points, and to have given her chemicals for use in treating letters containing messages in invisible ink. In October 1962 the female agent collected at Skripov's request a parcel concealed near a grave in a Sydney cemetery. ASIO found it to contain a Canadian passport for a person named Huha, a former Czech national, plus a photograph of another person. At the end of December, Skripov instructed her to deliver a rapid message-sender, for attachment to a wireless transmitter, to a person who would meet her in Adelaide. That person did not appear, and the agent returned to Sydney to report to Skripov. After refusing to reply to Skripov's written requests in invisible ink to return the message-sender, ASIO stopped the entrapment process and Skripov was forced to return to Moscow.[7] The embassy claimed that the 'materials' released by ASIO proved nothing and that they seemed to have been prepared with a view to hindering the development of friendly relationships between the USSR and the Australian people. The press suggested that the Adelaide recipient did not appear because he smelt a trap or was warned by someone in ASIO.[8] In a Moscow broadcast in English on 21 February 1963, it was announced that on the flight from Australia, Skripov's aircraft made an unscheduled stop at Darwin because of the fear that a bomb was on board. While waiting in the airport terminal, Skripov was approached by an intelligence agent 'with an Oxford accent' and invited to remain in Australia with promises of money, a two-storey house and a motor car. Skripov refused and returned to Moscow and obscurity.[9] Generally the affair passed with little public comment and it was perhaps a measure of the maturity of both the government and ASIO that they resisted the temptation to make it into a divisive and unproductive repetition of the Petrov affair.

ASIO, DISSENT AND THE VIETNAM WAR

ASIO received a considerable fillip from Australia's involvement with the US in the Vietnamese civil war. Its staff numbers increased, it moved into a specially constructed high-rise building at 469 St Kilda Road, Melbourne, and the numbers of specialized areas within it increased. This general expansion led to a similar growth in the Special Branches of the State police forces which became official adjuncts to ASIO performing the surveillance work ASIO itself could not perform. It was the growth in public dissent against Australia's involvement in the war that led to ASIO's expansion.

Until 1966 the popular mood in Australia favoured the war. The Labor Party opposed the war, but it could not obtain an electoral mandate to withdraw. Like the government, ASIO was ideologically and organizationally in favour of the war. In considering itself to be the fourth arm in the defence of Australia, it naturally shared the public expression of the government's policy that Communism must be met and defeated wherever it challenged Western liberalism.

The Menzies government took Australia into the Vietnamese civil war by becoming captive of its own rhetoric. Such rhetoric stretched back into pre-Second World War years, as outlined in previous chapters, and stressed the dangers of Communism at home and abroad. The more practical reason for joining the war was that the Menzies government wanted the US to become more committed in the South Pacific in the hope that it would defend Australia against possible threats from Indonesia or China. It expected that by committing troops to Vietnam the US would commit itself to Australia. This was a cynical position because the government in those years oversaw burgeoning wool sales to the Soviet Union and expanding wheat sales to China even though it refused to recognize the Peking government. Dissent against the war became more pronounced after April 1965 when the Menzies government sent the first of three infantry battalions to Vietnam to defend the Saigon regime in the civil war.

As an agent of the government, ASIO pursued the dissenters against its war policy. The anti-war activists were concentrated in university student bodies, women's groups, particularly among mothers, and church and trade union groups. Smearing these people as Communists was an obvious response by the government and its supporters. The CPA by then, however, had split into three factions with fewer than 1,500 active members. Much of the protest was driven by self-interest because selective conscription to serve overseas had been introduced in November 1964. As more middle-class youths were forced into military training, their families began questioning the necessity for the war. The research, writing and publishing to explain the causes of the war, dating back to French colonization of Indo-China in the nineteenth century, was undertaken by university staff and students. Their self-interest was also obvious because students could become eligible for service in Vietnam upon graduation. This stimulated the establishment of the Draft Resisters' Movement based around Australia's universities. Because draft evasion was an offence against Australian law, ASIO became more closely involved in watching the offenders and worked with the Australian Federal Police Force to have them apprehended.[10] ASIO was able to maintain this surveillance in universities because it had already engaged part-time agents among academic staffs in Australian universities. It also recruited trusted students, such as those serving in University Regiments and who were members of the university Liberal Clubs, to report on university anti-war activities. At the wider public level, ASIO recruited people to infiltrate the Communist and anti-war groups. Typical of these part-time agents was Phil Geri who was recruited by ASIO in 1963 to work in his large, rural town of Bendigo in Victoria. He was a working-class youth employed as a medical technician in the local hospital and proudly serving part-time in the Citizen Military Force (CMF), the then title for Australia's militia. He believes that he was selected for recruitment because the army could guarantee his non-left-wing credentials. His discharge from the CMF was arranged by ASIO because he had to assume the identity of an anti-war working-class activist and join the local Communist Party, then comprising approximately ten elderly people. This false identity created deep personal conflicts because he actually supported Australia's fighting in Vietnam. This self-conflict became poignant when the remains of a close friend who was killed fighting in Vietnam were brought by the army to be buried in Bendigo. He could not attend the funeral for fear of compromising this false identity.

Phil Geri attended State conferences of the Party, reporting all details to his case officers and identifying the delegates from the large library of photographs of CPA members. On one occasion he was shown 800 photographs in order to identify 400 delegates. In 1970 he organized an anti-war march in Bendigo attended by the Labor parliamentarian, Dr Jim Cairns, who by then was a national leader in the anti-war cause. Geri had to provide weekly reports to his case officers who travelled the 70 miles to Bendigo to meet their part-time agent under clandestine conditions.[11]

By the late 1960s the anti-war groups had loosely joined to form a Moratorium Movement which, like its US counterpart, held meetings and marches seeking the temporary cessation of fighting in order to achieve conciliation and settlement of affairs in Vietnam by other means. The Moratorium's marches in 1970 and 1971 often involved tens of thousands of people, and such events were monitored by ASIO and the police Special Branches. Photographs were taken and movie camera films were made of such events. The photographers, by necessity, were located in prominent positions, and it was this open surveillance that seemed most to annoy those middle-class people who made up the bulk of the marchers.

At these marches and rallies the power of the state was predominant. State police mounted high on horsesback, Australian federal police in identifiable white motor cars, Special

Branch officers trying to disguise themselves as ordinary citizens were obvious at such events. Whereas most people accepted the presence of the uniformed police, even if their crowd control methods were heavy-handed, the presence of the 'political police', as ASIO came to be known, was greatly resented. In Melbourne this mood led to political activists establishing in 1973 the Committee for the Abolition of Political Police (CAPP). Its members turned the tables on ASIO agents by photographing them as they left ASIO buildings, discovering their residential addresses and publishing this information in pamphlet form.[12] Such actions were later to become illegal.

Much of this resentment against ASIO was concentrated in ALP ranks. The new wave of middle-class people who joined the Labor Party added their dissatisfaction with ASIO to that existing in the ALP since the Petrov affair of 1954. Parliamentary members of the Party were disturbed to find that ASIO had withheld naturalization from particular Italian and Greek migrants who were active in ALP branch affairs. The Party took up their cases during the term of the Whitlam Labor government and naturalization was granted. Two of these men were subsequently elected as Labor members to the Parliament in Victoria.[13] This growing indignation against ASIO welled up at the 1971 national conference of the ALP, the national policy-setting organ of the ALP, finding expression in a motion to dissolve ASIO. It was opposed by the shadow Attorney-General, Senator Murphy, and went to a tied vote, to be defeated only by the chairman's casting vote. An alternative policy was adopted of having the Attorney-General report annually to Parliament on the functions of ASIO and appointing an administrative tribunal to establish regulations by which ASIO and other organizations should be governed.

It was generally accepted that the Labor Party would be elected at the end of 1972 and the debate at this ALP National Conference was not without its point. Had it then been known that ASIO employed journalists to write articles about the evils of communism for release to the Australian press, particularly the right-wing *Bulletin* published in Sydney by the Packer family, the outcome of the Conference might have been more positive.

This releasing by ASIO of cover stories to selected members of the Australian press about its quarries demonstrates the confidence ASIO held about its social and political role. It was clearly in the unique position of collecting and holding information about Communists and other left-wing activists that no journalist could discover. Given that ASIO perceived its function as holding the line against Communist subversion it was not surprising that it was discovered in 1974 to have distributed 67 sets of briefing papers to the Australian press between 1962 and 1972.[14] Inspection of a sample of these papers indicated that 54 per cent were about the Communist Party, 36 per cent were about what was then labelled the 'new left' and 6 per cent related to the right wing of Australian politics. Colonel Spry's successor as Director-General of ASIO, Peter Barbour, told the new ALP government that releases to the media ceased in 1970.[15]

This did not seem to be a truthful account of events because a well-known Sydney journalist, Bob Mayne, reported in March 1973 that he had been approached by Peter Coleman, editor of the *Bulletin* and a Liberal member of the NSW Parliament, and the ASIO agent, E.O. Redford, to edit a journal to be known as *Analysis*. This was to publish information provided by ASIO designed to discredit political radicals, including left-wing members of the ALP. Some days later he was given dossiers on five left-wing people resident in four Australian states. The scheme was never realized, but it demonstrates the degree of importance that ASIO placed on its record collection as a means of influencing public opinion.[16]

ASIO AND THE USTASHI TERRORISM

A brief analysis of the Ustashi terrorism provides interesting insights to the operation of ASIO. The Ustashi was dedicated to the overthrow of the Yugoslavian Communist government and despite its terrorist activities in Australia such as bombing Yugoslav embassy buildings and airline premises, ASIO seemed reluctant to constrain its leaders to any extent. This reluctance reflected the policy of the Liberal coalition government to defend the Ustashi against criticism and condemnation as it engaged in its campaign of terrorism. Another factor was the existence of Yugoslav intelligence organizations operating unofficially in

Australia, monitoring the Ustashi organizations as they plotted and trained to challenge the Yugoslav state.

By watching the Ustashi, ASIO could catch glimpses of the Yugoslav intelligence in operation and observe them applying KGB techniques in which they had been trained by the Russians. One report had five intelligence agents positively identified by ASIO and 17 suspected agents. These were members of Sluzba Bezbednosti (SB), the military intelligence service and Drzavna Bezbednosti (DB or UDBa) the State Security Service.[17] The Menzies government and ASIO probably considered that the cost of local terrorism, so long as it was kept at a low level, was a sufficient price to pay for gaining insights into the local operations of a Communist intelligence service. Although Yugoslavia was not attached to the Soviet monolith and its destabilization was not part of the programme of Western intelligence, the temptation for both ASIO and the Menzies government to keep even a mildly Communist government off balance was probably another factor leading to the toleration by ASIO and the government of this Croatian terrorism.

The Ustashi itself was founded in the early 1930s as a fascist body by Ante Pavlic, a Zagreb lawyer. After the invasion of Croatia by Italy and Germany he was appointed dictator of Croatia and began killing and torturing the Serbian and Croatian people. At the end of the war he fled to Argentina and established the Croatian Liberation Movement. After the fall of his protector, President Perón, he fled to Spain, then governed by the dictator, General Franco, and died there at the German Hospital in 1959 aged 70.[18] Ustashi leaders also entered Australia disguised among the 200,000 displaced persons who arrived between 1945 and 1951. Other senior Nazi collaborators responsible for the deaths of many of their fellow nationals arrived from Hungary, the Baltic republics, Romania and the Soviet Union. They had escaped to the West with the retreating German forces and remained concealed in the refugee camps. The Allied intelligence officers knew of the identities of some of them from the records supplied by the liberated countries, but they helped them to escape to Canada, the US, Australia and Britain.

These former Nazi collaborators were despatched by Allied intelligence to overseas countries to provide a pool of intelligence specialists who could later be used against targets in their former countries, that is those then governed by Communists in East Europe and the Soviet Union. The US State Department, aided by the expertise of George Kennan, established an elaborate plan known as Bloodstone to help whisk former Nazis, who were often involved in the extermination of the Jews, to the US to aid in the development of this anti-Communist intelligence operation.[19] Approximately 500 ex-Nazis slipped into Australia, although to what extent Brigadier Fred Galleghan, head of Australia's Military Mission and charged with preventing this outcome, consciously assisted this programme is difficult to quantify.

Two Ustashi leaders, father and son Joseph and Srecko Rover, arrived in November 1950 among the 30,000 Yugoslav immigrants who arrived in Australia between 1945 and 1964. Srecko immediately began organizing an Australian division of the Ustashi. He established a Croat-language paper, *Hrvat*, which was observed by ASIO, as were other Ustashi activities in Perth, Adelaide and Sydney. The Serbian Yugoslav groups also expressed alarm at the arrival of the Ustashi in Australia and while the regional ASIO officers reported anxiously on these developments, Colonel Spry perceived no threat and wrote that 'the Ustashi's political propaganda would not constitute a security threat to Australia'.[20] Indeed Rover was viewed as being of no security threat and after ASIO provided a security clearance he was permitted to become an Australian citizen on 28 November 1956. Other immigrants with left-wing backgrounds did not receive the same co-operative treatment.

Although the Ustashi split into two groups, one, led by Rover, named the Croatian National Resistance with the Croatian acronym HNO, and the other, led by Fabijan Lovokovic, named the Croatian Liberation Movement with the acronym HOP, it continued with its programme of violence and terrorism. A new group devoted more intently to terrorism emerged early in 1961, known as the Croatian Revolutionary Brotherhood (HRB). This body recruited and trained members in weapons-handling and terrorism at the Croatian Catholic Welfare Centre conducted by Father Rocque Romac at Woollhara, NSW. In 1963 nine members travelled to Europe and on 4 and 5 July conducted a sabotage raid in Yugoslavia near Trieste.[21] The Yugoslav intelligence agents in Australia proved to be effective because these terrorists were captured and jailed for six to 14 years. The HOP also conducted training camps in terrorist tactics and on 2–4 January 1963 some 100 men were found in a camp near Wodonga in Victoria wearing Ustashi uniforms. They mixed with an army armoured squadron training nearby and posed for photographs striking a military pose. The Menzies government treated the matter very lightly, rejecting the argument that the army was compromised by its association with a terrorist organization.[22]

The Yugoslav government complained to the Australian government in 1963 of such incursions being planned in Australia but, in a parliamentary statement on 27 August 1964, Prime Minister Menzies, far from announcing a crack-down on these terrorist organizations, actually praised them, saying that 'it could be expected that they should hope for the establishment of an independent Croatia'.[23] Thereafter Ustashi terrorist incidents flourished. Yugoslav embassy and consular offices were bombed as well as Yugoslav airline offices. Those opposing the Ustashi had their homes bombed and themselves attacked while the government stood idly by. Because the Ustashi appeared to enjoy the tacit approval of the government, other Yugoslav migrant groups became deeply concerned in their attempts to defend themselves. In February 1970 Vladimir Rolovic, a Yugoslav intelligence expert, visited Australia to present a report to the government showing that the HRB was controlled by Rover.[24] In April 1971 it was discovered by ASIO that Rover's other group, HNO, was allied with Soviet intelligence as a means of destabilizing President Tito's government.[25]

In July 1972 the HRB launched another terrorist raid on Yugoslavia with 19 men, most of whom were killed in gunfights with Yugoslav border guards. Nine of these had been Australian residents. Rover denied any implication in this affair. The Yugoslav government again complained to Australia, but Senator Ivor Greenwood, the Liberal Party's Attorney-General, announced that there was no evidence of organized groups of Ustashi terrorists operating in Australia.[26] Such comments ignored the large body of evidence held by ASIO and the Australian Federal Police proving the contrary. Indeed on 22 August 1972 the Federal Police raided Rover's home in Melbourne and found evidence firmly involving Rover in that terrorist action. The Yugoslav government sent an *aide-mémoire* to the Australian government on 16 August 1972, giving complete details of Ustashi activities in Australia as they related to incursions into its country.[27] Bombing outrages against Yugoslav targets continued into 1972. This brought to 26 the number of such attacks since 1963, but the government refused to accept that they were conducted by the Ustashi.

In commenting on these events, Gough Whitlam, Prime Minister between 1972 and 1975, remarked:

> If communists rather than anti-communist organizations had been thought responsible for the incidents I have described, all the Liberal Attorneys-General would have been active in pursuing and prosecuting the perpetrators but none would have been more frenetically active than Greenwood [the Attorney-General and the minister for ASIO]. The Ustasha [sic] had enjoyed immunity under [the Australian Prime Ministers] Menzies, Holt, Gorton and McMahon.[28]

ASIO AND THE ALP GOVERNMENT 1972–75

After functioning under a sympathetic and supportive non-Labor government for 22 years, ASIO found itself in December 1972 having to live with a Labor government (led by Gough Whitlam) whose membership had been critical of ASIO since the days of the Petrovs. To this was now added resentment against ASIO's snooping on the Vietnam war dissenters and its seeming tolerance of Ustashi terrorism. Colonel Spry had retired from ASIO in 1970 on reaching 60 years of age and its new Director-General was Peter Barbour who had been a long-serving ASIO agent. He was born in 1925 into a family of educators; his father had been warden of the Melbourne University Union and a classicist, and Peter had studied Latin and German there before joining the Australian Army during the war. He returned to the university to study for a Master of Arts degree in German, but before its completion he was approached in April 1951 with an invitation to join ASIO as an analyst. It was an example of the tap-on-the-shoulder recruitment technique used by ASIO to ensure that it obtained the 'right' and 'reliable' type of person. He was among those ASIO agents sent

Three sombre intelligence agents lunching in Australia in 1967. From left, Anatoli Golitsyn, a KGB defector, Mrs Spry, Colonel Charles Spry, Director-General of ASIO, and James Jesus Angleton, head of counter-intelligence in the CIA. It is not known how much ASIO shared Angleton's fetish that all Soviet defectors before and after Golitsyn were false. (Tom Mangold photograph)

overseas disguised as immigration officers to prevent Communists migrating to Australia. He worked in Holland and Italy on these duties.

In 1959 Barbour was posted to the Canberra office where as head of B2 (counter-espionage) he had an ASIO woman agent entrap the Soviet diplomat and KGB agent, Ivan Skripov, in 1963. This boosted his career prospects and led to his becoming director of the Canberra office in 1964. The following year he returned to Melbourne to become Deputy Director-General and then Director-General in 1970.[29] B.A. Santamaria, who was an unofficial leader of the right-wing political activists in the Catholic church in Australia and not without influence in ASIO, deeply regretted the retirement of Colonel Spry. He said that the new leadership 'did not believe Marxism was the prime threat' to Australia to the same extent as Colonel Spry.[30] Santamaria was exaggerating, because no shift occurred in ASIO policy, although Barbour did not show the same trusting confidence that Spry placed in the famous KGB defector, Anatoli Golitsyn. This defector captured the imagination of James Jesus Angleton, the chief of counter-intelligence in the

CIA. He blindly accepted the defector's claim that the Soviet defectors previous to him were false and that Soviet moles had infiltrated all Western intelligence agencies, including ASIO. He came to Australia twice after his defection in 1961 to be embraced by Spry. It has been suggested that Barbour's premature retirement from ASIO in 1975 was hastened by his refusal to accept uncritically Golitsyn's allegations about a mysterious Soviet mole in ASIO.[31]

By late 1972, when the ALP government took office, ASIO had a staff of approximately 400 people with an annual budget close to $5 million. It maintained officers in overseas postings, conducted a branch office in Papua New Guinea and had close affiliations with Western intelligence agencies. But to many Australians it was perceived to be a strongly politicized body. On 13 October 1972, on the eve of the change of government, retired intelligence officers met in premises near the ASIO headquarters in Melbourne to discuss the ramifications of a Labor government on the intelligence world, which ASIO officers were reported to have attended.[32] On the day after the election, Sunday 3 December 1975, great activity was observed at ASIO headquarters and a journalist queried whether there was more to this apparent dedication of ASIO officers to such energetic work on the Sabbath.[33]

THE MURPHY 'RAID'

With the extra-parliamentary party of the ALP calling for changes to ASIO and concern within the parliamentary party over the way in which ASIO had become so politicized in its functions and outlook, it was clear that ASIO would have to be made more accountable for its actions. The method for achieving this outcome was not discernible at that time and in any case the new government was more preoccupied in making changes on a wide range of public and administrative issues.

The first challenge to the power and secrecy of ASIO occurred in an almost accidental fashion and it was related to that issue over which the ALP had previously been frustrated in achieving any insight or change. This was the continuing terrorism being conducted by the Ustashi and which the Liberal government seemed quite unwilling to check. The issue came to a head in March 1973 when the Yugoslav Prime Minister, Dzemal Bijedic, visited Australia following an invitation from the previous government. Croatian national groups opposed Bijedic's visit and the Attorney-General, Senator Lionel Murphy, called for reports from the Australian Federal Police, then under his ministry, on the degrees of security that could be guaranteed to the Yugoslav Prime Minister. The alarming reply was that the police could provide no such guarantees, even while he was in Canberra. The belief that Senator Murphy and the ALP held about the Liberal government and its Attorney-General, Senator Ivor Greenwood, protecting the Ustashi from surveillance and prosecution by the Federal police now seemed to be confirmed.[34]

Murphy, however, anticipating problems with ASIO on this topic, had Kerry Milte, who had been superintendent in charge of the Crime Intelligence Unit of the Federal Police, but was then a practising barrister, attached to his staff as a consultant.[35] Milte had become an expert in Croatian and Ustashi affairs when serving with the police. At one stage he had interviewed Srecko Rover in an attempt to warn him off any dangerous exploits, only to be told by Rover that he should telephone ASIO who were quite familiar with Rover's status.[36] The declaration of the Federal Police about Bijedic's safety, plus the discovery by Murphy that some members of ASIO and other departments monitoring Croatian affairs were slow to disown the policy of the previous government on Croatian affairs, led him to visit the Canberra office of ASIO on the night of 15 March. Dissatisfied with what he found there, he flew with Milte and some Federal Police officers to ASIO headquarters in Melbourne the next morning. Federal Police in Melbourne entered the ASIO building to seal particular filing cabinets to await the arrival of the Attorney-General. Files were inspected by Murphy and after addressing staff he returned to Canberra.[37] The Bijedic visit went ahead although his trip to Port Kembla had to be abandoned for security reasons.

The response of ASIO to this visit from its minister was immediate. The *Canberra Times* of the following day carried a comment from a 'State police officer' about the visit – clearly a euphemism for an ASIO spokesperson. He emphasized the importance of the international connections that ASIO had

211

established and the suspicion with which those bodies viewed the Labor government:

> For several weeks both British and US intelligence agencies had been withholding from their Australian counterparts much of the information they traditionally supplied until they ascertained the new Government's intentions for the security service. ASIO was held in high regard by other forces because of its ability to keep things to itself . . . Now that it was known that an outside force had been through the ASIO files its sources of information would probably dry up completely.[38]

The Liberal Party leapt to the defence of ASIO with its parliamentary leader, Billy Snedden, declaring that 'the Government was trying to destroy ASIO and the first step towards destroying it was to discredit it'.[39]

It was not known what ASIO reported to the overseas intelligence bodies, but four years later James Jesus Angleton, commenting on the visit, reported that for a month after the 'raid' the few top CIA officials who knew of the Australian security crisis debated the merits of cutting intelligence off from Australia. The then director, James Schlesinger, 'finally decided to keep the relationship going'.[40] By this time Angleton had been forced out of the CIA and while his remarks may have reflected some of the alarm that ASIO had been able to arouse in the CIA administration, they could be taken more as an expression of his deep dislike of the Australian Labor Party government which dated from 1972.

A later Director-General of ASIO, Harvey Barnett, claimed with a certain degree of hyperbole that the event 'sent shock waves round Australia and the western world. For a cabinet minister to intrude in such an undisciplined and peremptory way . . . caused grave concern at home and abroad'.[41] Whatever the reputed seismic effects of Senator Murphy's actions the terrorism ceased after the NSW and Federal Police made numerous raids and seized quantities of gelignite and arms from private homes.[42] ASIO worked hard at liaising with the Attorney-General and a senior ASIO officer, Don Marshall, was placed on his staff. He was an agent Senator Murphy was prepared to trust.[43] In 1978 the police and ASIO were still observing and the police arresting immigrants alleged to have been involved in terrorist activities. In August 1991 Vitor Misimovic, who appeared to be a double agent working for both the Yugoslav Intelligence Service and ASIO, revealed his exploits in those events of 1978.[44]

ASIO AND ACCOUNTABILITY

The vociferous response to the visit by the Attorney-General to ASIO headquarters clearly demonstrated to the ALP that ASIO considered itself, and was considered by others, to be far more than an intelligence agency of the Australian government. An editorial appearing in the *Canberra Times* soon after the angry parliamentary debate, launched by the Opposition in response to Senator Murphy's visit, reflected much of the sullen anger among ASIO and its friends over that political action. The journalist who wrote it clearly had links to ASIO officers. In his editorial warning to the government he declared that the visit was 'an object lesson in how not to wield the instrument of power in the future'. The editorial concluded gravely: 'The greatest loss in the whole affair is that Australia's prime intelligence gathering organization has suffered damage from which neither it nor any successor can hope to recover in the short term.'[45]

The campaign against the Attorney-General over the visit intensified thereafter. The Senate, where the government lacked a majority, established a select committee on the initiative of the Democratic Labor Party – comprising the right-wing Catholics who split from the ALP – to investigate the matter as a means of embarrassing the government. Barbour was called before it, but he confessed that Senator Murphy had not overstepped his authority. It was clear to the government by then that ASIO had its firm defenders among the former government and that information could have been flowing to these and newspapers from ASIO sources.[46]

The most startling example of ASIO's perception of its seeming independence of the government came late in March 1973 when a Queen's Counsel of the Victorian Bar was paid to produce an opinion on the Attorney-General's visit to ASIO which argued that the Minister had no jurisdiction or power over ASIO and could not demand to enter its premises or view its files. This opinion argued that the Attorney-General could possibly be prosecuted for committing a common law misdemeanour for improperly influencing Barbour not to carry out his lawful duties. The QC remained anonymous, but his fee seemed to have been paid by present and previous ASIO agents who circulated his opinion among selected Opposition members to fuel their attacks on the government over the matter.[47]

The corporate independence shown by ASIO staff towards the elected government and the demonstration that it was able to mobilize its contacts in the press and the legal world to underpin that independence produced a threat that the government could not ignore. With the extra-parliamentary members of the ALP having already called for some curtailment of ASIO, it was not surprising that Prime Minister Whitlam established a judicial enquiry into ASIO. He was slow in implementing this decision and did not announce it until April 1974 when outlining this policy at the general election. Even then it was not until 21 August 1974 that he finally announced the appointment of a judge of the New South Wales court of appeal, Bob Hope, to conduct the Royal Commission into not only ASIO but the other intelligence agencies such as ASIS, the Joint Intelligence Organization (JIO) and the Defence Signals Division (DSD). These were included because the government had not known of their existence, with the exception of JIO, until taking power and wished to discover more about them. The outcome was that Hope recommended the expansion of ASIO giving it increased powers, human resources and money. And Whitlam by then was not only out of government but soon to be out of Parliament after his party failed to be returned at the general election of December 1977.

Whitlam did have one important impact on ASIO: in September 1975 he had Barbour transferred to become the Australian Consul-General in New York and appointed a judge from the Industrial Court, Ted Woodward, in his place. These appointments represented an important development in government–ASIO relations. They demonstrated that ASIO was indeed subordinate to the government and in spite of the institutional support ASIO obtained from the Australian press and legal opinions from the Melbourne Bar, the Prime Minister could unilaterally institute dramatic management changes if he had sufficient reason. For a brief while it appeared that ASIO, like other public administrative bodies, was on tap and not on top.

It is not clear why Barbour was replaced. One account has it that, on his visit to Washington, Hope was informed that ASIO had been penetrated by the KGB and that US and British intelligence who knew of this could find no reliable way of informing Whitlam.[48] It is difficult to believe that the US or Britain could have not sent a senior intelligence agent to Australia before then to inform Whitlam of the penetration. It was probably less a KGB agent and more likely a Yugoslav Intelligence Service (YIS) double agent who had been recruited by ASIO on the assumption that he was a Croatian nationalist. Vitor Misimovic, mentioned above and used unwittingly by ASIO to penetrate the Croatian terrorist organization as late as 1978, also appeared to be a double agent. A more believable account is that Barbour was removed through the agency of some of his staff who took a dislike to his management techniques and his attempts to work with Senator Murphy. Using the circumstances in which he made an overseas trip, this staff group reported the matter to the CIA. The CIA reported the matter to the government. It was probably not the first time that an intelligence chief has been deposed by a faction of his own staff.

The new Director-General, Ted Woodward, was born in Victoria in 1928, the son of an army officer, Eric Woodward, who served with distinction during the war and who was appointed as governor of NSW between 1957 and 1965. Ted studied law at the University of Melbourne, was married at 22, and raised a family of seven children. He joined the University Regiment in 1949 and transferred to military intelligence as a part-time officer in 1951. His military experience was to stand him in good stead. He sat on numerous boards of inquiry and was a judge of the Australian Industrial Court when Whitlam appointed him to ASIO. This appointment represented not only a further demonstration of Whitlam bringing ASIO under control, but also of his reinstituting principles, established by Chifley and Dr Evatt, of placing ASIO under the direction of a judge rather than an intelligence officer. He also re-introduced the plan of a fixed tenure for the directorship, and the ASIO Act was amended to provide that Woodward would lose no judicial privileges or income during the term of his appointment from early 1976 until it expired in September 1981.[49]

ASIO AND THE CIA

These changes were probably the maximum extent to which a Labor Prime Minister could exercise government authority over ASIO by this stage. Whereas other government institutions were being made more accountable and power was being devolved to the public, as with the Australian Assistance Plan to distribute government funds among voluntary groups in Australia, ASIO was becoming more independent of governmental supervision. This was because of ASIO's clandestine incorporation into the Western intelligence club insights which the Prime Minister himself glimpsed on the eve of the dismissal of his government by the Governor-General, Sir John Kerr, in November 1975. The ASIO–CIA connection, for example, was seen by Whitlam only by chance. Between Barbour's removal and Woodward's appointment, Whitlam had appointed to be head of ASIO F.J. Mahoney, a senior officer in the Attorney-General's Department, who had assisted Senator Murphy in his campaigns to check Ustashi terrorism. Mahoney passed a seriously worded cable sent by the CIA to ASIO during this time. It was very revealing about the ASIO–CIA connection and probably would not have been seen by the Prime Minister if it had not been for the loyalty of Mahoney to the elected government.

The circumstances behind the sending of the CIA cable arose from Whitlam's twice announcing in November 1975 that one of the Opposition parties, the Country Party, and its leader, Doug Anthony, had received financial aid from the CIA. This aid came via Richard Stallings, who had been director of the CIA-operated Pine Gap satellite transmission station established in the centre of Australia near Alice Springs. The government was then under attack from the Opposition because it had been exploring the possibility of raising a large petro-dollar loan in the Middle East. The Opposition seemed to have access to information derived from teleprinter transmissions. The treaty concerning the Pine Gap facility was also due for renewal

Structure of ASIO in 1978

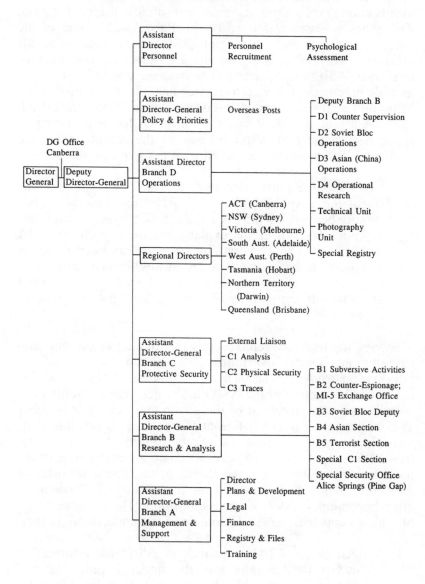

in December 1976, following discussions starting in December 1975.

The CIA was alarmed by the statements of Whitlam about its agents and nervous about its important satellite listening station. Ted Shackley, who was head of the East Asia division of the CIA, summoned the Washington ASIO representative to his office on 8 November and gave him a seriously worded message to send to ASIO headquarters. The message was to be regarded as a 'demarche on a service-to-service link'. It complained about Whitlam's statements and claimed that it could 'blow the lid off' the CIA listening post. It said that 'the CIA feel it necessary to speak also directly to ASIO because of the complexity of the problem'. The message concluded with the grave warning:

> The CIA feels grave concern as to where this type of public discussion may lead. The DG [Director-General ASIO] should be assured that CIA does not lightly adopt this attitude. It is a frank explanation of a problem. CIA does not feel that everything possible has been done on a diplomatic basis and now on an intelligence liaison link they feel that if this problem cannot be solved they do not see how our mutually beneficial relationships are going to continue.[50]

Mahoney immediately referred this threatening communication to Whitlam. It bore overtones of a ban on the flow of US information to Australia such as occurred in 1948 and which led to Chifley's establishing ASIO in the first place. Events were overtaken by the dismissal of the government on 11 November 1975 and its subsequent defeat at the polls. It is possible that, were Mahoney not acting as Director-General at the time, this interesting 'service to service' communication would not have become public, let alone shown to the Prime Minister of Australia. Whitlam commented on the message in Parliament after becoming Leader of the Opposition. He remarked that Shackley's approach to ASIO contained the understanding that

> Implicit in the CIA's approach to ASIO for information on events in Australia was the understanding that the Australian organization had obligations of loyalty to the CIA

itself before its obligations to the Australian Government. The tone and content of the CIA message were offensive; its implications were sinister. Here was a foreign intelligence service telling Australia's domestic security service to keep information from the Australian government.[51]

Shackley has since informed an Australian writer that the briefing to the ASIO representative was done following authorization from above. He implied that it could have been the Director of CIA, William Colby, or Secretary of State, Henry Kissinger, or indeed the President. Kissinger, he signalled, was the most likely.[52] It must have been disappointing to Prime Minister Whitlam that however much he tried to bring ASIO under firmer government control and accountability the closeness and secrecy of the brotherhood of intelligence organizations made such a goal unachievable.

Following the implementation of much of the Hope report giving it more power, money and staff, ASIO continued on the same path it had followed from 1949 of pursuing the 'Communist menace'. Of the 384 ASIO staff working in surveillance, 159 were watching Soviet and East European activities and 117 were watching Asian, mainly Communist actitivies. This included observing the intelligence officers reputedly posted to the new Vietnamese embassy to watch those migrants who had formed part of the Saigon junta and wished to continue the civil war. ASIO still watched the Croatian terrorists, but watched even more closely the Yugoslav intelligence agents watching the Croats. ASIO was quite unable to shift its focus away from the almost disappeared Communist Parties which were to collapse totally a few years later. Soviet affairs still held a fascination for ASIO agents. Like Justice Hope they too were caught in their own time-warp. They were still watching the so-called Soviet-sponsored and barely visible peace movements and trade union links as they had been doing since the early 1950s. Selected ASIO agents continued to enjoy overseas appointments with 30 then being posted mainly in Europe. Internal changes in ASIO at this time included the transfer in 1977 of Harvey Barnett from ASIS to ASIO as deputy to Ted Woodward with a view to grooming him to become the Director-General and the transfer of the senior agent, Colin Brown, to London.[53] ASIO expanded greatly following the implementation of Hope's report. Its staff increased from 400 in 1972 to 700 in 1980 while funding increased from $5 million in 1972 to $13 million in 1980.

NOTES

1. CCF Spry to Secretary, Department of Defence, 8 Nov. 1952, A45954/17, Item[37].
2. Soviet Property, A1838, Item 1500/1/3/27.
3. Peter Wright with Paul Greengrass, *Spy Catcher* (New York, 1987), pp. 84, 85.
4. Spry to A.H. Tange, 10 Jan. 1956, A1838/2, Item 1500/1/3/28 Pt 1.
5. *Canberra Times*, 3 Feb. 1963.
6. Richard Hall, *The Secret State: Australia's Spy Industry* (Sydney, 1978), p. 75; 'ASIO's Lawless Years' in *Nation Review*, 2–8 Dec. 1976.
7. Declaration of Russian Diplomat Persona Non Grata. Statement by the Minister for External Affairs and Attorney General, The Hon. Sir Garfield Barwick, QC, MP. A1838/T184, file 69/1/3/9 Pt 2.
8. *Bulletin*, Sydney, 6 Feb. 1963.
9. Transcript of Broadcast 18.30 GMT 21.2.63 in A1838/T184, file 69/1/3/9 Pt 2.
10. See Barry York, *Student Revolt! La Trobe University 1967–73* (Campbell, ACT, 1989).
11. Peter Ellingsen and David McKnight, 'The Sufferings of an ASIO Spy', *Age*, Melbourne, 29 April 1991.
12. 'List of ASIO Staff Members Past and Present'. issued by CAPP, May Day 1980; *Campaign for the Abolition of Political Police*, pamphlets, no authors, or publishers. Publication dates *circa* 1974, 1975. Copies in State Library of Victoria. See also Joan Coxedge and Gerry Harant, *Security Threat – The Urgent Need to Abolish Secret Agencies* (Melbourne, 1974).
13. CPD, 18 Sept. 1979, p. 1217.
14. Gough Whitlam, *The Whitlam Government 1972–1975* (Ringwood, 1985), p. 166.
15. 'How Secret Police use the Press and Vice Versa' in *New Journalist*, No. 23, August 1976, pp. 3–8.

16. *National Times*, Sydney, 19–24 March 1973.
17. *Nation Review*, 3–9 Nov. 1977.
18. ASIO Position Paper, 1 Oct. 1967, Croatian Liberation Movement, Hrvatski Oslobodilacki Pokret – HOP, Document A 6, p. 4. Croatian Terrorist Activities in Australia, papers tabled as Ministerial Statement by Senator Murphy, Australian Parliament, 27 March 1973.
19. Christopher Simpson, *Blowback: America's Recruitment of Nazis and its Effects on the Cold War* (New York, 1988), pp. 111–13.
20. Mark Aarons, *Sanctuary: Nazi Fugitives in Australia* (Melbourne, 1989), p. 229.
21. Commonwealth Police, Crime Intelligence, Report on the Croatian Revolutionary Brotherhood, Hrvatska Revolucionarno Bratstvo, Document A 7, p. 4. Croatian Terrorist Activities in Australia, papers tabled as Ministerial Statement by Senator Murphy, Australian Parliament, 27 March 1973.
22. CPD, 23 May 1963. For photographs see Document B7 in Croatian Terrorist Activities in Australia, papers tabled as Ministerial Statement by Senator Murphy, Australian Parliament, 27 March 1973.
23. Statement by the Prime Minister, the Rt. Hon. Sir Robert Menzies, Kt, CH, QC, MP in the House of Representatives on Thursday, 27 Aug. 1964. Document A1 in Croatian Terrorist Activities on Australia, papers tabled as Ministerial Statement by Senator Murphy, Australian Parliament, 27 March 1973.
24. *Nation Review*, 23–29 March 1973, p. 685.
25. Aarons, *Sanctuary*, p. 256.
26. Ibid., p. 258.
27. Document A15, Croatian Terrorist Activities in Australia, Papers tabled as Ministerial Statement by Senator Murphy, Australian Parliament, 27 March 1973.
28. Whitlam, *The Whitlam Government*, p. 171.
29. *Age*, 26 Nov. 1975.
30. David Armstrong, 'ASIO in Need of Intelligence', *Bulletin*, 24 May 1983.
31. Richard Hall, 'The Strange Case of KGB Defector Anatoliy Golitsin and the ASIO Mole', *Financial Review*, Sydney, 22 April 1987.
32. Mungo MacCallum, 'The Face of ASIO', *Nation Review*, 24–30 Aug. 1973.

33. William Martin, 'ASIO's Busy Weekend', *Nation Review* 24–30 Aug. 1973.
34. Hall, *The Secret State*, pp. 81–4.
35. See Document A10 for report of K.L. Milte to J.M. Davis, Commissioner Commonwealth Police on Activities of Extremist Groups in the Yugoslav Migrant Community, 16 Feb. 1970.
36. Report of Superintendant K.L. Milte, Interview with Srecka [*sic*] Blaz Rover, 16 Feb. 1970, document B9. Croatian Terrorist Activities in Australia, papers tabled as Ministerial Statement by Senator Murphy, Australian Parliament, 27 March 1973.
37. *Herald*, Melbourne, 17 March 1973.
38. *Canberra Times*, 17 March 1973.
39. *Canberra Times*, 20 March 1973.
40. Adele Horin, 'ASIO 'Raid' Jeopardized CIA Co-operation – Spy Chief', *National Times*, 13–18 June 1977.
41. Harvey Barnett, *The Tale of the Scorpion* (Sydney, 1988), p. 201.
42. *Canberra Times*, 2 April 1973.
43. *Age*, 26 Nov. 1975.
44. Paul McGeough, 'Fall Guy Breaks Silence Over ASIO's Terrorist Trap', *Sydney Morning Herald*, 26 Aug. 1991.
45. *Canberra Times*, 7 April 1973.
46. Jack Jones, 'Through A Murphy Looking Glass', *Nation Review*, 10–16 Aug. 1973.
47. For a copy of the QC's opinion see Hall, *Secret State*, pp. 232–5.
48. Hall, *Secret State*, p. 94.
49. *National Times*, 31 October–5 Nov. 1977.
50. Brian Toohey and Dale Van Atta, 'New Light on the CIA Role in 1975', *National Times*, 21–27 March 1982.
51. CPD, 4 May 1977, pp. 1519–23.
52. Brian Toohey and Marian Wilkinson, *The Book of Leaks* (Sydney, 1987), p. 97.
53. *National Times*, 31 October–5 November, 1977, p. 1.

10

ASIO in the 1980s

Harvey Barnett succeeded Ted Woodward in August 1981, thus overturning Whitlam's and Chifley's ideal of having a judge in charge of ASIO. Hope had already recommended against this principle with the comment that it would preclude an intelligence officer becoming Director-General and 'making a career in ASIO'. He seemed to ignore the reality that various government departments have 'outsiders' appointed to heads of them and the same principle could apply to ASIO.[1]

Harvey Barnett was born into what was then a prosperous family of shopkeepers in Albany, Western Australia, on 25 December 1925. He was educated at a private Church of England school near Perth where he was a boy soprano and later identified deeply with church ideals. He joined the Australian Navy during the war working as a seaman coder in naval signals. After the war he returned to the University of Western Australia to study for a Bachelor of Arts degree and after its completion left for Germany to teach English at a school in the Black Forest. He developed his lasting hatred of communism at this school through listening to the accounts of life in the German Democratic Republic (East Germany) from students who had come from there.[2] Returning to Australia, he became a teacher at Scotch College in Perth for two years until 1957. It was then that he received that irresistible tap-on-the-shoulder and an invitation to join the arcane world of intelligence. It was not ASIO, but Dick Casey's outfit, ASIS, that he was invited to join.

Barnett was sent to the Asian outposts of ASIS starting with Singapore in 1961 where the the ASIS office was contained within the British Far East Land Forces command. He met his wife

Harvey Barnett, head of ASIO, with fellow ASIO agent attending the Royal Commission into the Combe–Ivanov affair. ASIO mistakenly assumed Ivanov to be exclusively KGB. He did have some expertise in trading affairs which is why David Combe was negotiating with him. He was still expelled. (*Canberra Times*)

there, Deirdre Hartnett, who also worked for ASIS. She was the daughter of the wealthy industrialist, Sir Laurence Hartnett. The Australians were fully integrated into this British intelligence base and for a while Barnett conducted both the Australian and British operations in Thailand and Indo-China from that centre. After Singapore, Barnett and his wife were posted to Jakarta in Indonesia in the early 1960s.[3] Indonesia was an excellent training ground for Barnett. It contained the largest Asian Communist Party (PKI) outside China with three million members, and the Soviet Union conducted one of its largest embassies there, complete with a KGB contingent. President Sukarno governed its large population by delicately balancing the PKI, the large Muslim community and the US trained army in a temporary national accord. In addition he was receiving aid from the US, the Soviet Union and China. This delicate balance was upset in what some commentators suggest was a CIA-planned destabilization operation. While that coup was actually proceeding, ASIS staff in the embassy established a radio link using morse code to a RAN vessel standing offshore relaying reports to Canberra. Barnett's wartime naval radio skills may again have been of some benefit.

In 1973 Barnett was appointed to be head of training in ASIS, where spies and others were coached in trade craft.[4] By 1977 he had transferred to ASIO and became Director-General in August 1981. It was his first-hand experience of the KGB operatives in foreign fields, his deep animosity towards Communism and, because of its close connections to ASIS, his firm loyalty to the CIA, that Barnett brought to his new job in ASIO.

During the 1980s ASIO grew in stature, partly as a result of the implementation of the Hope report recommending larger funding and the employment of more professional staff, and partly by its removal later in 1986 to a new and impressive ASIO headquarters built specially for it in Canberra. This site was adjacent to Australian defence headquarters and served as a visual reminder to the claim by Sir Frederick Shedden in 1949 that ASIO was the fourth arm of Australian defence. Funding for ASIO increased from $13 million in 1980 to $39.2 million by 1989. The staff increased in a lesser proportion over that period from 700 to 734.[5] Either ASIO concealed an increased number of staff elsewhere or spent the additional money on new equipment such as the new generation of fast computers.

WATCHING THE KGB

The 1980s was the decade of new technologies accompanied by the deeper specialization of knowledge accompanying that development. The decade brought a greater tolerance of different opinions, lifestyles and cultures. The Communist Party could no longer be portrayed as a national problem by the government. China and the Soviet Union were becoming more prosperous and the changes in culture and booming consumerism were affecting social values in the USSR as much as they were in the West. ASIO reflected this burgeoning growth in professionalism. More university graduates were employed and its work routine consisted less of sitting in the back of dingy trade union halls reporting the speeches of CPA candidates in union elections and more of watching the KGB agents in Canberra as they drove about in their stylish cars and dined at expensive restaurants. The parsimonious era of the Petrov years was light years behind. The ASIO cars were just as stylish and the expense accounts of the ASIO as necessarily large as those of the KGB agents. The KGB, CIA and ASIO agents knew each other in the small Canberra community.

Lev Koshliakov, first secretary at the embassy and assumed to be KGB, had arrived in 1978, and on occasions when he was being followed by ASIO agents, embarrassed them by pretending to make homosexual advances to them. When a new first secretary (political), Valeri Nikolayevich Ivanov, arrived in June 1981, ASIO did not consider him to be a KGB officer. He was born in Moscow on 27 September 1947, spoke good English and had worked at the Soviet Trade Office in London for three months in 1974. As part of his duties as political officer he attended conferences of all political parties, including the Young Liberals and he usually drove the embassy car to these interstate meetings. His duties led him, like Petrov, to mix with the Australian–USSR Society. His English language skills and interest in travelling about Australia, together with his comparative youth, persuaded ASIO to alter its assessment and to consider him a KGB officer. Further information about Ivanov was obtained following the defection of a KGB agent, Vladimir Kuzichkin, in Iran in June 1982. He provided information to MI5 which led to dozens of Soviet officials being expelled from European and Asian countries. He was brought to Australia in March 1983 to identify Ivanov personally and he assisted in preparing the ASIO case for the Royal Commission following Ivanov's expulsion on 22 April 1983.[6] As a means of collecting more information about him, ASIO bugged the house with hidden microphones on 8 July 1982 while he and his wife and daughter were away in the USSR on annual leave.[7]

AUSTRALIAN–SOVIET TRADE

There had been trade links with Russia before the First World War and these grew rapidly during the war as the Czarist government purchased large quantities of lead from Australia, sometimes through Japanese firms. The Soviet Union purchased sizeable quantities of wool in the late 1920s and early 1930s mainly through the London markets because the British government gave the USSR trade credits and Australia continually refused to allow Soviet imports as a means of balancing this one-way trade. In the years after the Second World War wheat and wool exports to the Soviet Union greatly expanded under the auspices of the Australian Wheat Board and the Australian Wool Board which were both forms of statutory authority.[8]

Meat exports to the USSR also grew during these years through the agency of the Australian Meat Board and the Soviet foreign trade organization, Prodintorg. However, this trade tapered off by 1973 and 1974 and when it resumed in 1975 and 1976 it was conducted by Heine Bros in Australia and through its Australian manager in Moscow, Lawrence Matheson. The ostensible reason for a private trading firm's assuming control of the meat trade was that it could conduct a barter trade. For a short while Matheson negotiated between Soviet and Australian smelting organizations with a view to using Soviet techniques in Australia. Eventually Matheson took over all the business of Heine Bros and established his own firm, Commercial Bureau (Australia) Propriety Limited, in 1976. The Russian name was

Kommerchesko Byuro (Australia).[9] Another and more shady reason for the privatization of this meat trade seems to have been the growth of corruption in the Soviet Union whereby Mafia style groups were able to gain some control over meat imports and sales in the USSR. Such unorthodox arrangements would also have been of financial benefit to Matheson. Other aspects of this unorthodox trading affected Matheson because the KGB was involved in these trading arrangements through a Soviet overseas puchasing agency, known as State Committee for External Economic Relations, the Russian name for which was Gosudarstvenniy Komitet Po Vneshnim Ekonomicheskim Svyazyam (GKES). Matheson, by being involved in this KGB-run organization, seemed also to be connected with ASIO, making him perhaps a double agent. GKES had an office in Australia that had come under ASIO's observation.[10]

THE THIRD MAN – LAWRENCE MATHESON

Matheson was born on 25 April 1930 as Lawrence Phelan. He changed his name in June 1948 after he joined the Australian Navy in 1947 as a seaman. He was taught Russian for a year at the Australian Air Force language school at Point Cook and was commissioned as an officer in approximately 1959. He left the navy in 1968 to join the Department of Trade and later was posted to Vienna and Moscow to assist in the development of Australian–Soviet trade. After establishing his new firm, Commercial Bureau, with his new father-in-law, Dr Michael Salvaris, his co-director in Melbourne, the meat export business prospered with Matheson importing Russian vodka and some machinery to Australia to offset partly the trade imbalance in Australia's favour which stood at $649,925,000 by 1982. Between 1976 and 1981 beef and mutton valued at $230 million were exported to the USSR mainly through Matheson's firm which gave him a profit of nearly $1 million per annum. He managed to conceal his profits from the Australian taxation office because his company accounts lodged in Melbourne show him actually making a combined loss of $367,685 from 1976 to 1979.[11] His relationship with ASIO has also been surrounded with mystery. As a Russian speaker with entrée to the KGB and Soviet trading circles, which handled hard currency transactions, Matheson could have provided valuable information for ASIO to pass on to other Western intelligence agencies. He would also have been under an obligation to the KGB to give them information about the West.

With the profits from meat-exporting, Matheson moved into other ventures. These included exporting cheese and butter to the USSR and joining with the Soviet Ministry of Fishing, Sovrybflot, to establish a joint company, Asmarfish. Matheson invited another firm, Henry Jones (IXL) then controlled by John Elliott, to conduct this large-scale fishing operation off the Tasmanian coast with a Soviet fishing fleet of 100 ships. A Soviet-made floating dry dock was to be installed in Hobart to service the fleet and profits of $2.154 million from Asmarfish were anticipated. This scheme fell through in January 1980 when the Fraser-led government placed an embargo on trade with the USSR, except for wheat and wool, in response to Soviet troops being sent to Afghanistan. Matheson's magic touch seemed to fade in other enterprises at this time. Butter supplies could not be obtained in sufficient quantity for the USSR and the cheese Matheson sold failed to meet Soviet standards. His income fell drastically and he had to sell real estate into which he had invested millions of dollars at a loss.[12]

To add to Matheson's woes a former employee, Bruce Fasham, had left Matheson to establish his own firm, Pacific Commerce and Trading Coy. Pty. Ltd. (Pactra) in Sydney, taking with him much of the business and the employees. He began negotiations to sell a Soviet-made hydrofoil to the government in New South Wales.[13] Matheson, in an attempt to win back his failing Soviet trade, employed David Combe, a former national secretary of the ALP, but who then was conducting his own public relations and government lobbying business in Canberra. Combe's brief was to negotiate with Soviet trading officials during his planned visit to Moscow in November 1982. The representations made by Combe were successful and he reported to Matheson that he was viewed favourably in Moscow and should spend finance on promoting Soviet–Australian relations, as he had done some years previously on a Soviet art exhibition in Australia.[14]

Matheson was cheered by the report and his fortunes looked likely to recover with the election of the Hawke Labor government which had promised to lift the Fraser government bans on

Soviet trade if elected. Matheson hoped to re-establish the huge fishing enterprise which his former employee, Fasham, looked to be about to capture and over which Matheson had obtained a judgement from the Supreme Court of Victoria in his (Matheson's) favour. He gave these documents, including the original Soviet contract, to Combe on 25 March 1983 so that Combe could use them in Canberra to influence the government and to help Matheson re-start his fishing enterprise. Combe showed them to his contact at the Soviet embassy, Valeri Ivanov, hoping to influence Soviet support in Australia for Matheson.[15] Combe had held earlier discussions with Ivanov after meeting him through the Australian–USSR Society. He spoke good English and knew the political and trading bureaucracy in Moscow. The Soviet trading official in Canberra, Yuri Dashevsky, spoke no English. It was unfortunate that Combe selected Ivanov to negotiate through. It led to ASIO putting him under surveillance and to his becoming the centre of a Royal Commission, and then to the destruction of his public relations and lobbying business.

THE RISE AND FALL OF DAVID COMBE

David Combe was born in Adelaide, South Australia, on 26 April 1943. After completing an arts degree at the University of Adelaide he became active in Labor Party affairs in South Australia and later became national secretary of the party in Canberra in 1973 after the election of the first Labor government for 23 years. He was a popular and efficient officer and became a close friend of the senior Labor Party figures. He resigned from that position in July 1981 to establish his own lobbying business which received a great fillip in March 1983 when the Labor Party was elected to office. Business perceived him as the most influential lobbyist then working in Canberra.[16]

ASIO had maintained a file on David Combe since the late 1960s. It contained reports of his participation in demonstrations against Australia's involvement in the Vietnamese civil war and of the first trip he took to the Soviet Union in 1974. Information was added to it concerning the cruise he and his wife took in 1976 on the Russian cruise ship *Leonid Sobimov*, including the incorrect information that the fare was paid by the Soviet Union.

David Combe, national secretary of the ALP (left), receiving books on US labour from US ambassador Hargreaves in 1977. ASIO portrayed Combe as critical of US defence and foreign policy towards Australia. The smallness of this gift would not have influenced Combe at all. (*Canberra Times*)

231

In fact he paid for the fares himself, although he was given improved accommodation on the ship when he was recognized as the ALP national secretary. This was one of the many errors of fact that ASIO recorded in the Combe dossier. Also wrongly recorded was the consultant's fee he charged Matheson for work in the USSR. It was $2,500 plus expenses of $500, but ASIO recorded the fee as $5,000. Another error recorded was that the fares for Combe and his wife, Meena Blesing, to travel to Moscow in November 1982, when he lobbied on behalf of Matheson, were paid by the Soviet government. Combe's fares from Singapore to Moscow and back were paid by the Soviet government because he was a guest of the Australian–USSR Society to celebrate the sixtieth anniversary of the USSR. His return fare from Sydney to Singapore was paid by the Society. Combe paid for his wife's fare.[17]

ASIO was also concerned at Combe's ideological unreliability. Like many supporters of the ALP, he was sceptical of the Liberal coalition government's reliance on the ill-defined US–Australian alliance. Many in the ALP perceived it as one between a small country and a superpower where the interests of the smaller, by simple necessity, would always be subordinate to the larger. While in Opposition the ALP members could remain critical of the alliance, but on forming the government of Australia, the pragmatism of office compelled the abandonment of such convictions. Combe remained unconvinced that the CIA was not involved in the events surrounding the dismissal of the Whitlam government by the Governor-General in November 1975. He published an analytical article in the *Bulletin* in January 1982 with the title 'The CIA's Role in Labor's Downfall'. This was clipped by ASIO and added to his file as further support for the ASIO judgement that Combe was as suspicious of the CIA as he was of US foreign policy. He discussed these topics of the CIA and Labor's downfall with Ivanov in an ASIO-bugged conversation of 4 March 1983 and offered to give the diplomat press clippings on the subject. ASIO viewed such actions as confirming Combe's disloyalty.[18]

The unfortunate Combe could not escape ASIO's ideological condemnation. In 1982 he agreed to provide an interview for inclusion in the television documentary film, *Allies*, made by an independent Australian film company about the dominance of US defence and intelligence links over Australian government policy. The film was less about alliance and more about subordination. Historians, diplomats, political scientists and politicians all participated, but ASIO judged it as being 'part of a KGB backed disinformation operation'. Barnett went as far as to claim that it was trying to undermine 'Australia's intelligence service and hence in one view Australia's security' and that it was 'critical of Australia's own agencies'. ASIO claimed that it was backed with Soviet funds.[19] Again this was incorrect. The money for its production was raised entirely in Australia as documents lodged in the Department of Home Affairs to claim the film-making tax concession showed.

After hearing some of the details of what Combe did during his visit to Moscow in 1982, partly through its agent planted in the Australian–USSR Society and partly through its tap on the Soviet embassy's and Ivanov's telephones, ASIO placed Combe under closer scrutiny. He came under the close surveillance of the senior ASIO agent known as M. He was in charge of the B3 section dealing with the Soviet bloc research and analysis although he had no Russian language skills. He was then 42 years old and had 12 years' experience in security and intelligence work with over five years working for ASIO. Significantly, the B branch was also responsible for liaison with the large CIA satellite listening station at Pine Gap in central Australia. The Combe-style suspicion of CIA motives would have been regarded suspiciously in that environment.[20]

ASIO acquired a full report of the progress of Combe's involvement in Australian–Soviet trade and his involvement in other events through eavesdropping on a dinner party given by the Ivanovs for the Combes on Friday 4 March 1983. This was on the eve of the election which returned the Hawke Labor government. Mrs Combe was too busy to attend and remained at home. The dinner lasted over three hours and Combe drank during and after the dinner. Mrs Ivanov, an engineer, spoke no English, and the two men discussed a range of events. Combe, eager to extend his knowledge of Soviet–Australian trade matters, collected as much information from Ivanov as possible about the government and Communist Party officials who were responsible for these matters in Moscow. Ivanov was very knowledgeable on the topic.

Both men agreed that trade with Australia would expand, that Matheson could restore the fortunes of his business and that Combe might be engaged as consultant to the Russians on Australian trade matters. Other topics of conversation dealt with the impending change of government in Australia, the inefficiencies and corruption in the USSR, the Afghanistan war, Jewish emigrants, the CIA and the Whitlam government's dismissal and the film, *Allies*, then being made in Australia. Discussions about Russian food and drink occupied the lighter side of the conversation. As Combe became more jovial he began humorously to outline what grand offices he hoped to be offered by the new Labor government and how his business would grow in customers and income because of his closeness to the ALP. He looked forward to becoming rich in the following years. The ASIO transcript of this lengthy dinner party was subsequently released by the Royal Commission.[21] What else of the Ivanovs' domestic conversation was recorded over the months the microphones were in place has not been divulged.

The Ivanovs' daughter appeared to be watching a television programme in the lounge near the dining room. Combe, having a deep and resonant voice, was fully recorded but Ivanov, having a soft voice which rose and fell, was only partly recorded. The transcript was pored over by the ASIO agents and M, the Combe expert. The ASIO reports portrayed the conversation as indicating the existence of a serious security threat. Combe, for example, was seen as offering his services to the Soviet Union which would lead to his entrapment by the KGB. The inaudible parts of Ivanov's conversation were not ascribed to the distance of the microphone from the point of coversation but to Ivanov's intention of concealing significant parts of the conversation from his ASIO listeners. The television was not being used as a source of entertainment, ASIO decided, but as a cunning means of countering the recording of the conversation. ASIO regarded it as a first-class example of KGB trade craft. Both the topics and techniques of the evening's discussion were considered by ASIO as the positive development of a large scale spying operation by the KGB through Ivanov.[22] ASIO had constructed an espionage incident out of this suburban dinner-party.

ASIO AND THE COMBE–IVANOV AFFAIR

The surveillance of Combe and Ivanov was thereafter intensified and in March 1983 ASIO listened to Ivanov making a luncheon appointment with Combe for 21 March at the Lakeside Hotel. The lunch was observed by ASIO agents who sat close to the table with ears twitching. Although it could not be electronically recorded, ASIO argued that it was definitely a clandestine meeting. Its basis for this assertion was that the two men selected a table opposite the entrance door to the restaurant.[23] Another conversation between the two, recorded by ASIO microphones on 3 April 1983, when Combe again visited Ivanov's house, was not accorded the same high priority by ASIO as the dinner party conversation of 4 March. On 3 April, Combe delivered papers to Ivanov that dealt with Matheson's attempt to recover the Asmarfish business from Fasham, his former employee, by Supreme Court action. This conversation demonstrated that Combe's relationship with Ivanov was purely for commercial reasons. The conversation also revealed considerable information about Matheson's business which ASIO was unwilling to have aired. The transcript of this conversation was released by the Royal Commission in a greatly abbreviated form with the names of Matheson and other commercial firms expunged.[24] The question remains of why ASIO did not transcribe this conversation more quickly and prepare a comprehensive transcript of it. After being recorded it was sent to Melbourne to be placed with a large number of tapes awaiting what ASIO claimed was 'translation' even though the conversation was all in English. It was not impossible that ASIO was so intent on proving a case of a planned Combe–Ivanov espionage plot that it conveniently disregarded other evidence showing that the relationship was purely business.

For example, it can be seen, even from the heavily censored transcript, that Ivanov in his remarks to Combe was knowledgeable about the background to the Asmarfish project:

> It would be marvellous, much easier for us to have a base in Tasmania or, say in Adelaide or Melbourne. We are sending our ships for fresh water to New Zealand another, say, 1,000 miles. We have other bases in Singapore, a long

distance. So the tankers must go with our fleet with our, say, trawlers to New Zealand water. It would be much easier to have such handy.[25]

Contrary to this and other evidence, ASIO remained intent on classifying Ivanov as KGB and allowing him no credit for the slightest expertise in trade matters. Barnett rejected outright the notion that Ivanov would have had knowledge of trade matters. 'One might say', he declared, striving to belittle the fact, 'that it is almost ludicrous for Mr Ivanov, a KGB line PR officer, to be involved in any discussions about trade, a matter I would have thought, in which he was quite incompetent.'[26]

ASIO believed that its case for Ivanov being a KGB spy was greatly strengthened by a revelation made by Ivanov when taking leave of Combe after the meeting on 3 April. He told Combe outside the house (away from the ASIO microphones) that Soviet diplomats were being expelled from various countries and that similar action could be taken against him. Combe could be implicated, he said, and warned that Combe's phone could be tapped by ASIO. He recommended that they communicate in the future by meeting at each other's premises.[27] This comment suggested that Ivanov did not appreciate that his own home was bugged. How did Ivanov know of a telephone interception that was not then installed? ASIO considered it to be a typical case of Soviet disinformation since the phone was not then bugged.[28] David Marr argues that Ivanov heard it from Koshliakov who heard it from the journalist, Bill Pinwell.[29] Combe was greatly angered at the news and although finding it difficult to believe mentioned it to several of his friends, including Matheson. Matheson immediately retailed it to ASIO with his own embellishments indicating that the two men agreed to establish a clandestine relationship which ASIO could not monitor. ASIO chose to believe Matheson's incorrect version of the arrangements rather than Combe's account of it even though Matheson built his elaborations on the original Combe explanation. It was predictable that ASIO would prefer Matheson's exaggerations to Combe's factual account. It sought at every turn to make events far more dramatically clandestine than they actually were.[30]

The unfortunate Combe was to be firmly condemned by ASIO for not having reported Ivanov's warning. It was made to count against him despite the fact that ASIO agreed there was no evidence of clandestinity. It was unlikely that if he had reported it ASIO would have moderated its deep suspicion of him. By that stage ASIO had clearly judged him and found him wanting. This was demonstrated in the ASIO claim that it had earlier considered approaching Combe and warning him off Ivanov. ASIO claimed to have consulted no fewer than five of his friends who all agreed that he might overreact if warned and advise Ivanov that he was under surveillance – a fact, of course, already known to the diplomat.[31] ASIO refused to divulge the names of the friends. It could have fabricated the story of the intended approach as a means of rebutting the accusation that ASIO had failed to rescue Combe from an embarrassing situation that ASIO was observing and was itself playing a role in. A more likely explanation for not intervening in the situation was that ASIO did not wish to lose the opportunity of observing the techniques by which the KGB established and maintained a clandestine relationship. It was a situation not greatly dissimilar to the entrapment operation of another KGB agent, Ivan Skripov, in 1963. The incident also demonstrated the politicized role of ASIO. It knew that it was still held in odium in ALP ranks and was greatly reluctant to expose its workings to a leading Party activist for fear of being accused of still living in the Cold War past.

During April 1983, Barnett appears to have decided to have Ivanov expelled and Combe isolated. He claims that he reacted in response to the Ivanov–Combe plan to avoid using the telephone. But such a claim is questionable because the plan for clandestinity was made on 3 April. Matheson's retailing of it would have taken some days to filter through the ASIO bureaucracy and Barnett would not have learned of it until about 5 April. Barnett made an appointment to see Prime Minister Hawke on 5 April to reveal the affair to him and have Ivanov expelled. But before then he had the B3 section prepare an *aide-mémoire*, or memory jogger as he called it, for use in his interview with the Prime Minister.[32] This passed through seven stages of drafting which would have occupied some days. The reality appears to have been that Barnett decided on action in the middle of March and that the bugging of the 3 April meeting, which clearly indicated that Combe and Ivanov were interested only in trade discussions – not espionage – was ignored. Indeed, as ASIO acknowledged, the tape of the bugging languished in the ASIO transcription pool until 22 April and was not actually read until 28 April.[33]

Hawke could not meet Barnett on 5 April, and because of an important national economic conference he had to wait 15 days until 20 April. It can be inferred from Barnett's acceptance of this delay that he did not then regard the matter to be of the national importance he later ascribed to it. Armed with his much edited *aide-mémoire*, Barnett flew to Canberra on 20 April to meet his Prime Minister at 4.45 p.m. ASIO was now to be catapulted into a position where some of its innermost workings were to be publicly exposed.

Barnett's visit to Canberra was the first occasion that a Director-General of Security had gone to his Prime Minister with an account of KGB spying from the Soviet embassy in Canberra since Colonel Spry and George Richards took Petrov's documents to a probably forewarned Prime Minister almost exactly 29 years previously. On this second occasion the Prime Minister had not been forewarned of the intelligence exposé that Barnett had prepared for him.

The case laid before Hawke looked bad for Combe: he was money-hungry, he accepted free trips from the Soviet government, he was anti-CIA, he had allowed himself to be ensnared by the KGB with whom he had appeared to establish a clandestine relationship.[34] Hawke swallowed the whole story. He asked for no proof or documents or even the sighting of the much-drafted *aide-mémoire*.

Hawke was new to his political career. He had worked as a trade union advocate and had been President of the Australian Council of Trade Unions, a type of federation of all trade unions in Australia. He seemed to lack any knowledge about the history of ASIO and was disadvantaged by not having been in Parliament in 1978 when the ALP firmly opposed the legislation that the Fraser government introduced to extend the powers of ASIO. Hawke was also highly critical of the KGB. He had some experience of Soviet officials he believed to be KGB when he visited Moscow in 1970. He went there as a senior figure of the International Labour Organization and on behalf of the Israeli government to have Russian Jewish emigrants given permits to travel to Israel. He was deeply and emotionally disturbed in failing to achieve his goal. Hawke, unlike other ALP leaders, lacked any critical attitude to the various US governments and the alleged anti-CIA stance of Combe would have disturbed him.

Although convinced of the guilt of the two men as described to him, Hawke was obliged to refer the matter to the National and International Security (NIS) Committee which discussed it over two days. Barnett was asked to have papers and officers sent from Melbourne to brief the committee. The important role of Matheson and his intelligence and trading connection were not revealed by Barnett. The Deputy Prime Minister, Lionel Bowen, however, knew something of Matheson and his ASIO connections through the Fasham imbroglio, but still ASIO refused to divulge all its information.[35] It refused to allow the Cabinet members to read the suitcases of documents it brought to the Cabinet room and the ministers were forced to sit at the foot of the Cabinet table while Barnett read extracts from the ASIO transcripts of the Ivanovs' dinner party. Barnett defended his refusal to allow ministers to read the files by referring to the precedence he regarded as evolving from the effect of the Murphy raid of 1973. He quoted the remedy proposed by Mr Justice Hope in his 1977 report on that situation. This was to the effect that while the Attorney-General might be allowed to visit ASIO offices he must not be allowed to read the material.[36] Indeed Barnett carried in his pocket a copy of paragraphs 363 and 365 of Hope's report which contained that direction. 'There were suitcases full of them [files] over the Cabinet room,' declared Barnett when decribing the scene in the Cabinet room:

> I could think of nothing worse than to have Cabinet ministers picking up ASIO files and flicking through them and getting nowhere, and it has always been my philosophy and I believe the philosophy in western intelligence services that minsters normally should not have access to raw intelligence files of a security service.[37]

The outcome of the meetings was that Ivanov was declared *persona non grata*, without any reason being given and Combe was barred from having connection with government members, thereby destroying his business. On Barnett's recommendation Combe's telephone was tapped by ASIO to ensure, as he explained, 'That there were no untidy ends left over and that Mr Combe, you know [sic] had not got himself into a state where some other KGB officer might have contacted him.'[38] The ban on Combe's lobbying activities soon became public and was raised in Parliament. Prime Minister Hawke, without consulting his ministers, referred the matter to Mr Justice Hope to be added to his Royal Commission in the following legal phraseology:

> To inquire into . . . all circumstances, including the actions of the government, surrounding the expulsion from Australia of Mr Valeri Nikolayevich Ivanov, First Secretary, embassy of the Union of Soviet Socialist Republics, and the involvement of Mr Harvey David Mather Combe in those circumstances.[39]

JUSTICE HOPE'S ROYAL COMMISSION

It is difficult to generalize about why Royal Commissions are established in Australia. Part of their function is to act as the means for disposing temporarily of embarrassing political issues. By the time the Royal Commission is held and its report becomes available, political tempers have cooled and the topic at issue no longer bears the same relevance. The Royal Commission into the Combe–Ivanov affair was one of this category. The NIS committee had over-reacted to ASIO's information which was itself an over-reaction, based on Matheson's distorted report, to what it perceived to be a threat of clandestinity being established between Ivanov and Combe. Caught in the middle of this confused decision was David Combe who was perceived by normal observers to have done nothing more than to have acted on behalf of a client who was attempting to re-establish his trading business links with the Soviet Union.

In retrospect, the sensible action would have been to have had a senior legal figure in the Attorney-General's Department review the case and declare that no national security issue was at stake, particularly with Ivanov expelled, and that David Combe could resume his normal lobbying work. In fact the Attorney-General, Senator Evans, had called for a report from the Secretary and Acting Deputy Secretary of his Department in the middle of the NIS committee meetings. Their report

Mr Justice Bob Hope, Royal Commissioner into the Combe–Ivanov affair, was a guru in intelligence affairs because of the several official inquiries he had undertaken into the Australian intelligence agencies. (*Canberra Times*)

declared that Combe had committed no offence.[40] It is likely that if Barnett had raised his security concerns directly with the Attorney-General the affair would not have blown up to such large proportions. The government would not have over-reacted. The affair could have been settled within his department. At the time, however, these senior Labor Party members were properly aware that Barnett and his ASIO had to be treated with great caution. The Petrov affair may not have been fresh to many of their minds, but they would have all been aware that had Barnett reported all this to Prime Minister Fraser some weeks previously, they might well have not been seated on the government benches. Barnett and ASIO were politically dangerous. The Labor ministers knew that they had to be treated with great caution and respect.

It was fortunate for the deeply troubled and underinformed Cabinet committee members, bluffed by ASIO officials into accepting that they must not read the files, that a ready solution was at hand. Mr Justice Hope had already been invited to open another Royal Commission and it was into his lap that their leader was able to dump this embarrassing affair. By this tactic the

Cabinet ministers avoided a possibly damaging confrontation with ASIO. As a result of this decision, Hope's brief was expanded so that he reported on three points: the circumstances of the Combe–Ivanov affair; the operation and efficiency of the various security agencies; and the need for legislative change to ensure proper accountability of the security agencies. He began the Combe inquiry first; it opened on 1 June 1983 and closed on 14 October 1983.

THE ASIO CASE

The brief for the inquiry was to establish that the government had acted properly in relying on the security advice of ASIO, and further that ASIO had presented the best security advice it possessed at the time to the government. As a measure for ensuring that neither of these organizations was cast in an unfavourable light, both the government and ASIO had leading barristers engaged to defend their interests. There seemed to be an agreement, in which Hope was involved, that Matheson would not have to reveal publicly his trading and intelligence alliances with ASIO or the KGB. His evidence was given in closed session and any mention of his activities was expunged from publicly released transcripts. He too had a barrister in the Royal Commission to attend to his interests.

It was David Combe who quickly became the centre of the inquiry. Unfortunately for him it became a trial in which he had to justify himself and his actions. The government, ASIO and Matheson quickly established that their actions had been conducted in the best interests. The Cabinet ministers forming the NIS committee were all called to give evidence and justify their actions. They were helped through this unwelcome and embarrassing event with the cool and efficient support of the barrister representing the government. He was later to be appointed as a judge of the Australian High Court.

ASIO based much of its attack on Combe on the comments made by him at the Ivanovs' dinner party on 4 March and recorded by the ASIO microphones. ASIO laid great emphasis on the boasts made late in the evening by Combe after he had become very relaxed with dinner drinks. ASIO interpreted

Combe's expectation that he would become wealthy in his lobby-ing business as an indication of being a security risk. 'I would say', remarked Barnett, 'that one of the greatest concerns of a security service today is the person who is on the make for money, is venal in some way, has shown himself to be venal.' 'This can often be', he added as a means of justifying ASIO's actions, 'an indicator to the sort of person who can be cultivated by a hostile intelligence service such as the KGB.'[41]

The far more innocuous conversation dealing with trade matters and recorded by the ASIO bug in Ivanov's house on 3 April was also used by ASIO to justify its actions. It claimed that the giving of business documents represented the 'small hook approach' of the KGB. The cunning Soviet agent, explained the wordy Barnett:

> will very gladly accept documents and they can be completely overt, they do not have to be secret documents. And once one set of documents had been given it is easier to ask for another set of documents and before long it is the usual technique of a KGB officer to be seeking, from those who have the appropriate access, for nationally classified documents.[42]

ASIO determinedly clung to the argument that Ivanov could know nothing about trading matters. Any dent in its argument that Ivanov was anything less than KGB would lay it open to the obvious challenge it had over-reacted to a situation that was not as threatening as a more objective assessment would have revealed. 'I do not believe', Barnett categorically declared, 'that he had any interest at all in improving in detail, trade relations. He is a KGB line PR officer and they are totally given to providing political intelligence.'[43] Barnett had previously explained to the NIS committee that if Ivanov had any claims to commercial expertise, it was only for an ulterior motive:

> Ivanov's claimed interest in improving trade relations can be interpreted as an ancillary objective at best. His intent must be to secure Combe's services as a KGB asset providing

243

information and forecasts [of] the Labor governments [*sic*] activities, assisting KGB access to key members of the labour [*sic*] party and influencing government policy to the Soviet advantage.[44]

ASIO was desperate to conceal Matheson's trading and intelligence links with the Soviet Union. This necessity forced it into adopting a stance before the Royal Commission of pretending to be ignorant of the details of Australian–Soviet trading arrangements. As part of the Western intelligence brotherhood, ASIO had links with COCOM which was the Coordinating Committee of the Consultative Group. This Group had been established in 1949–50 by the US, UK and West European countries to stop Western trade with the East in goods that could be considered in any way strategic. Transit trade and exports from neutral countries were also to be stopped by COCOM.[45] ASIO closely watched Soviet trade for these reasons. Combe's defence counsel was eager to show that Combe was negotiating normal commercial matters with Ivanov about which ASIO would have had extensive knowledge. Barnett, however, while agreeing with Combe's counsel that trade occurred between the Soviet Union and various bodies in Australia, answered with the disclaiming phrase: 'I could not claim to be any sort of expert on it.' He had previously responded about trading matters involving Matheson: 'Normally that is a commercial matter that we would not be over-zealous about covering.'[46] Barnett was caught out when he claimed to know only vaguely about the Asmarfish arrangements established by Sovrybflot. 'Yes,' said Barnett coyly, 'I knew about them in broad terms.' Did he know that it was the heads of this agreement that Combe handed to Ivanov? 'Yes,' he replied. 'Have you read them?' Combe's counsel asked. With the truth about ASIO's trade expertise starting to show, Barnett replied confusedly, 'Yes, not – I have glanced at them'.[47]

Because the Royal Commission resolved itself into a trial of David Combe, his counsel had to adopt the tactic of contesting the evidence of ASIO because it became the basis of the 'prosecution's case' against him. Combe's counsel challenged ASIO by arguing that if Ivanov was such a clever KGB agent, he would have guessed that his house was bugged and he would not have discussed important Soviet political and commercial matters at the famous dinner party. Not so replied M, 'He would have designed the evening to minimize that risk.'[48] The dropping of his voice and switching on the TV set in the adjacent room was part of this risk minimization, he blandly claimed. If the meeting was to be so clandestine, replied Combe's counsel, why did the KGB-trained Ivanov not arrange an outdoor barbecue away from the ASIO microphones which were in the house? 'Mr Ivanov, as a Russian, I think is much less familiar with barbecues than most Australians,' answered M. But he had lived in Australia for some years and knew about barbecues, hinted the barrister. 'The traditional style of Russian entertaining is to sit around a table indoors and to eat and drink through the evening. There are cultural differences,' doggedly asserted M, who was clearly unwilling to surrender one inch of the ASIO position that Ivanov was clever and devious.[49]

Agent M adhered loyally to the ASIO argument that Combe was being entrapped by Ivanov. He was not simply discussing trade and business affairs with the Russian, as a layperson might assume. The layperson would be misled, argued ASIO, because the entrapment process was clear only to the trained eye of an ASIO officer like M. 'There is no reason why even a well experienced intelligence layman such as Mr Combe should have identified that [entrapment] process as going on at all?', asked Combe's counsel. 'No', M replied loyally and finally.[50] As the Royal Commission continued it became apparent that in spite of ASIO's assertions about KGB entrapment and clandestinity, David Combe stood accused of trying to make money by helping Matheson restore his faded fortunes and of becoming light-headed and boorish through consuming dinner wines at a Soviet diplomat's dinner party. The question arises of why was such a hue and cry set off by the Combe–Ivanov affair. The short answer is that ASIO wanted to catch a Soviet spy. This was reflected in the statement made by Barnett when urging the Prime Minister to have Ivanov expelled with full publicity:

> In making that statement I said I would like to make it clear to the Prime Minister that I had an interest in that ASIO for a long time had been accused of not having detected a Soviet spy and that personally it would suit me if some publicity to this effect were to ensue.[51]

ASIO got its spy, but at some cost of attracting wider scepticism and more public ridicule about its continued existence.

JUSTICE HOPE'S REPORT

Predictably Justice Hope reported in December 1983 that the government and ASIO had done no wrong, that Ivanov was KGB (the evidence for which he withheld) and, most pointedly of all, that David Combe had all but become Ivanov's spy. Hope swallowed whole the ASIO proposition that Combe was putty in the hands of the devious Ivanov:

> I have concluded that one of the purposes of Mr Ivanov's cultivation of Mr Combe was illicit, and that to draw this inference from the evidence is not mere speculation. No doubt Mr Ivanov intended to use Mr Combe as well for legitimate purposes, as, for example, in the overt promotion of Soviet/Australian trade. However, he also intended, if possible to use Mr Combe to obtain and to hand over to him information and documents illegitimately, and in the interests of the Soviet Union, and to act, wittingly or unwittingly, as an agent of influence. I reject the view that Mr Combe's access to Ministers and their staffs was so limited that he could not achieve any of these objectives even if he were so minded.[52]

It was an astonishing claim by the judge. David Combe, a man who had fought his way up the political ladder of the Labor Party, experiencing more the gall of three electoral defeats rather than the fruits of victory, was by Hope's assessment, the subject of easy manipulation by this Russian Svengalian figure, four years his junior. Such parts as this of the Hope report bore more the mark of a novelist than a judge.

The report also repeated the interpretations of events as they had appeared before the Royal Commission. Hope continued to conceal the truth about the mysterious Lawrence Matheson. Just as his presence and evidence at the Royal Commission were veiled in secrecy, so was Hope's account of his involvement in the affair confined in the report to four short and relatively uninformative paragraphs. The most important questions about him went unanswered as they had at the inquiry. How, for example, this Australian citizen was able to have himself accepted by the Soviet trading hierarchy, not to mention the KGB trading organization, the judge did not disclose. Nor did the judge reveal how Matheson was able to install himself in an office suite in the heart of Moscow, on Leninsky Prospect, with an apartment also in Moscow and a dacha on the Black Sea. Matheson's position as a possible double agent with links to the KGB and ASIO were not touched on. Nor was His Honour prepared to reveal in his report how the mysterious Matheson was able to purchase and maintain houses in Delphi, Greece, in the fashionable Toorak, in Melbourne, and a stylish country estate at Mount Macedon outside Melbourne in which he also housed his art collection worth $2 million.[53]

In sharp contrast, David Combe's bugged dinner-party comments were combed through line by line in the body of Hope's report. Words or phrases were highlighted that could be used to demonstrate his venality, his indiscretions and his lack of judgement. And then the whole transcript was added as an appendix to the report. His financial and private affairs were revealed in fine detail and his personality analysed by the judge in amateur psychological terms. The conversation recorded on 3 April by ASIO, where the two men discussed business affairs, was passed over in the report as it had been at the royal commission. Hope shared ASIO's strategy of playing down the fact that Combe and Ivanov were basically interested in promoting Australian–Soviet trade. He therefore ignored much of the content of the 3 April transcript. Hope uncritically accepted the ASIO allegation that Combe had tacitly agreed to a clandestine arrangement with Ivanov after the diplomat had warned Combe on 3 April that his telephone was being tapped. By turning reality on its head, Hope actually accepted Matheson's elaborations on what Combe had told him about the telephone bugging as being more accurate than the account of Combe. Like ASIO, Hope wanted to believe the clandestinity theory because it confirmed Ivanov as being KGB. Hope blandly declared of this crucial event: 'I am satisfied that Mr Ivanov's proposal as to how he and Mr Combe should meet after 3 April was substantially as recounted by Mr Matheson.'[54] A third-hand account bore more weight for the judge than the direct account by the participant. Thus did hearsay replace evidence.

Hope's siding with the ASIO account of events was not surprising. He was more knowledgeable and thereby more committed to intelligence work than perhaps Barnett himself. The insights obtained by him in his visits to overseas intelligence organizations and his knowledge of the Australian intelligence agencies made him pre-eminent in that field. But in his global tours he had not visited the USSR. His lifelong belief in the existence of a monolithic Soviet state directed by a group of Communist Party officials through the powerful and ubiquitous KGB was never challenged. Unlike Combe and many other Australians who had travelled in the USSR, Hope's ideas about the 'evil empire' never had to confront the reality. He was never witness to the lazy bureaucracy, the low technology and absence of modern institutions that marked much of Soviet life and which gave the obvious lie to the widely held Western belief that the USSR was a superpower. Hope and ASIO were still clinging to the belief that the USSR was a highly organized imperial power about which the West should be constantly on its guard. And this was at the time when the cracks in this artificial edifice, which led to its total collapse (and that of the KGB) were obvious to the trained eye.

The mistakes made by ASIO about Combe earned it a slap over the wrist from Hope with the proverbial feather duster.[55] But this expensive five-month-long inquiry did little to silence the critics of ASIO. Like the Petrov affair nothing of substance came from the Combe affair as the critics had predicted. The inquiry would have collapsed entirely were it not for an apparent unspoken collusion between the commissioner and those counsel representing the government and ASIO to keep pressing the empty argument that Combe might at some distant time be manipulated to give Cabinet secrets to the KGB. It was a naive argument and a serious reflection on the character of Cabinet members. In such an unlikely eventuality it would be the Cabinet ministers as well as Combe who would be put on trial for spying.

As with the Petrov affair, there were winners and losers, although fewer of both. The legal counsel prospered. Knighthoods were no longer being issued, but judgeships and admission to become Queen's Counsel, which gives the right to charge higher fees, were allocated to legal practitioners involved. Matheson died of cancer in June 1987. The ALP and many in the Labor government were deeply concerned at Combe's treatment. His lobbying business had been permanently ruined. But the left groups of the Party took up his cause at the ALP national conference in July 1984 and a resolution was adopted in his favour. The following year his business skills were put to use by the government when he was appointed Australian Consul General and Trade Commissioner at Vancouver, Canada.[56]

Harvey Barnett maintained, long after he took early retirement from ASIO, the ASIO argument that the clever Ivanov would have manipulated Combe into becoming a spy. 'To my mind,' Barnett wrote in the book giving his account of the affair, 'he was within a hair's breadth of entering the grand gallery of KGB spies, along with Philby, Burgess, Maclean, Fuchs . . . I like to think ASIO saved him from such a fate.'[57] For Barnett there was little difference between Britain in the 1940s and Australia in the 1980s.

In fact the Combe–Ivanov affair reflected badly on ASIO. It convinced many in the ALP and in the government that the long-established policy of making ASIO more accountable should be quickly implemented.

NOTES

1. Royal Commission on Intelligence and Security, Fourth Report, Vol. 1, pp. 177–8.
2. Harvey Barnett, *Tale of the Scorpion* (Sydney, 1988), p. 190.
3. Brian Toohey and William Pinwell, *Oyster: The Story of the Australian Secret Intelligence Service* (Melbourne, 1989), p. 67.
4. Ibid., p. 158.
5. Barnett, *Tale of the Scorpion*, pp. 220–21.
6. Laurie Oakes, 'ASIO spoke to KGB Defector Over Ivanov', *Age*, 30 April 1984.
7. 'Royal Commission on Australia's Security and Intelligence Agencies', Transcript of Proceedings (hereafter Transcript), p. 882, 4 July 1983.
8. See F.M. Cain, 'Some Aspects of Australian–Soviet Relations,

1800–1960', in *Journal of Communist Studies*, Vol. 7, No. 4, March 1992.

9. George Munster, 'The Third Man in the Combe-Ivanov Equation', *Sydney Morning Herald*, 6 Feb. 1984.

10. Transcript, pp. 497–8, 23 June, 1983; *Royal Commission on Australia's Security and Intelligence Agencies, Report on Terms of Reference (C)*, Australian Government Publishing Service (Canberra, 1983), p. 60.

11. George Munster, 'Matheson Casts His Net – In Political Waters', *Sydney Morning Herald*, 7 Feb. 1984.

12. George Munster, 'Moscow Says Nyet to a Rescue Bid', *Sydney Morning Herald*, 8 Feb. 1984.

13. David Marr, *The Ivanov Trail* (Melbourne, 1984), pp. 79–85.

14. See Meena Blesing, *Was Your Dad a Russian Spy?* (Melbourne, 1986), pp. 22–3 for copy of Combe's report.

15. Transcript, pp. 500–2, 23 June 1983.

16. Blesing, *Russian Spy?*, p. 1.

17. Transcript, p. 819, 30 June 1983.

18. Transcript of dinner conversation in Appendix to 'Royal Commission on Australia's Security and Intelligence Agencies'.

19. Transcript, p. 435, 29 June 1983.

20. Transcript, p. 921, 4 July 1983.

21. Transcript of dinner conversation, op. cit.

22. These judgements appear in Transcript, pp. 471–501, 23 June 1983; pp. 837–45 30 June 1983; pp. 1013–182, 5 and 7 July 1983.

23. Transcript, p. 908, 4 July 1983.

24. Transcript, pp. 476–507, 23 June 1983 examines Barnett on his knowledge of Matheson's business arrangements. The transcripts are heavily censored to remove any mention of Matheson or the Commercial Bureau. By careful answering of counsel's questions, Barnett was able to escape revealing his and ASIO's knowledge of Matheson's business.

25. Transcript, p. 471, 23 June 1983.

26. Transcript, p. 439, 26 June 1983.

27. Transcript, p. 3923.

28. Transcript, p. 683, 29 June 1983.

29. Marr, *The Ivanov Trial*, pp. 175–6; See also Transcript pp. 5645–71, 4 Oct. 1983 for Pinwell's heavily censored account.

30. See ibid., fn 48, p. 348 for a brief explanation of Matheson's account.

31. Transcript, pp. 393–5, 22 June, 1983.
32. Transcript, p. 921, 4 July 1983.
33. Transcript, p. 845, 30 June 1983.
34. Transcript, pp. 836–937, 30 June 1983.
35. Marr, *The Ivanov Trail*, pp. 205–6.
36. Transcript, p. 794, 30 June 1983.
37. Transcript, p. 800, 30 June 1983.
38. Transcript, p. 717, 29 June 1983.
39. Report of Royal Commission.
40. Exhibit 23, papers of 'Royal Commission on Australian Security and Intelligence Agencies'.
41. Transcript, p. 732, 29 June 1983.
42. Transcript, p. 507, 23 June 1983.
43. Transcript, p. 501, 23 June 1983.
44. Transcript, p. 840, 30 June 1983.
45. See Philip J. Funigiello, *American–Soviet Trade in the Cold War* (University of North Carolina Press, 1988), for the most recent book on COCOM.
46. Transcript, pp. 497–8, 23 June 1983.
47. Transcript, p. 826, 30 June 1983.
48. Transcript, p 1015, 5 July 1983.
49. Transcript, p. 1017, 5 July 1983.
50. Transcript, p. 1174, 11 July 1983.
51. Transcript, p. 626, 28 June 1983.
52. *Royal Commission on Australia's Security and Intelligence Agencies, Report on Terms of Reference (C)*, p. 104.
53. David Elias, 'Laurie Matheson, Millionaire', *Age*, 21 July 1983.
54. *Royal Commission, Reference (C)*, p. 94.
55. Ibid., Issue 5, p. 212.
56. Blesing, *Russian Spy?*, pp. 212–19.
57. Barnett, *Scorpion*, p. 130.

11

ASIO and Accountability

The 1980s were marked by a series of legislative measures in Australia and other countries by which greater accountability was demanded of government departments and their officers. These developments in Australia saw the appointment of Ombudsmen, Freedom of Information Legislation, an Administrative Appeals Tribunal and other such measures. These administrative and legal changes were made partly as a result of institutional changes that became popular in Western democracies and partly because governments sought to distance themselves from dispute-settling between a better informed public and an enlarged governmental administration.

ASIO could not escape from these demands for greater public accountability. The Hawke government introduced a series of legislative changes in the 1980s to achieve those ends. For the Hawke government it was more than just making ASIO accountable to Parliament. The government sought to shed responsibility for having to defend ASIO's actions, but more importantly it sought to distance itself from the repetition of embarrassing events that marked the Combe–Ivanov affair discussed in the previous chapter.

THE FIRST ASIO ACT

ASIO's first legislative enactment in 1956 followed in the wake of the Petrov affair. Its intention was not to make ASIO more accountable, but to make it less vulnerable to dismantling by a possible Evatt Labor government. Indeed by endowing the

Director-General with considerable power, this initial legislation made ASIO less accountable. ASIO was then functioning under the terms of the original charter given to Justice Reed by Prime Minister Chifley on 16 March 1949 and modified by Prime Minister Menzies on 6 July 1950 on the appointment of Colonel Spry. Both charters made the Director-General subordinate to the Attorney-General, while also allowing him access to the Prime Minister.

By the time of the Petrov affair, ASIO and the Menzies-led government had developed a strong symbiotic relationship. The electoral tactic of Menzies (discussed in Chapter 5) of casting Communists out of trade unions, the public service, the arts and universities had popular support. But it relied entirely on the wide-sweeping and efficient work of ASIO. By this time ASIO would have had a staff of 200 with an unquantifiable number of part-time agents and informers planted in the trade unions, the political parties, immigrant groups and elsewhere. The attack in 1954 by Dr Evatt on ASIO for its agency in promoting the Petrov affair demonstrated to ASIO that if Dr Evatt were to become Prime Minister both the Menzies image of liberalism and the future of ASIO would be seriously at risk. Colonel Spry and his staff could be dismissed and Menzies' involvement in ASIO's work exposed.

The answer was to replace the impermanent ASIO charter with legislation. To this end Spry wrote to Prime Minister Menzies on 15 October 1954, when the Royal Commission was little more than half-way complete, seeking approval to make ASIO more permanent. 'I feel that in view of the various attacks which recently have been made upon the Organization, I should raise with you the matter of its constitution. I believe there is room for doubt as to the legal position of the Organization as a Commonwealth body and of its staff as permanent employees of the Commonwealth.'[1] Menzies agreed with Spry's concerns and accepted his offer to prepare legislation to establish ASIO permanently.

Nothing further happened until October 1955 when Dr Evatt renewed his attack on ASIO following the tabling of the report of the RCE. Spry, again alerted to the impermanency of ASIO, repeated his plea to Menzies for support as follows:

I am, however, becoming concerned at the viciousness of Dr Evatt's attacks upon ASIO and that unenlightened people may believe what he says. In view of the virulence and falsity of Dr Evatt's attacks, I do feel that he has not only jeopardized my own career as a loyal servant of the Crown but also that of my colleagues. This is a shameful situation, which I feel should not be left unanswered.[2]

However shameful the good Colonel may have considered events, the Menzies government was firmly ensconced in office by December 1955 with a greatly enlarged majority thanks to the Petrov affair. Dr Evatt's attacks on ASIO and Petrov led the right-wing Catholic members of the parliamentary Labor Party to sever their already tenuous connections with the ALP and to switch support to the Menzies government. ASIO was a sacrosanct institution for these Catholic members. It was their one barrier against godless communism. Menzies and ASIO were now safe from any Evatt-led attempt to demolish their organization. But still Colonel Spry wanted his legislation. He wrote to a more imperturbable Menzies on 13 January 1956 with a copy of a draft bill to establish ASIO. Aware that Dr Evatt appeared no longer to be a problem for Menzies, Spry marshalled a new argument that was actually to stand ASIO in good stead for another 40 years. This was the 'overseas ASIO connections' argument. ASIO was inviolate because it was the trusted repository of information from the Western intelligence brotherhood, Spry claimed in the following deathless prose:

By all friendly countries we are accepted as a permanent body, and their information is freely supplied to us on that basis. The extent of the information is, frankly, surprising and it is a continuing source of gratification to me. But I am quite certain that any suggestion of a doubt of the continued existence of the Australian Security Intelligence Organization would seriously affect the supply of secret information not only to the Australian Security Intelligence Organization, but also to other Government Departments and instrumentalities.[3]

The Colonel's sting was in the last line – a clear allusion to the US embargo on all classified information imposed on Chifley's government in 1948. Along with his draft bill, Spry sent a second reading speech for use by the Prime Minister in presenting the bill to Parliament. It was used by Menzies and referred again to the Evatt-led opposition to ASIO. But it did not emphasize the 'overseas connection' argument except to claim that the US had legislated for the establishment of its intelligence services.

> The attacks made on our own Security Service during the course of the Royal Commission on Espionage have convinced the government that it is necessary for the protection, and therefore also the efficiency of the Security Service to take a similar step in Australia.[4]

Spry's bill was a very brief document. It decreed that the ASIO body established in 1949 should continue and that it be under the complete authority of the Director-General. It did not state to which minister the Director-General was responsible. The Director-General was to collect intelligence and distribute it, as he considered 'in the interests of security'. He was to work with 'such Departments and authorities of the States and of other countries', a coy euphemism for Australian police forces and overseas intelligence agencies. He was to hire and fire staff who were expressly excluded from the powers of the Public Service Act which then laid down all the conditions for employment and payment of the public servants. Conditions of remuneration and employment for ASIO agents were to be determined by the Director-General in consultation. Existing agents hired by Spry were retained but could be offered new employment conditions. ASIO employees were to be permitted to join the Commonwealth Superannuation Fund, thereby gaining a pension on retirement.[5] Spry's earlier concern about an ALP government dismantling ASIO was met by clause 12 of the bill which declared that the employment of the Director-General and other officers was not to be terminated at will. The Cabinet minister, William McMahon, later to be a Liberal Party Prime Minister, best expressed Spry's and the government's intentions behind the ASIO legislation at that time:

> The general purpose of this bill is to ensure that loyal and honest servants of the Commonwealth, who have effectively done a job, are given proper security of tenure in their

employment, and that they shall not be lightly dismissed at the whim of persons who feel that in the past, by destroying the authority of Communists in this country, they may have destroyed one, two or perhaps a few more political reputations.[6]

This legislation now guaranteed the continuation of ASIO and the secrecy of its large dossier collection. The parliamentary Labor Party seemed to accept that ASIO was here to stay, but that it must be made more accountable by insisting on the following inclusions: that there be ministerial responsibility for ASIO in Parliament; that ASIO officers have the same rights of appeal for promotion and against dismissal as other public servants; and that there be provision for appeals by people against adverse security assessments. Dr Evatt, in seeking redress for wrong ASIO assessments, suggested the type of Appeal Tribunal he had established during the war for internees whereby its officers could inspect army records and explain to the detainee the reasons for internment. E.G. Whitlam, who was to become Prime Minister 16 years later, offered the principles behind the US Loyalty Boards as an example of how people could clear their names in circumstances where faulty documentation was used against them by intelligence bodies. These novel responses to an important institutional development were not appreciated by the government. It refused to accept the ALP's amendments, and the matter of ASIO's accountability had to wait the formation by Whitlam of his own government.[7]

THE FIRST HOPE REPORT ON ASIO

Whitlam had reportedly decided in 1971, before his government was elected the following year, to have a royal commission conducted into the intelligence organizations and to invite the New South Wales judge, Bob Hope, to head it.[8] Whitlam had set on this course after the near defeat of the resolution to disband ASIO at the Launceston national conference of the ALP in 1971. Whitlam was impressed by Hope whom he knew from his years at the Sydney Bar. He was also impressed by Hope's liberal outlook as demonstrated by his accepting the presidency of the

Australian Council for Civil Liberties in New South Wales for two brief years. Hope appeared to be different from the usual run of conservatively minded judges in Australia. However, Hope was already engaged on the Committee of Inquiry on the National Estate which prevented him from starting the inquiry on intelligence organizations until August 1974.[9]

Both the delaying of the inquiry and the appointment of Hope proved to be mistakes for Whitlam. Hope took too long to conduct his inquiry and did not present his final report until October 1977, long after the Whitlam government lost office. Hope toured overseas visiting the British and US intelligence centres, he listened to the Australian intelligence community and heard a few public submissions.

Mr Justice Hope was asked by the Whitlam government to examine the following five aspects of the Australian intelligence community: enquire into the history of Australian intelligence and security services (this was completed by engaging an historian, Jacqui Templeton, to complete a history which was not released); make recommendations on the intelligence and security services which Australia should have; make recommendations on administrative review procedures; review the question of responsiblity; make recommendations on other matters raised by the Prime Minister. Hope issued several reports, but the exact figure is unclear because most were secret or ultra-secret. What was labelled as his third report was issued in April 1977 with the sub-title Abridged Findings and Recommendations.[10] His fourth report was issued at the end of October 1977.

At a time when other countries were examining their intelligence organizations and questioning their rationale, Hope recommended the strengthening of ASIO's legislation and the expanding of its powers. If Whitlam had wished to obtain a report recommending a more accountable ASIO, he selected the wrong man from the wrong occupation. Judges by profession are necessarily people of fixed ideas and while they may seek individually to keep abreast of changing times, the nature of their profession compels them to keep their vision fixed on the past. Their judicial role in society is to maintain the social values of a previous age and to adapt or interpret them in seeking solutions to contemporary legal, moral or constitutional problems. A good illustration of how Justice Hope was influenced by this practice was to be seen in his construction of the philosophical justification for the continuation and expansion of ASIO. In 50 pages of tortuous logic where he debated these points with himself, he relied significantly on the relevant statements about ASIO made 25 years previously. The ministerial directions to Justice Reed and Colonel Spry in 1949 and 1950, together with the comments of Prime Minister Menzies at that time when the Cold War was well under way, were mined for their intellectual rationale. The partisan comments of the Royal Commissioners into the Petrov affair 20 years earlier were quoted as self-evident proof that Australia was always facing Soviet espionage activities.[11]

Hope showed no realization of the ultimate power and responsibility of Parliament and the government ministers for the conduct of state affairs. He firmly shared the view of ASIO that its secretive nature and design put it in a class apart from all other government departments. In passing judgement on the visit by Attorney-General Murphy to ASIO headquarters in 1973, Hope claimed that the minister was entitled to visit ASIO premises, but not to inspect the files without the Director-General's consent. He went on to recommend that the law should exempt ASIO from ministerial direction. This was to apply particularly in the question of to whom ASIO was to give its intelligence information or how it was to exchange its intelligence with other nations. Ministerial advice on such matters was not to be sought and decisions were to be made solely by the Director-General.[12]

Hope wanted ASIO isolated from parliamentary supervision by recommending against the proposal to have a standing parliamentary committee scrutinizing ASIO. He also opposed the suggestion that ASIO should provide an annual report to Parliament. Security was his excuse. 'So much of ASIO's work is secret, very little of real value to Parliament, which is a public forum, could be provided', he stated. Ministers, he further recommended, were to be excluded from the making of any judgement about what was 'a security question'. That matter was to be left solely to the Director-General.[13]

Mr Justice Hope did not wish to see ASIO made more accountable as other Western governments were seeking to achieve for their intelligence agencies. In fact Hope wanted to expand the number of targets ASIO could bring into its sights. These were terrorism and agents of influence. They were simply new names for old concepts. Terrorism was the armed campaign by minorities against their enemies. This was more pronounced in those countries where Arab nationalists believed they could attack with a certain impunity their Israeli or Zionist foe. However, the terrorism already experienced in Australia, that of Croatian terrorism, was viewed mildly by Justice Hope. 'This type of activity in Australia', he calmly remarked, 'may not affect, in any direct way, Australia's security, but it may have a very prejudicial effect on Australia's relations with a foreign power'.[14] The other new threats, disinformation and agents of influence, Hope embraced more firmly. 'Agent of influence' was simply a new term for the Cold War smear of fellow-traveller. The new exponent of the term was the editor of the *Reader's Digest*, John Barron, whose book, *KGB: The Secret Works of Soviet Secret Agents*, had been published in 1974. Hope quoted approvingly from this publication as if it were an authoritative text. He decreed that disinformation be added to those targets of espionage, subversion and sabotage against which ASIO was guarding Australia.[15]

On the question of the ASIO–CIA connection, which had been brought into sharp focus on the eve of the Whitlam government's dismissal, Hope chose to perceive no misuse of authority. However, it was revealed in May 1983 that Hope added a highly secret supplement to his fourth report dealing with the more shady aspects of ASIO. In addition he had issued a super-secret supplement in December 1976 detailing facts he had extracted from a highly reluctant ASIO about its connections with the CIA. ASIO agents had met CIA agents in a safe house near Washington to discuss Australian intelligence questions. Ostensibly discussions were also conducted about the possibility of Soviet moles operating in ASIO.[16]

On the credit side, Hope did recommend the establishment of a Security Appeals Tribunal to allow people to appeal against their wrongful security assessments, but this was only meeting Whitlam's original request to advise on the provision of administrative review procedures. He also suggested that ASIO streamline its vetting procedures which absorbed so many of its resources. He reported that in the previous five years 344,456 security checks had been made, but only 484 adverse assessments (0.7 per cent of the total) produced. He suggested that total vetting of all public

259

servants and associated people was not required. He had discovered that of the Australian government departments 18 claimed that their staffs had access to no sensitive material, seven to partially secure material and five to highly classified material.

THE SECOND ASIO ACT

The Fraser government took two and a half years to absorb all of Hope's recommendations and it was not until 25 October 1979 that it introduced the amending legislation for ASIO. The Cold War had practically ceased by this time and the issues of civil liberties had become more pronounced. But the new ASIO bill reflected few of these changes. Its principal organizational function was to provide legally for the activities such as telephone-tapping and mail-opening which it had previously conducted under the very broad powers of its 1956 Act, then over 23 years old. What it had previously done with perhaps questionable legality, it could now do with certainty. Indeed the attempt to detail all the specific powers that ASIO could now legally exercise required an entirely new bill to replace the 1956 Act. Whereas the first Act occupied five pages, this new one ran to 36 pages, although 18 of them related to the establishment of the new Security Appeals Tribunal (SAT).[17] This SAT was the sole acknowledgement to the demands of a more aware public for some check on the powers of ASIO. It was what the Labor Party had sought to have incorporated in the first ASIO Act in 1956.

To give it due acknowledgement, SAT was the first occasion on which a common law country had attempted to provide a statutory framework regulating the making of security assessments and to provide a right of appeal by individuals to an independent judicial tribunal against an adverse security assessment. It applied only to Australian government public servants and immigrants seeking naturalization. It did not apply to security assessments made of other people such as State public servants to which there could have been an ASIO input. The SAT consisted of three people who had experience in public service or immigration matters. The SAT would call for ASIO to state its case, in camera, the appellant would state his or her case, also in camera, and the SAT could then announce its decision which would be final and overrule any assessment made until that stage. It had the potential to be a flexible and useful system for forcing ASIO to be totally accountable for security assessments. In 1983 it was to give a ruling which was to provide a significant challenge for much of the ideology upon which ASIO believed it was founded.[18]

The remainder of the bill provided for the bugging, mail-openings and the entry and searching of premises to be now legal when authorized by a warrant from the Attorney-General that could be extended to six months' duration. ASIO was now officially authorized to pass on to State police forces or the Customs Department or ASIS information of a criminal or spying nature it might come across in its snooping operations. ASIO thereby expanded its work to watching drug-smugglers and criminals, and collecting economic intelligence. ASIO was also sanctioned to become a more secretive body. Agents publicly divulging information were to be heavily fined or jailed. Publishing a known ASIO agent's name was also to be heavily punished with imprisonment for one year or a $1,000 fine. The public ridiculing of ASIO by organizations like CAPP was thereby suppressed.[19] Journalists, historians, whistle-blowers and the public were all warned off any probing of ASIO affairs. ASIO agents were not involved in dangerous situations as CIA or ASIS agents may have been. They planted informers in the target groups being watched. Elements of the police operated similarly. But ASIO considered itself to be a cut above the work of the constabulary and demanded a veil of secrecy. The only visible remnant of ASIO and its 400 staff was to be not a ghostly smile like that of the Cheshire cat, but an enigmantic one-line entry in the telephone directory.

The question raised by the Murphy 'raid' about who was really in charge of ASIO was left unresolved by this new bill. The Director-General was to be 'subject to the general direction of the minister', meaning the Attorney-General. However, he remained independent of the minister in three specific areas. These were: whether information should be collected on an individual; whether any particular information should be passed to other agencies including foreign intelligence agencies; and the nature of the information to be passed to any other Commonwealth authority.[20] This could be translated to mean that the minister could be bypassed by the Director-General whenever he chose. The concern held in ASIO of the danger of a sceptical Evatt-like minister or a questioning Murphy-like minister had to be planned for.

The Labor Opposition sought to make ASIO more accountable and agreed to support the measure if the government added the following nine amendments. These were that a periodical judicial audit into ASIO be conducted; that the minister be fully informed on matters of the administration of ASIO; that the leader of the Opposition be regularly briefed on ASIO actions; that the auditor-general conduct regular audits on ASIO's accounts; that the definition of 'security' be narrowed to prevent misapplication; that the periods of time for which warrants could remain active be reduced; that SAT hear appeals against retrospective security assessments; that all people having adverse security assessments be notified; and that the penalties for divulging names of ASIO officers be applied only when security was seriously prejudiced.

The government left the defence of its measures in the hands of its back-bench members indicating that it viewed Labor's amendments with contempt. The government did accept two small suggestions of Labor: that the leader of the Opposition consult regularly with the Director-General and that he receive copies of the secret annual reports of ASIO. The government members adopted the argument of all previous non-Labor governments that ASIO was an important fourth arm of defence, that Labor's amendments would 'effectively emasculate' ASIO and that Australia's enemies could only benefit from open discussion of ASIO's activities. The suggestion of a judicial audit was opposed because of the implication that some judges, who might be selected by a Labor government, could not be trusted. 'I can think of a couple of judges', said Kevin Cairns, a government MP from Queensland, 'whose names would only have to be dropped for the security organization to be in shambles within a week'.[21]

Many of the Labor Party speakers were senior members who were knowledgeable about ASIO's lack of accountability from their own experiences when previously in government. Barry Jones, who was to become Minister of Science in the next Labor government, likened ASIO to a collection of Keystone Cops and asked the question: 'If the entire staff of ASIO went on long service leave for 12 months without anyone knowing, would anything change in Australia?'[22] That Justice Hope recommended against any role for Parliament in supervising ASIO and that the government refused to make this provision as well, caused concern in the Labor Party ranks. Dr Blewett, formerly a political scientist at Flinders University in Adelaide, condemned Justice Hope for this failure in the following terms:

> I think it must be said of Justice Hope that he is rather cavalier about Parliament....He dismisses the notion of a supervisory committee being provided by Parliament. Further he argues that Ministers should not respond to parliamentary questions on ASIO. In addition he opposes provisions to ensure the presentation of an annual report by ASIO to Parliament, and he is against adequate financial information on ASIO – he says none of these things are possible and that Parliament cannot play a role – but at the same time he maintains that ASIO has a role in supervising individual politicians. We need to think a little more about that relationship. Unfortunately, because of what Justice Hope said, in this Bill the Government gives no role whatsoever to the Parliament. The Labor Party believes that it is necessary to involve Parliament in the supervision of ASIO.[23]

For ideological and historical reasons, ASIO remained under the patronage of the Liberal and National Party coalition. Even though the Cold War had ebbed the historical reliance of each on the other remained. The Labor Party's proposals were rejected, but their implementation became a high priority for a new Labor government.

The succeeding years actually witnessed a lessening of ASIO's accountability marked by a series of court judgments placing ASIO's actions beyond questioning even by the High Court. This remarkable situation arose through a series of challenges brought to the Court between 1979 and 1982 by the Church of Scientology in an effort to stop ASIO maintaining surveillance of its activities and passing on the information to such bodies as the special branch of the NSW police. Mr Justice Aickin refused this request saying that the ASIO Act shielded ASIO from any review by the courts and that the ASIO officers were like a group of individuals in that they could maintain a surveillance on any people as a private person could. The court implied that the Crown, with all its vast powers, could act in the same way as an individual. The Church of Scientology appealed to the High Court again in 1981, but Justice Wilson ordered that the claim be struck out, saying that ASIO's actions were not justiciable. The Church then appealed to the full bench of the High Court which gave its judgment in November 1982, but because the Court divided two–two in its judgment, Wilson's order remained. Two judges, including Justice Murphy, who supported the appeal, declared that ASIO's actions were not above judicial scrutiny. On the other hand, Chief Justice Gibbs, who opposed the appeal, raised the important question whether ASIO would soon lose all effectiveness if its actions were scrutinized.[24]

What the High Court gave with one hand, the SAT took away with another. A decision of the Security Appeals Tribunal on 1 June 1983 effectively pulled from under ASIO one of its oldest and strongest rationales for existence, that of preventing communists who worked in the Australian Public Service obtaining access to government secrets. A young man in the Department of Trade, who was both a Catholic and a Communist, had been denied a security clearance by ASIO in June 1982, but the Tribunal overruled this action in a landmark decision, holding that the Communist Party was not 'revolutionary' in the sense of seeking to overthrow the state and that members were simply seeking to advocate a 'particular political and ideological view'.[25] A perception which had ruled ASIO and its preceding surveillance bodies for 66 years now had to be abandoned. Some of ASIO's supporters were startled by this decision, as were, no doubt, many of its staff. The planned removal of ASIO's headquarters from Melbourne to Canberra was coming all the closer at this time and many of its staff resigned and collected their superannuation rather than leave Melbourne. How much the tribunal's decision contributed to these resignations is hard to say.

The Labor Party was elected to government on 5 March 1983 with the intention of providing greater accountability for ASIO. It was forced to take action in this regard sooner than expected as a result of one of Justice Hope's very secret

Management Structure of ASIO in 1990

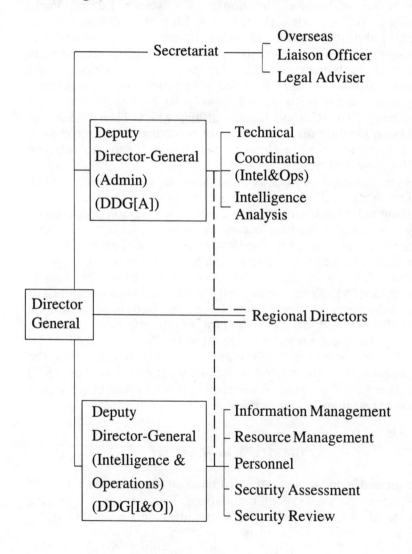

reports from his mid-1970s inquiry somehow being leaked to the press. This report examined various allegations including the ones that ASIO had formed a secret alliance with the CIA, passing on information it had collected on Australians, and had also burgled the house of a senior Liberal Party minister, William McMahon. On 5 May the *National Times* began publishing these and other items in that report. The newly elected Prime Minster, Robert Hawke, immediately informed Parliament on 12 May that Justice Hope would conduct another inquiry into the several intelligence agencies. This was ostensibly to be a follow-up to his report five years previously. The Combe–Ivanov affair, which Harvey Barnett had been bottling up for what could be considered three critical weeks, was revealed to Hawke on 20 April. It too was referred to Hope on 6 May.

Hope disposed of the Combe–Ivanov affair before turning to review ASIO early in 1984. In February 1984 the ALP extra-parliamentary party presented a 26-page submission prepared by a special Party committee consisting of senior federal ministers, back benchers, branch members and the national secretary. The submission reflected the Party's platform and made recommendations. These were that the National and International Security Committee (NISC) be permanently established with a secretariat; that a Security Commissioner be established as a combined ombudsman, auditor and inspector of all intelligence bodies; that a Joint Parliamentary Committee for National Security be established to oversee ASIO and the other bodies; that the Opposition be fully briefed on security affairs; and that ASIO recruitment and training be widened and ASIO staff become part of the Australian Public Service.[26]

THE SECOND HOPE REPORT

The second Hope report into ASIO was an extensive document of 398 pages making 93 recommendations.[27] In an action reflecting the mood of greater openness about intelligence organizations, the government released the report to the public with two chapters on the Management and Personnel Administration deleted. The report was completed in December 1984 and the government released it in May 1985 with a commentary on what it proposed to do about its recommendations. The ensuing legislation did not appear until May 1986.

Much of this second report was expressed in the same legal philosophical prose of Hope's first report. It never failed to use a lengthy convoluted paragraph where a short sentence would have sufficed. Little of explicit information about ASIO appeared through the wordy fog. However, readers did discover that ASIO refrained from numbering the pages in its files, thus making page location difficult. But it probably made removal and substitution of other pages easier. Files were kept on members of Australian Parliaments (consisting of nearly 800 people) which were reviewed annually by senior ASIO officers and the Director-General.[28] This gem of information was squeezed into Hope's discussion about the necessity, which ASIO wished to avoid, of depositing its files more than 30 years old with the Australian Archives. It is uncertain whether this telling fact appeared because it escaped the eyes of the report checker or whether the support of the MPs concerned was being subtly recruited to support ASIO's bureaucratic struggle to keep its files out of the hands of Australian Archives and hence out of public view.

Other pieces of ASIO operational information were that trade unions and their active members were no longer kept under surveillance.[29] Nor was ASIO any longer keeping a close watch on universities. However, contact was maintained with 'talent spotters' and a nebulous group of academics described as those 'who help with general field inquiries'.[30] ASIO agents under-taking part-time studies at universities were instructed not to dally near the student union buildings to collect political pamphlets. This was to remain the duty of the secretive 'helpers'. Hope revealed also that dossiers or files were not opened on Austra-lians; instead 'intelligence collection programs' (ICPs) were insti-tuted relating to person or persons.[31] ASIO had now embraced the era of the euphemism.

Former themes were revisited by Mr Justice Hope. His concept of agent of influence enumerated in his first report was given another airing. This time it occupied 17 long paragraphs of the judge's prose. The ALP in its submission claimed that this loose concept had no application in ASIO's work. It was a bait His Honour could not resist. But he was no more able to clarify his concept behind the title than seven years previously.[32] Nor had Hope's opposition dimmed to the establishment of a parliamentary committee to oversee ASIO. On this occasion, however, in the face of the ALP submission favouring that development, he was tactful enough to say that he would leave the final decision on the matter to Parliament itself.[33] His opposition to people other than intelligence agents being appointed as the Director-General of ASIO had diminished after seven years. He was now prepared to see such appointees drawn from people with 'proven managerial ability, not necessarily from security or intelligence background, as well as professional intelligence officers and judges'.[34] The confusion in expression perhaps reflected his subconscious attachment to intelligence agents still being the principal candidates.

With all its limitations, the report did provide the Australian public with its first glimpse of the role of ASIO in national affairs. However, it threw little light on what actually occupied the 700 staff and on how they expended their annual budget of $30 million.

Administratively speaking, the report signalled a significant shift in the general operations of ASIO. Hope had silently accepted that the 'Communist menace' and threats of subversion could no longer sustain the ASIO edifice. The public's acceptance of ASIO as being relevant in the mid-1980s had been heavily eroded. Indeed, as Mr Justice Hope bitterly observed, ASIO had now become the butt of criticism and lampooning.[35] The public perceived the 'ever-present threat' of the 1950s and 1960s as no longer evident. China had joined the world of Coca-Cola consumers, the Soviet Union was on the verge of significant re-ordering. At home the CPA had all but disappeared and its newspaper *Tribune* was about to cease publication. ASIO's original rationale for existence, that of keeping the public service, the defence force and the inflow of immigrants free of Communist infiltrators, was no longer relevant. On figures published in the Hope report, showing that 20,122 employees in the public service were vetted in 1983 with no adverse reports and 20 qualified reports, it was difficult to justify expenditure on this type of operation. But it was still to be continued.

There were new administrative factors compounding the question of ASIO's relevance in the post-Cold War society. Government employment had rapidly declined in the face of economic slump, the military forces had taken over their own vetting work and the Security Appeals Tribunal (SAT) was upholding appeals because ASIO's evidence was of low standard. In migrant affairs, the Department of Immigration was conducting its own checking arrangements and the overseas ASIO agents were infrequently called upon to communicate with their local intelligence counterparts to obtain dossiers. Hope actually hinted that foreign agencies were no longer willing to provide details about their nationals.[36] Immigration from the USSR and Communist Poland had also increased. It was unlikely that ASIO had contact with the KGB or Polish intelligence about these immigrants. Hope concluded that the need for ASIO agents serving overseas for vetting purposes be reviewed.[37] Thus ended an ASIO tradition stretching back for 30 years. What was ASIO to do now?

Hope urged that all was not lost for ASIO. It could expand into other areas of work. The most prominent of these was counter-terrorism. Australia was fortunate in having no warring factions importing their differences and continuing their animosities, but the potential was always there. The Croatian problem had diminished and the violent manifestations of the Ustashi were disowned by the more moderate leadership of the Croatian immigrant groups. But other migrant groups such as the Vietnamese, Lebanese and Turks contained hostile factions requiring monitoring. In this new form of security work, ASIO had to share the territory with the army, the Australian Federal Police (AFP), with its intelligence branch of 200 people, and State police forces. To make matters worse, ASIO's role was confined to collecting intelligence, not conducting operations. The Federal Police had a higher profile because they did both. The police also had established close connections with their overseas counterparts and Interpol in Paris with its X-25 data transmission network known as Criminal Intelligence System (CIS).

Hope pointed to another new territory for ASIO to explore, but it had already expanded into it. This was known as protective security and jocularly referred to as installing burglar alarms in government buildings. The burgeoning electronics industry had produced a range of alarms and detection devices of which ASIO's agents kept abreast. ASIO had developed the marketing technique of offering a security package to its public service customers which neatly combined the physical, administrative and personnel elements.[38] But here too it faced competition. The Defence and Foreign Affairs departments had their own security units which installed their electronic monitoring devices. Hope was understandably ambivalent about pushing Australia's spy-catching force into this semi-commercial activity. He reminded ASIO that its burglar alarm installation activities must complement and not detract from its charter to guard national security. His final recommendation was that the government should give the burglar alarm business to the government's property-holding department with ASIO providing specialized input.[39] This did not come to pass, and ASIO actually expanded its expertise in this area by becoming the authority in testing and endorsing the large array of electronic devices coming onto the market. It also established a team to sweep public offices to detect bugs.[40]

Another growth area for ASIO, on which Hope complimented it, was that of producing threat assessments against VIPs. Such assessments applied to VIPs visiting Australia and Australian government VIPs travelling abroad. Here again ASIO was trespassing on Federal Police territory since it was that police force which supplied the bodyguards for all VIPs. ASIO, however, held the legislative authority to tap telephones of ethnic groups who might wish to demonstrate against visiting VIPs whom they opposed in their homelands and continued to oppose after migrating to Australia. This facility gave ASIO a legislative advantage over the Federal police. ASIO's brief to monitor politically motivated violence ensured that ASIO would retain a good proportion of the VIP guarding business. In the year ending June 1989 ASIO provided 700 specific threat assessments for the protection of VIPs.[41]

Hope recommended that ASIO expand this telephone-tapping power. He noted that ASIO could pass on to the police information about criminal activity it overheard during telephone interceptions. Such criminal activity was confined to that punishable by imprisonment from six years to life.[42] The normal ASIO agent, unschooled in the law, was unable to discriminate between criminal offences. The easier solution was adopted of presenting the Federal Police with all the transcripts and allowing them to make the judgements about the level of criminality. Such a solution conflicted with the wording of the Act, and

Hope recommended that it be changed. The relevant clause was amended and the jail sentence criterion replaced with the more general phrase 'indictable offence'.[43]

THE THIRD ASIO ACT

The bill to amend the ASIO Act was presented to Parliament on 22 May 1986. It incorporated most of the amendments sought by the Labor Party in its submission to the Hope Royal Commission. The definition of ASIO's targets was changed so that less emphasis was placed on subversion and more on politically motivated violence. This change represented a move away from Cold War phobia to the more pressing security problem of Australia where ethnic migrant groups were tempted to maintain hostilities against each other within Australia. ASIO was to monitor discreetly those possible tension points and pass information to the police forces when appropriate.[44] Another significant amendment was that ASIO was to collect foreign intelligence. This widened the powers that ASIO had previously possessed.[45] An overriding clause was also added making it clear that ASIO had no power to limit the right of a person to engage in lawful advocacy, protest or dissent.[46]

The vexed question of ministerial authority was now settled. The Director-General was to be subject to the minister's direction and he could override the Director-General's decision about who was to be watched and to what organization the information was to be disseminated. But this had to be in writing and a copy given to the Inspector-General of Intelligence and Security. ASIO had to keep a record of intelligence so collected and communicated.[47] The Labor Party had accepted the concept that if there were to be a civilian security organization, it must be guarded against the possibility of manipulation. ASIO's pursuit of ALP opponents of the Vietnam war was clear in the minds of the parliamentary members.

The power of the minister was further strengthened by the Attorney-General being authorized to issue guidelines for the functioning of ASIO. These guidelines were to be laid before each house of Parliament, with secret sections deleted where necessary. With firmer ministerial control in place ASIO could

271

now be permitted, with ministerial direction, to co-operate with authorities of other countries capable of assisting ASIO.[48]

The Joint Parliamentary Committee, twice opposed by Hope, was provided for and consisted of seven parliamentarians. But it could only consider matters referred to it by the minister or either house of Parliament although it could suggest to the minister what it should be investigating. It was hedged about with restrictions and fines for members and staff divulging ASIO's secret information.[49] It represented an important if limited break-through in providing for parliamentary supervision and inspection of ASIO's activities.

The establishment of the office of Inspector-General of Intelligence and Security was contained in a separate parliamentary act. The Labor Party had requested the appointment of such an officer in its submission and Hope had agreed to this proposal.[50] Hope seemed to appreciate that an Inspector-General was the lesser of two evils. ASIO escaped the attentions of oversight agencies that other government departments were exposed to. These included the Ombudsman, the Freedom of Information Act, the Administrative Appeals Tribunal and the Human Rights and Equal Opportunity Commissioner. Hope appreciated that an Inspector-General's office, hedged about with security limitations, would be preferable to having the secretive ASIO accountable to this much wider range of external review authorities.[51] The necessity to qualify accountability with heavy secrecy was uppermost for Hope. The ensuing legislation provided that the Inspector-General was to be guided by the Human Rights Act.

The role of the Inspector-General was to ensure that ASIO in particular and the other intelligence organizations, ASIS, DSD, JIO and ONA, did not interfere unnecessarily with the privacy of Australian citizens or permanent residents. He was to act in response to complaints from individuals or the Attorney-General or on his own volition. He was given wide powers to summon people to give evidence or to demand documents. He was to investigate contraventions by ASIO or any impropriety. He could also investigate the grievances of ASIO agents – a move to stop them seeking redress through publicity. His investigation of agents' complaints regarding promotion, discipline, remuneration or the like could only be undertaken if they had first been aired before ASIO's own grievance resolution arrangements. He had to advise the Attorney-General when he was about to investigate an ASIO problem and he had to give a copy of his report on the complaint to the Director-General for the ASIO head to comment upon. His term of appointment was limited to three years and he or his staff were liable to be fined or jailed for divulging ASIO secrets.[52]

In the parliamentary debate on the bill, the Liberal and National Party Opposition firmly resisted the changes. The resulting debate witnessed a revival of a tribal loyalty towards ASIO that the non-Labor forces had always displayed. Its manifestation was all the more remarkable because by this time most of the members of the non-Labor alliance had been replaced by younger members, many of whom would have been about 10 years old when ASIO was established. One of the more voluble opponents of the change was M.J.R. MacKellar, a former agricultural scientist from Queensland. He evoked the ghost of the Petrov affair to demonstrate how ASIO was the effective guardian against Soviet espionage. He displayed a grasp of some of the detail of the affair although he miscast Wally Clayton as the 'key operator' in the alleged Soviet spy network.[53] MacKellar would have been 16 years old at the time of the Petrov affair and his evocation of those events probably owed more to the Party folk memory of the affair than to any accurate details of its history.

The parliamentary debate marked a reversal of political party roles but the continuation of party policies. Whereas on previous occasions when ASIO legislation was amended, the Labor Party as the Opposition had sought to widen the accountability of ASIO against non-Labor's refusal, this occasion witnessed non-Labor, now as the Opposition, continuing to maintain its resistance to such changes albeit ineffectively. But the opposition to these amendments also had an ideological basis. Non-Labor was reacting to the government's changes partly from ideological instinct, which demanded that it rally to ASIO's defence, and partly from the deep suspicion of the Labor Party's motives, which non-Labor had perceived to be firmly opposed to ASIO. Non-Labor was automatically convinced that the Labor modifications were intended to hamstring ASIO. The deputy leader of the Liberal Party, N.A. Brown, who had been a Melbourne barrister before becoming an MP, reflected his party's deep suspicion of any Labor Party tinkering with ASIO. 'I would not trust the Australian Labor Party as far as I could kick it,' he firmly declared, 'as far as its having anything to do with the security services of this country is concerned'.[54]

Non-Labor disliked the concept of the Inspector-General's office. However, because Hope had recommended it the Opposition gave it token support, but it imposed a sunset restriction limiting the office to three years' duration. This move was defeated. Non-Labor disliked even more the Joint Parliamentary Committee perceiving it as a means for Labor Party MPs acquiring inside knowledge of ASIO's working. It could not stop the provision but promised to abolish it on being elected to office.

THE FUNCTIONING OF ASIO'S ACCOUNTABILITY PROCEDURES

By late in 1986 ASIO had become accountable to the three different institutions representing judicial, administrative and parliamentary elements. The concerns of the Parliamentary and extra-parliamentary Labor Party resulting from ASIO's partisan involvement in the Petrov affair, opposition to the Vietnam war and the Combe–Ivanov affair would be satisfied by these changes.

Before discussing how these accountability provisions have functioned, it should be noted here that there have been three other administrative changes made within the bureaucracy affecting the autonomy of ASIO. These are the issuing by the Attorney-General of guidelines to ASIO, the presentation by ASIO of annual reports to Parliament and the establishment in the Attorney-General's Department of a section to monitor and advise ASIO on legal questions. This third provision was recommended in the second Hope report. It has functioned with a staff of ten officers most of whom are lawyers with strong experience in intelligence and human rights questions. The first mentioned arrangement has been exercised by the Attorney-General issuing a set of guidelines to ASIO on its functions relating to politically motivated violence.

The publication of the annual ASIO reports to Parliament had an interesting evolution. Since 1979 ASIO had been required to present secret reports annually to the Attorney-General. This allowed ministers some insight into ASIO's arcane world. In 1985 a brief extract of this report was published by the Labor Party Attorney-General, Lionel Bowen.[55] The ASIO Act was thereafter amended to provide for extracts from that confidential report to be presented to Parliament. These parliamentary reports have been published since 1988, but their highly generalized contents are not very revealing. Spy threats to Australia do not fail to be mentioned. These are euphemistically referred to as 'hostile foreign intelligence services'. ASIO has gravely declared that these 'cannot be quantified' (begging the question of whether intelligence services can usefully be measured), but it has judged them to be 'significant'.[56]

With large typefaces and generous margins, such generalized reports have filled out to more than 80 pages in recent years. ASIO has used these reports to advertise its complaints against historical researchers. ASIO has resented having to lodge its 30-year-old records in the Australian Archives Office. Each year it summarizes statistically the heavy load this requirement places on its two archival officers. In effect very little ASIO material has been released, signalling that ASIO intends keeping its secret history to itself.

The Inspector-General's office which opened on 1 February 1987 has had a considerable impact on ASIO. The first incumbent of the office was in search of a role, but his successor has managed to establish a viable presence. He has maintained a public office with a staff of five and has been available to hear complaints against ASIO. He has also pursued complaints that have appeared in the press. His small annual reports have provided more reliable insights to ASIO's functioning than the much-padded ASIO reports.

Some perception of ASIO's contacts with US intelligence agencies can be obtained in his 1990 report. The Inspector investigated a newspaper report of how ASIO had selected an Australian tourist for questioning from a party which had travelled to Cuba.[57] No feathers were ruffled, but it showed how ASIO, in its small way, has paid its dues to the US intelligence club. As with most post-Cold War intelligence organizations, the Inspector has reported that industrial conditions and future employment have become the abiding questions for intelligence agents. It is in his role as grievance officer that the Inspector has become involved in such issues. As a means of isolating its staff from the Australian public service unions, ASIO has established its own Staff Association.[58] Reflecting an understandably strong anti-union mood (radical unions and their leaders have been ASIO's quarries since it began) over one-third of the staff have refused to join even this very mild employee group. What small authority it might have exercised has thereby been further diminished. In these circumstances, it is to be expected that the Inspector will become more deeply involved in matters affecting the industrial relations of the ASIO staff.

The work of the Security Appeals Tribunal (SAT), the second watchdog of ASIO, has declined since it was established in 1979. The explanation for this lies in the narrowed range of public service staff ASIO has had to review together with ASIO's lower rejection rates for security clearances. The rigorous judicial standards demanded in previous years by the SAT has forced ASIO to be more certain of its facts when rejecting security clearances for people. This has led to fewer rejections being issued.

The third reviewing body of ASIO, the Joint Parliamentary Committee on ASIO, was slow in being formed because the non-Labor Opposition refused to nominate members to sit on it. This has reflected the Opposition's hostility to the Committee and its promise to dissolve it on being elected to office. The Opposition believed the Committee would become a device for the ALP probing into ASIO secrets. It was a continuation of the attitude of previous decades where non-Labor considered itself to be the progenitor of ASIO and its protector against ALP subversion.

The Committee was formed on 31 August 1988 and in December 1989 the Attorney-General referred to it the question of particular concern to ASIO and the other intelligence agencies. This was the obligation under the Archives Act of 1983 for all departments, including ASIO, to make their 30-year-old records available to the Australian Archives and the public. The Committee was to examine the question from several aspects. These included ASIO's position in relation to the Archives Act, the implications of privacy for those who had been under ASIO surveillance and how to maintain the secrecy of ASIO material. The Committee advertised for public submission and started hearings in October 1990.[59]

The concern driving ASIO's demand for change was the functioning of the Administrative Appeals Tribunal (AAT). This is a judicial body that has investigated and if necessary reversed decisions by government departments. Several appeals against ASIO for withholding material from archives have been heard by the AAT, but they have been dismissed. However, ASIO feared that an appeal might be upheld one day in the future. ASIO seized on this assumption to claim that it had lost control of its dossiers to this AAT which would ignore all security implications in ordering their release. It also sought to extend the 30-year rule to 50 years as a further means of delaying the public release of its dossiers.[60]

This perception by ASIO was again an over-reaction to a new situation. The release of ASIO files has always been hedged by significant restrictions. Unlike other departments, ASIO and the intelligence agencies retain their files of whatever age in their own secure headquarters. Special provisions in the Archives Act ensure that any record of security importance or material obtained from a foreign source is not to be released. In practice ASIO rarely releases intact files. It does not reveal what files it holds and, if it does choose to release one, it is thoroughly weeded down to a few folios, often containing no more than press clippings. The Archives office deletes all file numbers and agents' names before public release. No intelligence leak has occurred as a result of this expensive and intensive vetting procedure.

It was a situation where ASIO had responded to the public demands for open government with a Canute-like reaction. It naively demanded the replacement of the 30-year rule by 50 and rejected the authority of the AAT. ASIO's case to the Committee was presented by J.M. Moten, Director-General of ASIO, and two agents. Two years previously the government had passed the Privacy Act and appointed a Privacy Commissioner to guarantee the rights of all people to privacy. ASIO submitted to the Committee that the provisions of this new privacy legislation should be used to stop the public obtaining the release of ASIO dossiers. ASIO unblushingly confessed that the dossier had been compiled by the abuse of the principles of privacy in previous decades against both the target individuals and third parties such as neighbours or friends.[61]

However, it was not the privacy of the ASIO target that most concerned ASIO; it was more the need to keep secret the identity of its informants and part-time agents. Several hundreds of these had been employed by ASIO to snoop on their fellow workers, unionists and friends. Any revelations of this large informer network would embarrass ASIO as much as it would the informers. It is a problem that all intelligence agencies, both in the West and the East, have had to face in the post-Cold War era. For example, the effects of the release of the information about the informer network of the former East German intelligence service, Ministerium für Staatssicherheit (MFS or Stasi), has had an important impact on German politics. The latest count of the Stasi file collection is of 170 running kilometres.[62]

Following two years of inquiry, the Joint Parliamentary Committee reported to Parliament on 2 April 1992. Its main recommendation was that ASIO should continue to conform to the 30-year-rule. It met one of ASIO's demands, inspired perhaps by the revelations disclosed by the release of the Stasi files showing that husbands had informed on wives, that the identities of ASIO agents and their informers not be released until 30 years after their deaths. The Committee responded to an issue raised constantly during its hearings by historians and recommended that a special archives unit be established in ASIO, like other government departments, to provide for the quick release of documents for archival research.[63] The 14 recommendations made by the Committee would require the amendment of three Acts, including the ASIO Act, and given that the government is having to confront Australia's most serious post-war depression and that the Cold War has ended, it is unlikely that time will be found in the government's heavy legislative programme for any such amendments.

CONCLUSION

While a considerable amount of publicly available material has been generated about ASIO activities (Royal Commissions, inquiries and legislative debates) over its 40 years of existence, there remains widespread ignorance of what its 700 staff does with its annual budget now close to $40 million. This book has cast some light on what lies behind the public documents, but little on what goes on behind ASIO's heavily guarded doors.

Like many intelligence organizations, ASIO was a post-war phenomenon. It has been uncritically accepted as an element of Australian public administration. The legal, political, constitutional and administrative problems created by its existence and functioning have been tackled on an *ad hoc* basis as they have arisen. Indeed ASIO's incorporation into government administration has led to other government intelligence-based institutions being established to monitor actitivities in the areas of customs, immigration and taxation.

The history of civilian intelligence organizations has become an important episode in the functioning of government during the Cold War years. A history of their activities necessarily concentrates on their publicly observable behaviour. Such a study provides important insights to ideological, defence, foreign affairs, political and social histories of the last 50 years. Because such institutions are new to the post-war years their study provides fresh insights to the events of those decades.

However, a judgement at the micro-level about what use ASIO has been to Australia is not easy to make. Its presence may have helped governments to focus more clearly on the Soviet or Chinese threats to Australia which, in retrospect, can be seen to have been more imaginary than real. Certainly ASIO has had an interdependent relationship with non-Labor governments. ASIO provided the rationale and the non-Labor governments provided the rhetoric to fan the embers of the Cold War which might otherwise have become extinguished. It may have created jobs in ASIO and ideological enthusiasm in the post-war years – but little else.

One use that ASIO possibly served, as we see from the reasons for its establishment in 1949, was to win the approval of the US Defense Department for Australia to be the recipient of its defence and technology secrets. With the defeat of the Chifley Labor government this rationale was removed. In any case it was a mood in the US administration that was based more on the typical instinctive dislike in US governing circles towards trade union-based political parties than any real fear of Soviet spying in Australia that led to the US embargo on sending information to Australia. The hindering of British high-technology defence developments was another important motive behind that stance. In succeeding decades Australia has been permitted to purchase

US high-technology weapons. It was less the presence of ASIO and more the fact that Australia was paying cash for this equipment and demonstrated a close alliance to the US that determined the sale of such technology to Australia. In any case the defence services conducted their own vetting arrangements which were more acceptable to US defence intelligence circles than ASIO's.

The central theme to ASIO's history is the tension between it and the parliamentary and extra-parliamentary parties of the ALP. It was a tension created more by the ALP's electoral weakness than by ASIO's partisanship with the non-Labor parties. This book shows that this friction produced more of a positive than a negative outcome. A study of those events provides important insights to post-war Australian history that would not have been available if the tension were not there. Another aspect of this antagonism was that it led to the establishment of a range of accountability measures that probably puts Australia ahead of other Western nations in their attempts to control their intelligence organizations.

What is the future for ASIO? Mr Justice Hope's second inquiry showed some avenues of activity ASIO could pursue as the end of the Cold War made it increasingly redundant. These should tax ASIO's ideological resources to the limit. Whereas it was able to activate a large informant network on what can now be seen to be a misleading interpretation of threats to Australia it will require a severe shift in direction to mobilize newer forces to confront the more important economic threats facing Australia. International criminal links, money laundering, tax evasion, underpricing of Australian resource exports and other economic threats to Australia could well become the more important focus of ASIO's powerful intelligence resources. It is a challenge to which ASIO could well rise.

NOTES

1. C.C.F. Spry to R.G. Menzies, 15 Oct. 1954, A2109, Item 72/100048.
2. Spry to Brown, Secretary, Prime Minister's Department, 21 Oct. 1955, A6213, Item RCE/G/7.
3. C.C.F. Spry to R.G. Menzies, 13 Jan. 1956, A1209, Item 72/100048.

4. Notes for Second Reading Speech by the Rt. Hon. R.G. Menzies, A1209, Item 72/100048.
5. Australian Security Intelligence Organization Act 1956, No. 113 of 1956.
6. CPD, 31 Oct. and 1 Nov. 1956, pp. 2019–20.
7. CPD, 31 Oct. and 1 Nov. 1956, pp. 2015, 2033.
8. David Marr, *The Ivanov Trail* (Melbourne, 1984), p. 269.
9. Gough Whitlam, *Whitlam Government* (Ringwood, 1985), pp. 171–2.
10. *Pacific Defence Reporter*, Sept. 1977, p. 47.
11. *Royal Commission on Intelligence and Security*, Fourth Report, Vol. 1 (Canberra, 1977), pp. 16–67.
12. *National Times*, 31 Oct.– 5 Nov. 1977, pp 11, 12.
13. *Royal Commission on Intelligence and Security*, Fourth Report, Vol. 1, pp. 55, 220.
14. Ibid., p. 66.
15. Ibid., pp. 16–17, 29.
16. Brian Toohey, 'How ASIO Betrayed Australia to the US', *National Times*, 6–17 May 1983.
17. See Australian Security Intelligence Organization Act 1979, No. 113 of 1979.
18. See Part IV of the Act.
19. See paragraphs 18 and 92 of the Act.
20. See paragraph 8 of the Act.
21. CPD, 18 Sept. 1979, p. 1210.
22. Ibid., p. 1237.
23. Ibid., p. 1214.
24. *Federal Law Review*, No. 3, 1980, pp. 102–8.
25. Nicholas Seddon, 'ASIO and Accountability' *Australian Quarterly*, Vol. 54, No. 4, 1983, pp. 362–81.
26. 'Submission by Australian Labor Party to the Royal Commission Australia's Security and Intelligence Agencies', presented by R.F. McMullan, ALP National Secretary, February 1984.
27. *Royal Commission on Australia's Security and Intelligence Agencies. Report on the Australian Security Intelligence Organization, December 1984* (Canberra, 1985).
28. Ibid., para. 7.39.
29. Ibid., paras 4.122 to 4.129.
30. Ibid., paras 4.130 to 4.133.
31. Ibid., para. 4.108.

32. Ibid., paras 3.17 to 3.33.
33. Ibid., paras 17.21 to 17.35.
34. Ibid., para. 16.16.
35. Ibid., para. 2.31.
36. Ibid., para. 10.11.
37. Ibid., para. 10.29.
38. Ibid., para. 12.13.
39. Ibid., paras 12.1 to 12.81.
40. *Australian Security Intelligence Organization, Report to Parliament 1986–87* (Canberra, 1988), p. 19.
41. *Australian Security Intelligence Organization, Report to Parliament 1988–89* (Canberra, 1990), p. 9.
42. Australian Security Intelligence Organization Act 1979, No. 113 of 1979, Section 18 (3) (2).
43. *Report December 1984*, para. 8.89; Australian Security Intelligence Organization Amendment Act 1986, No. 122 of 1986, Communication of Intelligence etc., Para. 10 amending Section 18.
44. Amending Act, 1986, Interpetation, Section 3.
45. Amending Act, 1986, Communication of Intelligence, etc., Para. 10.
46. Amending Act, 1986, Section 9.
47. Amending Act, 1986, Control of Organization, Section 5.
48. Amending Act, 1986, Guidelines, Section 6; see Attorney-General's Guidelines in relation to the performance by the Australian Security Intelligence Organization of its functions relating to politically motivated violence. Laid before Parliament, n.d.
49. Amending Act, 1986, Part V A. Parliamentary Joint Committee.
50. *ASIO Report*, December 1984, paras 16.76 to 16.102.
51. *ASIO Report*, December 1984, para. 16.78.
52. *Inspector-General of Intelligence and Security Act 1986*, No. 101 of 1986, *passim*.
53. CPD, 2 June 1986, p. 4386.
54. CPD, 2 June 1986, pp. 4373–4.
55. *Australian Security Intelligence Organization, Report to Parliament 1984–85* (Canberra, 1985).
56. *Australian Security Intelligence Organization, Report to Parliament 1988–89* (Canberra, 1990), p. 4.
57. Inspector-General of Intelligence and Security, Annual Report 1989–90 (Canberra, 1990), p. 13.
58. Ibid., p. 15.

59. Joint Committee on Australian Security Intelligence Organization, (Official Hansard Report), Canberra, ACT, 11 Oct. 1990.
60. *Joint Committee on Australian Security Intelligence Organization,* (Official Hansard Report), Canberra, ACT, 6 Dec. 1990, pp. 108–13.
61. 'Parliamentary Joint Committee on ASIO, Inquiry Into Aspects of Archives Act', Submission by the Australian Security Intelligence Organization, Feb. 1990, pp. 26–34.
62. *Intelligence Newsletter*, Paris, No. 165, 13 March 1991, p. 6.
63. *ASIO and the Archives Act, The Effect on ASIO of the Operation of the Access Provisions of the Archives Act.* Report of the Parliamentary Joint Committee of the Australian Security Intelligence Organization, April 1992. See F.M. Cain, 'The Right to Know: ASIO, Historians and the Australian Parliament' in *Intelligence and National Security*, Vol. 8, No. 1, January 1993, for an analysis of the Parliamentary Committee's investigation of ASIO's archival policy.

Index

45; contest with Defense
Department, 57–8; 112, 113,
119, 136–7; says Petrov typical
of disgruntled embassy staff,
125–6; 182; discounts RCE
findings, 189

Cabell, Major-General C.P., 80, 96
Cairns, Dr Jim, 202
Cairns, Kevin, 262
Calwell, Arthur, 62, 67, 182
Campbell, Colonel Eric, 15
Canberra Times, 211–13
Casey, Richard Gardner:
7; biographical details, 92;
possibly selected Spry as
Director-General, 92; work
in wartime intelligence,
93; establishes ASIS, 95;
connections with CIA, 95;
unexplained resignation from
politics, 96; 102; 'nest of
traitors' speech, 119; 136;
148; convinced of Soviet spy
ring in Australia, 149; 156;
involvement in Ollier affair,
184; 198, 223
Central Intelligence Agency (CIA):
reports government leak in
Australia, 40–1; publishes
anti-Australia monograph,
75; connections with Casey
in Australia, 95; appoints
representative in Australia, 96;
lobbies to stop disbandment of
ASIS, 96; 212, 215–16, 218,
225, 232, 259
Chandler, Herbert, 132, 136, 153
Chifley, Joseph Benedict, 1, 23,
34, 44–6; seeks explanation
from UK government for US
embargo on Australia, 48–50;
52, 53; announces Reed to
be first Director-General
of ASIO, 54; 55, 57, 62;
discussion with Hollis, 63,
135; accused of ignoring CPA
subversion, 67; 72; instructed

by State Department not
to use Shedden invitation as
demonstration of stronger
US ties, 73; preferred by US
Defense to Evatt as head of
ASIO, 78; 80, 81; defeated,
82; 85, 86; discussion with
Sillitoe, 135, 138; 218; 253; 279
Chiplin, Rex, 118, 119, 120, 141,
144, 153, 177
Church of Scientology, 263–4
Clayton, Walter, 136, 142, 149, 152,
153, 273
COCOM (Committee to Control
East–West Trade), 244
Colby, William, 219
Coleman, Peter, 204
Combe, David, 28, 229–30, 232–49,
252, 266, 274
Combe, Meena (née Blesing), 230,
232, 233
Commercial Bureau (Australia) Pty
Ltd, 227
Committee for the Abolition of
Political Police, 203, 260
Committee of State Security, *see*
KGB
Committee on Un-American
Activities, 29
Commonwealth Investigation Service,
22, 25, 48, 54, 90, 91, 97
Commonwealth Scientific and
Industrial Research
Organization, 49, 183
Communist Party of Australia
(CPA), 6; banned 1940, 17,
20–1; post-war activities,
24; exaggerated US reports
concerning, 67; Menzies
government attacks, 88;
legislation to proscribe 96–7;
plans to go underground 1950,
98; ASIO plans Party room
raids, 98; ASIO prepares
government paper to assist in
banning, 101; assumed links
with KGB, 153, 164; ASIO
continues surveillance, 219

INDEX

Communist Party Dissolution Act,
98; challenged in High Court,
99
Counter-Espionage Bureau, 2
Cowen, Myron M., 66; thwarts
Australia's case in Washington,
72–3; smears Evatt's reputation
in Washington, 75; undermines
Shedden's visit to US, 76–7;
replaced as ambassador to
Australia, 82
Croatian Liberation Movement
(HOP), 205, 206
Croatian National Resistance
(HNO), 206
Crow, Sir Alwyn, 77
Cypriot Communist Party, 105

Dedman, J.J., 48, 67, 70
Dening, M.E., 45–6, 47
Devanny, F.H. 11
Dixon, Sir Owen, 72
Document G, 181–2
Document H, 174
Document J, 173–4
Donovan, William J., 94
Drzavna Bezbednosti (Yugoslav
Intelligence), 205
Dulles, Allen Welch, 95–6

Eisenhower, Dwight D., 84–5
Evatt, Clive, 178
Evatt, Dr Herbert Vere, 12; lifts
ban on CPA, 18; establishes
diplomatic relations with
USSR, 26; policy towards
USSR, 29; Minister for
External Affairs, 45, 46;
pursues reasons for US
embargo, 51; defamed in
reports by US officials in
Australia to Washington,
65–9; particular target of
Ambassador Cowen, 72–5; 76,
77, 78, 79, 80, 81, 86; counsel
for trade unions, 99; 113, 117,
119; 144; suspects staging of
Petrov defection, 164; barred

from RCE, 173, 186; 174,
175, 177, 180, 185; letter to
Molotov about Petrov, 188;
rebuts RCE conclusions,
190; 252, 253, 254; ASIO
legislation, 1956, 256
Evetts, Lieutenant-General J.F., 33

Fasham, Bruce, 229, 230, 235, 239
Federal Bureau of Investigation
(FBI), 99, 139
Forrestal, James V., 51, 52, 68, 70, 73
Fraser, Malcolm, 229, 241, 260

Galleghan, Brigadier Fred, 206
Garran, Sir Robert (Randolph), 4,
10, 11
Garrett, Frances (née Bernie), 149;
gives information to ASIO,
June 1953, 152; 160, 182
Geri, Phil, 202
German Nazis in Australia, 14, 15
Gibbs, Mr Justice, 264
Gibson, Ralf, 12, 15
Golitsyn, Anatoli, 133, 209, 210
Gouzenko affair:
comparisons with Petrov affair,
40, 41, 65 125, 153, 160, 183
Gray, Gordon, 72, 77, 78, 79, 80,
82, 83
Greek Communist Party, 25
guided missiles, 31; development
post-war by UK and US, 32;
Australian–UK agreement
to build testing range,
33; US constructs its own
Banana River range, 34; US
restricts release of technical
information, 83

Hasluck, Paul, 136, 137, 139
Hawke, Robert J., 117, 229, 237–40,
252, 266
Harbin intercepts, 41–2
Harris, Colonel Collas G., 96
Harry, Ralph, 96
Healey, James, 66, 101, 103
Heine Bros, 227

287